Boss of Bosses

Also by Clare Longrigg

Mafia Women
No Questions Asked

Boss of Bosses

A Journey into the Heart
of the Sicilian Mafia

CLARE LONGRIGG

Thomas Dunne Books
St. Martin's Press
New York

THOMAS DUNNE BOOKS.
An imprint of St. Martin's Press.

BOSS OF BOSSES. Copyright © 2008 by Clare Longrigg. All rights reserved. Printed in the United States of America. For information, address St. Martin's Press, 175 Fifth Avenue, New York, N.Y. 10010.

www.thomasdunnebooks.com
www.stmartins.com

Library of Congress Cataloging-in-Publication Data

Longrigg, Clare.
  Boss of bosses / Clare Longrigg. — 1st U.S. ed.
    p. cm.
  Includes bibliographical references and index.
  ISBN-13: 978-0-312-53394-6
  ISBN-10: 0-312-53394-2
  1. Provenzano, Bernardo, 1933– 2. Mafiosi—Italy—
Biography. 3. Mafia—Italy—History. I. Title.
  HV6453.I83M3543455 2009
  364.1092—dc22
  [B]
                                                              2008039095

First published in Great Britain by John Murray (Publishers),
an Hachette Livre UK company

First U.S. Edition: April 2009

10 9 8 7 6 5 4 3 2 1

For Adrian

Contents

List of illustrations   ix
Acknowledgements   xi

Introduction   3
1.   Corleone bandits   12
2.   Palermo ambitions   28
3.   Love and title deeds   43
4.   Bagheria's feudal lord   53
5.   The split   67
6.   Family matters   85
7.   Goodbye Totò   100
8.   The regent   117
9.   A new strategy   129
10. A management handbook for the aspiring Mafia boss   144
11. Politics for Pragmatists   162
12. Treacherous friends   176
13. Letters home   188
14. Spies and leaks   202
15. Prostate trouble   217
16. The net tightens   233
17. The arrest   249
Epilogue   261

Sources and notes   270
Bibliography   286
Index   289

List of illustrations

1. Bernardo Provenzano after his arrest, Palermo, 11 April 2006
2. The sheep farm near Corleone where Provenzano was arrested
3. Bernardo Provenzano's first police mugshot, 1958
4. Bernardo Provenzano's second police mugshot, 2006
5. Provenzano leaving for his military service, 1954
6. The Corleone mafioso Totò Riina as a young man
7. Totò Riina feeding pigeons on holiday in Venice, 1970s
8. Saveria Benedetta Palazzolo, Provenzano's companion of thirty-seven years
9. Luciano Liggio, boss of the Corleonesi, in court, 1987
10. Vito Ciancimino, during his brief tenure as mayor of Palermo, 1970
11. Shoot-out in viale Lazio, Palermo, December 1969
12. The murder of General Carlo Alberto Dalla Chiesa and his wife, Emanuela Setti Carraro, 1982
13. Leoluca Bagarella, Totò Riina's brother-in-law
14. The bomb that killed Giovanni Falcone, his wife and their escort, May 1992
15. Giovanni Brusca, boss of San Giuseppe Iato, after his arrest, June 1996
16. Nino Giuffré, boss of Caccamo and Provenzano's right-hand man
17. Identikit picture of Bernardo Provenzano, 2002
18. Totò Riina's son Giovanni riding his motor bike around Corleone, 1994

19. Provenzano's sons, Angelo and Francesco Paolo
20. Part of a letter from Bernardo Provenzano to Nino Giuffré
21. The secret code used by Provenzano in his letters

Acknowledgements

I have to thank my great friend Rino Cascio, a brilliant journalist with whom I have been privileged to work, who has been a tireless, resourceful and knowledgeable researcher on this project – and always great fun.

I'd like to thank Linda Pantano for her help with research and, of course, the peerless staff of the Istituto Gramsci in Palermo. Thanks to Rino, Linda and Alberto for their wonderful hospitality.

Thanks to Piera Fallucca and Antonella Maggio for their ideas and Mafia tours.

Pippo Cipriani was incredibly generous with his time and knowledge. Salvo Palazzolo, author of two brilliant books on Provenzano, was a fount of ideas and information, and generous with help on documentation.

Thanks to Saverio Lodato for giving me permission to quote from his excellent books based on interviews with Tommaso Buscetta and Giovanni Brusca.

I'd like to thank the experts – lawyers, prosecutors and investigators – who agreed to be interviewed for this book, especially Alfonso Sabella, Nino Di Matteo and Michele Prestipino, General Angiolo Pellegrini and Rosalba di Gregorio.

Thanks to my agent Derek Johns, to Linda Shaughnessy, to my editor Rowan Yapp, and particular thanks to Roland Philipps. Thanks also to Ian Katz at *The Guardian*, who commissioned the article that set the whole project in motion.

I'd like to thank Emma Cook and Laura Longrigg for their comments on the manuscript, and Dani Golfieri for emergency translation. Thanks to Christine Langan and Christian Spurrier, Camilla

Nicholls, Amanda Sutton, Natasha Fairweather and Rick Beeston, and Denise and Charlie Meredith for their friendship and support. Thanks to Nigel Skeels for help with my website.

Heartfelt thanks to Helen and Bruce Buchanan. Thanks to my mother and sister Francesca for their constant support.

Finally, thanks to my husband, Adrian Buchanan, and my children, Patrick and Alice, who had to put up with my year-long absence.

Boss of Bosses

Introduction

'There's someone inside.'

The voice of Il Segugio ('Bloodhound'), one of the agents posted on the mountain, crackled over the radio. He had been watching the shepherd's hut day and night for over a week, looking for a sign of life. This was the signal his commander had been waiting for.

'We had been watching the sheep farm for days,' said police chief Giuseppe Gualtieri, 'and the door to the hut was always closed. Some days the shepherd arrived at seven in the morning and opened the door, but he never went in. He stood in the doorway, and sometimes it looked as though he was talking to the wall . . . it looked wrong somehow. We wanted to go up close at night and see what was in there, but then we thought, careful: if there was someone hiding in the cottage, we didn't want to risk frightening him off and destroying all our hard work. We would wait.

'One day we saw the shepherd standing in front of the cottage, fiddling with an aerial. We wondered, what's that for? Why would you need an aerial on an uninhabited house? It was a couple of days before the elections, so we were thinking, which fugitive takes a keen interest in politics?

'Shortly after that, a package was delivered to the cottage that looked like it could be a television set. We said, Oh my God! One of them comes up with an aerial, the other one turns up with a television, there's got to be someone living inside, and it could be Bernardo Provenzano.'

Early on the morning of 11 April 2006 the shepherd opened the door as usual, and just for a fleeting moment the observers up on the mountain saw an arm reach out from inside. It was all the proof they needed. The police unit got into position: the leader, Renato Cortese, moved up to a point 4 km away with eighteen men; the chiefs waited in the cover of the nearby forest.

'Go!' Bloodhound's voice came over the radio, loud and clear. Everyone knew what to do; they'd been rehearsing this moment in their sleep.

When Cortese burst into the little farm building, the old man tried to slam the door in his face, but he threw himself against it, smashing the glass with his fist. For a moment the old man looked like a trapped animal, then he composed himself to face his captor.

'You don't know what you are doing', he said in a low voice. He spoke quietly, with a strong Sicilian accent. Cortese thought he might be trying to say they'd got the wrong man. He checked for the scar on the old man's neck: there it was. He had been told of another identifying sign: the Boss would be wearing three silver crosses on a chain. Sure enough, they were hidden under his shirt. There was no doubt, it was Provenzano. After forty-three years on the run the Boss of Bosses had finally been caught.

'I looked into his eyes, and I knew it was him', Cortese said.

One of the agents, nicknamed 'the Director', had recorded the build-up to the arrest on a hand-held camera. Seeing the lens turned on him, Provenzano hid his face. When he finally lowered his hands, he was composed, fixing his visitors with a scornful expression, an inscrutable half-smile, offering his hand and his congratulations.

Outside the cottage the agents hugged each other and wept, whooped with euphoria and phoned their loved ones. In the midst of this scene of wild celebration Gualtieri followed Cortese into the hut. 'He wore a knowing smile, as though to say, "You think you've won, but you haven't. Capturing me doesn't change anything. Cosa Nostra isn't beaten." '

The place they found Provenzano, in the mountains above Corleone, was known as the 'triangle of death': a couple of miles away were the ravines and forests where Provenzano's earliest victims had met their violent ends. He had come home.

The massive international media coverage and frenzied analysis that followed Provenzano's arrest was largely due to the fact that, until that moment, very little was known about the boss of Cosa Nostra. He was one of the most powerful criminal leaders in Europe, and hadn't been seen in public for over forty years. The mystique that had built up around him made his arrest an object of fascination world-wide – yet even then there were no easy answers. People watching the news all over the world were shocked at the humble circumstances in which Provenzano was living: the tiny shepherd's hut reeked of rotting vegetables and urine, his diet of bread and onions . . . how had the Boss of Bosses, at the age of seventy-three, been reduced to this?

'He's living in this dump', said the Sicilian crime writer Andrea Camilleri. 'He's got candles, because maybe the electricity goes off . . . but he knows he's got power. He's a multi-billionaire. Provenzano is the living embodiment of the Sicilian saying *meglio commandare che fottere:* it's better to rule people than to screw them.'[1]

The old man living in a cramped shepherd's hut was, in spite of appearances, the centre of Cosa Nostra's operations. People sent for his advice, his blessing, his introductions, his judgement. 'People weren't looking for him to arrest him', wrote journalist Salvo Palazzolo. 'They were seeking him out to ask his considered opinion.'

Not one bulldozer moved without his say-so. Multi-million-dollar deals were made on his word. And all these instructions were contained in little Sellotaped notes, banged out on a manual typewriter and carried from hand to hand. After his arrest the hideout was searched inch by inch, every carrier bag inspected and noted down. But the more they found, the more mysterious, if anything, his personality became.

'You could think he was a peasant living in the country', observed assistant prosecutor Michele Prestipino, who had been on Provenzano's trail for eight years. 'He had all the props – the cheese, bread and onion, the simple pious lifestyle – he had constructed a whole rustic image, but then we discovered he had a wardrobe full of silk jackets, cashmere sweaters, clothes from the most upmarket stores in Palermo. He led us to think he's a rough countryman, when all the time – and this is my theory – he'd been staying in a massive apartment in the middle of Palermo, living the life of a bourgeois pensioner.

'He had seventeen cases containing his stuff: winter pyjamas, summer pyjamas, four vanity cases with manicure sets and very nice products. It was clear that living in this shepherd's cottage was not his normal life. His possessions, the products he uses, would not have seemed out of place in any professional's house. This was no peasant living rough.' Provenzano even had a battery-operated device for trimming nose and ear hairs: he was clearly not a man who lived his whole life among peasants.

'Provenzano is a chameleon', says Giuseppe Gualtieri. 'You'd see him in an immaculate suit in the finest drawing-rooms in Palermo, and he'd look as if he belonged there. You'd see him in the country, in an old pair of trousers and an anorak, looking like a shepherd. There are one or two collaborators who say they've seen him dressed as a priest – and apparently he looked the part. Provenzano's great skill is this ability to adapt . . . it is also his greatest weapon.'

From one viewpoint the cheesemaker's hut in Corleone was a perfectly calculated last staging post for the Boss of Bosses. The message implied by this improbably humble setting was: if this malodorous hovel is where the godfather has been holed up, the Mafia can't be as powerful as we thought.

Provenzano was acutely aware of the importance of messages and symbols in the Mafia's secret communication system, and of the uses of propaganda. Whatever message his circumstances sent out was intended.

Provenzano had rescued Cosa Nostra from disaster. He had taken over the organization when the Mafia's political connections were losing traction and its leaders were trying to impose their will on the state by means of extreme violence.

Under the leadership of Luciano Liggio, Provenzano and his brothers in arms had transformed the Corleone Mafia from a machine that guaranteed the status quo into an expansionist force determined to dominate Cosa Nostra. They broke every rule of the old Mafia and blew apart the families that had run Palermo for generations, with an audacity and savagery that had never been seen before. The partnership between Totò Riina and Bernardo Provenzano, who took over as joint leaders after Liggio's conviction, was greatly feared: Riina had muscle and determination; Provenzano had a political mind and contacts. And at the same time both were fugitives, scarcely known outside their own circles: under cover they wreaked devastation by setting families against each other.

But the differences between them became increasingly marked, and Riina, maddened with power, ceased to listen to his old friend. Provenzano remained in the shadows as Cosa Nostra waged war on the state, and as the tide turned against them, he began to keep his distance from Riina, building his contacts, counselling prudence, taking a long view. And when the strategy of violence backfired, threatening to destroy Cosa Nostra, Provenzano finally emerged to take control.

After years of political assassinations, internecine fighting and hundreds of arrests, the Mafia capos were disoriented. The soldiers were suffering from trauma, and many had 'repented' and confessed their role in the organization. These so-called *pentiti* were the greatest threat to Cosa Nostra. Terrible things had been done in the name of the organization, and it badly needed a new way forward.

'Provenzano became head of Cosa Nostra not because he was the last godfather left standing', wrote Michele Prestipino and Salvo Palazzolo, 'but because he was the only one capable of forging the new Cosa Nostra, adapting it to the demands of the time.'

Most mafiosi had never seen him. Investigators had long believed him seriously ill. More than once over the years since his disappearance in 1969, Provenzano had been pronounced dead. The most recent announcement had come just two weeks before his arrest, when his lawyer had made an extraordinary announcement. 'Bernardo Provenzano has been dead for years. The Mafia has created a phantom.'[2]

The conspiracy theorists and Mafia watchers puzzled over the significance of this. It seems his lawyer was announcing the death of the bandit who sowed terror in Corleone, the wild beast who killed at least forty people with his own hands, the unstoppable criminal known as 'the Tractor'. These were shadows, ghosts, the lawyer seemed to declare. The old Provenzano no longer existed.

The new model of the Mafia boss was a far more sophisticated version. 'The new founding father of Cosa Nostra, the great reformer', one recent book calls him.[3]

'Provenzano's role?' mused the Boss's former right-hand man, Nino Giuffré, on the witness stand. 'I could tell you exactly what it was: he gave the orders. But it was more complex than that. He came up with a new strategy for Cosa Nostra. He wanted to preserve the rules of Cosa Nostra, which had been corroded. And he had an impressive number of contacts in every area of Italian life.'

Provenzano's rescue of Cosa Nostra from the brink of defeat is an extraordinary story, from which the heads of corporations have much to learn. The culture he instilled, and his successful restoration of old values with new methods, could be a fruitful management guide in some industries – and I have included a chapter ('A management handbook for the aspiring Mafia boss') that lays out his guidelines for turning around a failing business.

Over the days that followed his arrest, satisfaction at the capture of the man who had been a persistent embarrassment to Italian justice was quickly replaced by angry questions about why he had been allowed to live freely for so long without ever straying far from home. It seems likely that his 'contacts' in high places allowed him to remain at large because he created an organization they could live with.

'He was protected by professionals, politicians, businessmen, law enforcers', said chief anti-Mafia prosecutor Pietro Grasso. 'We have found them all represented in our investigations, so we had to conclude that he was protected not just by a criminal organization but by entire sectors of society. I believe that it isn't a single politician who has protected Provenzano all these years but a political system.'

'Provenzano believed that Cosa Nostra could co-exist with the state, cohabit with it, that there was no need to destroy it', says assistant prosecutor Alfonso Sabella. 'He recruited followers among those who played a role in civil society, and infiltrated the organs of state with his own people. His philosophy was, I'll get inside the state and take what I can. I don't need to take it all.'

'He is the Mafia: they're one and the same', says Sabella's sister Marzia, also an assistant prosecutor. 'He is a great mediator. A little obsessive-compulsive . . . He is capable of great thinking. If he hadn't been a Mafia boss, he could have been a lawyer, a businessman. He doesn't give a damn about killing someone over an act of disrespect; he's much more concerned about making money.'

'He kept himself below the radar', recalls General Angiolo Pellegrini, a carabiniere who has spent years on Provenzano's trail. 'He rarely saw anyone, or let himself be seen. He didn't stick his head over the parapet. In the end the others all followed his line – they realized his ideas were right.'

Provenzano is the only Mafia boss we have come to know so intimately through his own words, and through the words (either intercepted or spoken on the witness stand) of his former friends and advisers. Other bosses before him have been revealed only through the words of their enemies.

We have access to a personal and political profile of Provenzano, thanks to his friend, traitor and unofficial biographer Nino Giuffré, boss of the mountain-top town of Caccamo (dubbed the Switzerland of Cosa Nostra, because so much Mafia money ran through it). Giuffré has revealed his likes and dislikes, his anxieties, ambitions, friendships, his pity and generosity. Men who would rather shoot than talk had to admire Provenzano's skilled mediation, his quiet authority.

There is, of course, a human story behind the political intrigues of organized crime – a story of friendship betrayed, of great personal loss, of relationships destroyed by the demands of Cosa Nostra: the officers working seven days a week on the trail of the fugitive, who sacrificed their personal lives for their duty; the boss's sons, who had terrible problems trying to create a relationship with their father and to lead their own lives; the wife, who stuck by her man through the years, only to be sent away, for the safety of her children; the old man, sick and alone, deserted by friends, betrayed by his closest advisers.

Giuffré has revealed details of how the long-term fugitives lived – sometimes in luxury, sometimes in reduced and pitiful conditions. He has recalled the small kindnesses they showed each other – a cake at Easter, boxes of citrus fruit at Christmas and their favourite pasta sauce. Under examination in court Giuffré was asked to interpret a note on which was written, 'Thank you for the bottles of sauce'. Was it code for money? A concealed weapon? No, Giuffré replied, the guy likes home-made tomato sauce, so I sent him some. Sometimes a bottle of tomato sauce is just . . . tomato sauce.'

Provenzano's family lived for years in western Sicily without ever being identified as the relations of Italy's most wanted. The boys grew up learning to live quietly, never drawing attention to themselves. Their father missed their teenage years almost entirely, which made it extremely difficult for them to revive a relationship with him in their twenties. He tried to make sure they did not follow in his footsteps, which inevitably created a painful distance between them.

I've always been fascinated by the human lives behind the Mafia, people living in a parallel society in which they do not have the freedom of choice that the rest of us enjoy. The family of a Mafia boss is required to obey the needs of an organization that, while giving them power and prestige, robs them of their loved ones.

Before Giuffré's revelations it was very difficult to get an understanding of Provenzano. Through his letters, the accounts of his consiglieri and close supporters we are beginning to get a picture of an extraordinary leader, and a complicated man, who transformed a violent beginning into a political career.

I arrived in Sicily in 1992, after the second major outrage of that terrible summer: the murder of Paolo Borsellino and five bodyguards. Palermo was on its feet, marching in protest, enraged, grieving, wounded. Women went on hunger strike in the throbbing heat of Piazza Politeama, demanding the resignation of the justice minister. We painted slogans on sheets to hang from balconies and carry through the streets.

In the following weeks, while working on a book about women in the Mafia, I interviewed many people who really believed that this time the Mafia had gone too far, that it had tipped the balance and that at last things were going to change. Women who had lived in Mafia families all their lives were taking the stand to testify against the killers who had ravaged their neighbourhoods and their families.

This was the situation when Bernardo Provenzano took over the organization, with public opinion turning against Cosa Nostra for the first time in recent memory; with mafiosi defecting in their hundreds.

But returning to the city over the following years, it was as though none of that popular uprising had happened. Investigators and magistrates felt abandoned by the state, which no longer offered them protection. The ruling classes had gone back to denying the existence of the Mafia and denouncing TV documentaries about Cosa Nostra as bad for Sicily's image.

I wanted to discover more about the man who had brought about this astonishing transformation and restored the Mafia's grip on Sicilian society. No one seemed to know anything about him. No one even seemed to agree on whether he played an important role or was merely a gunslinger. To have become so powerful while remaining in the shadows was an extraordinary achievement. It shows tenacity, humility, caution and calculation. To live as a fugitive relying on the generosity of others for forty years requires more than power: he commanded tremendous loyalty. Whatever one thinks of Provenzano's chosen career it is hard not to be impressed by the manner in which he rescued the organization from the edge of disaster.

I

Corleone bandits

ON A SPRING NIGHT in 1958 four horsemen galloped across a farm on the plain below Corleone and rode up to one of the barns. They crept inside carrying axes and shovels, and smashed the wine barrels, splintering the seasoned wood and releasing rivers of strong red wine.

The raiders worked for Luciano Liggio, a low-life peasant upstart and cattle rustler. They wanted this farm and were determined to drive the farmer off his own land.

The corn ripened and stood, growing darker, and no one dared to cut it. The local peasant workers had been threatened with death if any of them went to harvest that land. Finally the farmer and a few hired hands went out before dawn, working in fear and haste. But no one would thresh the corn, so it lay where it had been cut until Liggio's men came with their trucks, loaded it up and drove it away.

The vines with their purple grapes were smashed and burned. The cattle's water troughs, set in cement and fed with pipes from a spring, were stacked with explosives and blown up. One night the gang turned up at the farm store with a truck and held the guard hostage with his own hunting rifle while they loaded up seventy barrels of pecorino cheese. As a final insult they stole the rifle.

When the farmer had nothing left to lose, he finally called the police. The thieves, all of them well known in the local community, were rounded up and escorted to the station. So, at the age of twenty-five, Bernardo Provenzano got his first criminal charge, for stealing cheese.

The police mugshot shows a clean-faced young man in jacket and tie, with his curly hair carefully greased back and an insolent look.

This mugshot would be the only record of his existence for many years to come. It would be aged by computer, studied by psychological profilers, examined by investigators. His pale, deep-set eyes and prominent cheekbones, immortalized in that black-and-white photo, reveal little of the man except for his square-jawed peasant stock and his fearlessness. A cheese thief, and a good shot – he could shoot a hole in a coin thrown up in the air – he was known to his friends as Binnu.

The other members of Liggio's gang were: Giuseppe Ruffino, Liggio's lieutenant, who had the same violent streak; Calogero Bagarella, son of a Mafia family and the only one younger than Provenzano; and Giovanni Pasqua, Liggio's childhood friend and brother in arms. They would be joined by others, most notably Bagarella's younger brother Leoluca, and Salvatore (Totò) Riina, who became Provenzano's friend and running mate. All of them were ambitious, like their leader, to move beyond the confines of Corleone – of hunger, blistered hands and animal stench. To these young men the Mafia represented the only way to climb out of poverty, and in Liggio they had a leader whose ruthlessness gave them inspiration.

Binnu was silent and diffident; when they were waiting for orders or discussing their next move, he seemed moody and sullen, and always had a question or an objection to make. But once he had decided on a course of action, nothing would stop him. Totò was more sociable, teasing and ragging his mates, always ready with a put-down to make everyone laugh. He was the only one who joshed Binnu; the others kept a little more distance.

Liggio, an aggressive little man who suffered from a debilitating condition of the spine and a vicious temper, had no sentimental attachment to the rural poverty in which he was raised. As a teenager, realizing he would never get far as an illiterate farm-hand, he went to find the schoolmistress and told her she must teach him to read and write or he'd set fire to her house.

Like many young men who later became mafiosi, Liggio began his career as an estate guard, protecting the wealth of absentee landlords. In 1948 he murdered the young trade union activist Placido Rizzotto, who had been heading a campaign to defend peasants' land rights. Liggio marched his victim out into the rocky countryside, where he shot him and threw his body into one of the deep ravines at the foot of the mountains. Liggio's status rose with that cold-blooded murder: ridding Corleone of a troublesome advocate of peasants' rights went down well with a certain class of landowner. Provenzano was fifteen when Rizzotto was killed, and had been working among the peasants for over half his short life. He admired the way Liggio dealt with the problem and got away with it. He saw that the community, and the dead man's family, were powerless to raise a hand against the young mafioso.

Provenzano's other important model as a young man was the Mafia boss of Corleone, the eminent doctor Michele Navarra. An educated man from a middle-class family, Navarra was well connected in politics and industry, and wielded considerable power in the region. In Corleone, Dr Navarra was known as *padre nostru*, Our Father. He had many political friends but would not hesitate to switch allegiance from one party to another if it offered him an advantage – a lesson that was not lost on the young Provenzano. The talents he later developed for mediating between the Mafia and political power, switching between political parties, combining traditional values with forward-looking pragmatism, were all learned from Dr Navarra.

When Navarra began to receive petitions from farm owners across the county, begging him to put a stop to Liggio's gang's nightly raids, he ordered Liggio to stop stealing cattle. Liggio's response was to force landowners to sell their acres to him and to start a cattle ranch stocked almost entirely with stolen livestock and run by Provenzano, Riina and the others. They drove the illegally butchered meat down to the market in Palermo; Provenzano rode shotgun on the trucks, but once his boss had witnessed his cool-headed efficiency with a pistol, he became Liggio's best hit man.

The two young friends, Provenzano and Riina, were Liggio's lieutenants and bodyguards. They were both short: neither more than five foot six, but Binnu was strong and thick set, with a muscular neck and broad shoulders. Totò was shorter (his nickname was *u curtu*, 'Shorty'), with a lighter build and dark, shifty eyes. They both wore their thick, dark curly hair shaved at the nape and greased back. They were both extremely respectful of their boss and careful never to arouse his wrath.

'Liggio had a look that struck fear even in us mafiosi', a *pentito* later admitted. 'It took only the slightest thing to get him worked up, and then there would be a strange light in his eyes that silenced everyone around . . . You could sense death hovering in the air. He was changeable and moody as a child.'[4] From handling Liggio's capricious demands Provenzano learned the diplomatic skills that would become his greatest asset.

Liggio was determined to take on Navarra and the Palermo Mafia, and he found a way to do it: water. Cosa Nostra controlled the supply of water to the lemon and mandarin groves in Palermo's 'Golden Basin'. A proposal to build a dam to supply Palermo would bypass the Palermo bosses, and Liggio was determined to get his hands on it. The dam project became the central issue of a forthcoming election. Liggio dragged his young thugs off their horses, smartened them up and sent them out with leaflets campaigning for the candidate who supported the dam.

As far as Navarra was concerned, the dam would never be built: the projected reservoir would flood land belonging to his friends, but, more importantly, it would disrupt the Mafia's lucrative monopoly of the water system. He threw his weight behind the Christian Democrat candidate, who opposed the dam.

Next to Navarra, Liggio was a novice at politics. Hundreds of Corleonesi reportedly went blind on election day, so that Dr Navarra could accompany them into the polling booth and make sure they put their cross in the right place.

The Christian Democrats enjoyed a comfortable win, and Liggio was incensed. A long period of skirmishing between Liggio and Navarra erupted into open war. The feud between the two men laid waste to a generation of Corleonesi, with over fifty murders, twenty-two attempted murders and many more 'disappeared'.

Early one morning in June 1958 Liggio staged an ambush for Navarra. On the winding country road to Corleone, where pine trees measured out the miles and the verges plunged down into deep ditches, Liggio blocked the road with his car and lay in wait. When Navarra came driving along with another doctor, he was forced off the road and blasted by several guns. As the car was ripped full of holes, both doctors died in a storm of bullets and broken glass.

Gunning down Navarra was a reckless crime, and Liggio's men had to keep fighting or risk a revenge attack. Provenzano organized a meeting with a delegation from the enemy ranks, to demand they hand over the men who had shot at his master. They refused, knowing that they would have been making less a peace offering than a bloody sacrifice.

On a September evening the procession for the Madonna of the Chain was weaving its way through the streets of Corleone, the drums and trumpets playing, the people, some of them barefoot, droning their tragic hymns to the statue of the Virgin as she was carried around the town. Liggio's killers ran through the crowds, chasing Navarra's men. They were shooting back and forth, narrowly missing the screaming crowds, who crammed themselves into doorways and clasped their children to them. Several bystanders were hit. Three of Navarra's men were killed as they ran, but as the gunmen tried to escape, their route was blocked by the angry crowd, and Provenzano was shot in the head. He collapsed on the pavement, blood pouring from the wound. Ruffino stopped a passing car and lifted him into the back, ordering the driver to take him to hospital.

While he was recovering, Provenzano told the carabinieri he had been walking along, heading for the cinema and minding his own business, when something had hit him in the head and he'd lost consciousness. He had no idea what had happened.

He got away with it. Provenzano had begun to get a reputation for immunity: his fellow gang members, including his friend Totò Riina, had been arrested and served time in the reeking county prison. Not Binnu. He'd even got off military service after a brief stint in the air force, dismissed on medical grounds, with a glowing conduct report, after six months. In 1960 the police commissioner in Corleone proposed that he be put under special surveillance, and the Palermo court ordered that he be banished to the prison island of Ustica for four years. But he stayed in Corleone, and after a few months the order was withdrawn. This ability to evade the spotlight of investigation, while earning a reputation for ruthlessness and murder, was to become a great asset.

As far as Provenzano's family was concerned, the boy was doing all right. 'In the 1950s the Mafia was the only means they had to climb the social scale', says historian Salvatore Lupo. 'They did not join out of idealism, but purely material concerns: survival, affirmation and power, money. These are people from modest families. They've done well for themselves in the Mafia.'

Nino Giuffré, who worked as a teacher, recalled that when he was initiated into the Mafia, his boss said to him: 'Now you're a rich man indeed. You're already a Sicilian, and you'll be wealthy too.'

Binnu's parents were a poor peasant couple, Angelo Provenzano and Giovanna Rigoglioso. He was born in Corleone on 31 January 1933, the third of seven brothers and sisters. Peasant labourers in those days gathered in the chill of dawn and waited to be called by name, by the all-powerful farm managers. A day's hard work in the fields would scarcely bring in enough to feed nine, and the crowded house-hold was occasionally sullen with hunger. Binnu dropped out after the second year of primary school, semi-literate, and went to work in the fields with his father. While most boys his age struggled on for another few years in class, he was living on his wits at the age of seven.

His father died in 1958, when Binnu was already established as part of Liggio's notorious armed gang. His sisters, Rosa, Maria Concetta and Michela Arcangela, had all married local boys, but his brothers still lived at home, and his mother, who pressed and starched their shirts, barely knew where they were most of the time. Binnu would get home in the early evening and eat supper, then he would be out of the door.

She suffered a good deal from worrying about the company he kept, but at least he came home at night. Soon he would have to drop out of sight, and for the rest of her life she would see him only fleetingly, on secret visits.

On 9 May 1963 four men, Provenzano among them, met at first light on the edge of Corleone, shotguns slung over their backs. They were waiting for one of Navarra's men, Francesco Streva, who was living in hiding, but Binnu had information that he was due to pass that way. Streva was always armed, and extremely cautious. When Provenzano caught sight of him that May morning, he called out to him. Streva fired at the group and took off across the fields. The gang dispersed, and for the next few months they lived in hiding, staying with trusted family members, meeting after dark, plotting how to kill their enemies and avoid being killed. It was Provenzano's first taste of exile, and although he didn't go far from home, he experienced the profound loneliness and exhilarating freedom of living in hiding, which would become his daily reality.

Months later Provenzano contacted Streva, offering to meet for peace talks. They made an appointment early in the morning of 10 September, in the wooded countryside near Corleone. Above them lowered the imposing and craggy Rocca Busambra, an impenetrable hiding place for bandits and outlaws.

A local farmer taking out his flock heard shots and looked out across the field to see two men, one of whom he recognized as Provenzano, both carrying guns, making off towards the shadowy foot of the mountain. Later that day Streva's body was found in the woods, along-side two of his men.

The dead men's grieving relatives reported the murders to the police – an unusually drastic and risky move in such a small commu-nity. But the sense of outrage was high, and its target was Liggio's thugs, in particular Bernardo Provenzano.

The police reaction to the Corleone Mafia's activities had thus far been muted. Liggio himself, already a notorious criminal, had been served a polite request by the police to 'live honestly, respect persons and property, and observe the law'. But after the murders of Streva and his men, people who had been threatened and intimidated, robbed and driven off the land, finally rebelled and signed witness statements. A joint report by Corleone's police and carabinieri landed on the Palermo prosecutor's desk, accusing Provenzano of aggravated murder. In spite of numerous witnesses, when the first major case against Provenzano eventually came to court, he was acquitted. He had confronted his enemies face to face, been shot in the head, arrested and tried – it seemed nothing could touch him.

Provenzano's burning ambition was to make it in the city. Through their gradual takeover of the illegal meat market Liggio, Provenzano and the rest of the Corleone clan made the journey from their rural home town to the capital of Cosa Nostra.

Palermo was a busy, overcrowded town, swarming with country folk moving off the land and desperate to make a living. The narrow, noisy neighbourhood markets heaved with meat trucked in from the hinterland and fish freshly caught: swordfish with their great glassy eyes and fat tuna like rubber tyres. Stalls were piled high with huge fennel bulbs and fragrant tomatoes. Watermelons were piled up on street corners like bowling balls, the vendors calling out, *o molone!*

As an enforcer for Liggio's urban loan-sharking business, Provenzano came into contact with a better class of victim. The moneylending business was based in the centre of the old city, by the bronze lions of the Teatro Massimo. It became a massive money-laundering operation, and the businessmen who 'invested' money to be lent to clients at extortionate levels of interest included drug traffickers with links to American mobsters.

In the early 1960s Palermo was the scene of an outbreak of savage violence. War broke out over control of drug trafficking between two Palermo clans, the aristocratic and apparently respectable Greco family and the upstart La Barberas. They fought in the crowded streets and markets of Palermo and in other cities further afield; Angelo La Barbera was shot and seriously wounded in Milan. In Palermo mafiosi exchanged gunfire over bar tables; a famous gun battle was fought across a fish stall, blood mingling with ice and mussel shells flying as men dived for cover, firing from behind dripping swordfish and tuna.

The war reached its grisly climax when a car bomb killed seven policemen. An Alfa Romeo Giulietta had been abandoned with a flat tyre near Mafia boss Salvatore Greco's palatial villa in Ciaculli, a leafy outpost of Palermo. Responding to a tip-off, carabinieri sealed off the area and saw a crude device on the back seat of the car. Once the bomb had been defused, they searched the car for clues. One officer opened the boot, setting off a massive explosion. The Ciaculli bomb was calamitous: after years of impunity it brought down the full weight of the law against the Mafia.

Nearly two thousand arrests were made, and Liggio was captured the following year, in November 1964. After making a hasty escape from a Palermo clinic, he had sought refuge with two sisters, spinsters, in Corleone, who nursed him back to health. In a peculiar twist, one of the women had been engaged to a man Liggio had murdered, the trade unionist Placido Rizzotto. Liggio's 'possession' of his victim's fiancée was the ultimate insult.

The prosecutor who signed an indictment against Luciano Liggio and 115 members of the criminal underworld in response to the Mafia war was Cesare Terranova, a judge of great courage and diligence. Terranova also oversaw the creation of a parliamentary anti-Mafia commission, which delivered regular reports on the latest intelligence on organized crime. The state had finally mounted a co-ordinated response to Mafia violence that had made whole areas of Sicily unliveable.

After the crackdown the Mafia's ruling body was hastily disbanded, and the various families went to ground. Liggio ordered a cessation of all criminal activity. But once the killings stopped, the pressure from law enforcement let up a little and allowed the Mafia to regroup. It was a lesson that Provenzano did not forget and would later use to great advantage.

Terranova had understood that the Corleonesi's activities extended far beyond cattle rustling, murder and extortion. His report detailed the bloody years of the vendetta between Navarra and Liggio. But it also demonstrated how the Corleonesi had moved beyond their rural home in the shadow of Rocca Busambra, extending their insidious influence over Palermo and the rest of western Sicily, through their political contacts. They had, he explained, 'got control of areas ripe for development, by seizing key posts within the public and private administration'.

The trial took place in Calabria, to avoid any possible jury-rigging or corruption of magistrates. There was no court of law big enough to hold so many defendants and their lawyers, so the proceedings took place in a primary school. Among Liggio's protégés, Provenzano and Calogero Bagarella were still on the run, although Riina and Leoluca Bagarella, two angry young men, were in the dock. Strangely enough, the prosecution's star witness seemed to have suffered some sort of breakdown and, having denied everything in court, spent the rest of his life confined to a mental asylum. The trial ended in a raft of acquittals.

The following year Liggio and sixty-two others went on trial in Bari. Provenzano, Ruffino and Bagarella remained in hiding. Yet again Riina was in the dock; yet again the prosecution case was sabotaged. One prosecution witness, a Corleone barber who had seen Provenzano and the others firing at three of Navarra's men, retracted his statement in court and disappeared shortly after the trial. When the prosecution produced the shattered brake lights from Navarra's car, collected at the scene of the shoot-out, they realized the glass had been switched for another make of car.

Magistrates demanded life sentences for Liggio, Provenzano and Bagarella. But on 10 June 1969 the court acquitted every one of them on grounds of insufficient evidence (Riina alone was given a small penalty for receiving stolen goods). Provenzano and Bagarella were cleared of the triple murder of Navarra's men in the forest above Corleone. The judges claimed that the culture of *omertà* had made it impossible to prove anything against the defendants, and Liggio was cleared of murdering Navarra, for lack of evidence. This was in spite of a report by the carabiniere colonel Carlo Alberto Dalla Chiesa, warning that Liggio was 'to be considered one of the most dangerous elements that the province of Palermo has ever contributed to the history of the Mafia'.

Provenzano and Riina continued to work for Liggio, who now had a place on the ruling body, known as the 'commission', and behaved like a capricious child – they were continually having to smooth over problems he had needlessly created. Liggio liked to sunbathe naked, and when he was living on the run, in a villa lent him by a man of honour in Catania, disported himself on the terrace in full view of the neighbouring apartments. One sunny day he received a summons from the local police. Since there was already a warrant out for his arrest, he sent Binnu down to the station to find out what they wanted. Provenzano didn't know whether the police had identified the notorious fugitive; when he was told that the neighbour had merely made a complaint about Liggio's naked sunbathing, he was not amused.

Dodging a police hunt, Provenzano moved constantly around western Sicily, from the Mafia stronghold of San Giuseppe Iato, a traffic-choked little town in the hills inland from Palermo, to Cinisi, another Mafia fortress between the mountains and the sea. He was sheltered by mafiosi who knew that none of the locals, not the old men sitting in their circle of chairs in the square, not the heavily pregnant young mothers struggling with shopping and children, or even the local priest, would ever say a word about a stranger in town.

During the mid-1960s Provenzano was sought by police more assiduously than at any time during the next twenty-five years. The experience gained during this time on the run stood him in good stead when he later became Italy's most wanted. He understood how much people put themselves out to shelter a fugitive, and tried to return the favour with as much grace as he could muster. As he travelled around, moving at night and staying indoors most of the day, there were several close calls. In Castronovo, a small and secluded town high in the mountains north of Agrigento, he and his friends were ambushed by carabinieri. The stone-built town has a church in every square, where the people took cover from ricocheting bullets as the carabinieri pursued the outlaws through the streets, both sides firing as they ran.

Liggio moved to northern Italy, to make serious money, and Binnu followed him. Milan was becoming a major financial capital, and as the Mafia moved in, it gained a reputation as the New York of organized crime. Police got a tip-off that Binnu always drank his morning espresso at the same bar in Turin. They staked out the place for two weeks, but there was no sign of him.

The Corleonesi were almost all living on the run, moving around and dodging arrest warrants. This underground existence became one of their most feared traits: not even the other Mafia families knew who they were or what they looked like. This increased their fearsome reputation: you never saw them, you only saw the bodies in the aftermath of their passing. Provenzano's mystique grew: no one knew for sure whether he was just a hit man or held a more important role. The fact that he had evaded the authorities successfully while notching up several murders increased the mythology around him.

During these years the old city of Palermo was being consumed by a building boom that would see the destruction of much of the city's charm and most of its green spaces. The Palermo families were infiltrating local government and development companies to cream off a substantial fortune from the building frenzy. Power struggles between families culminated in a massacre that changed the course of Mafia history. And it was this terrible event that gave Provenzano his next big chance.

On 10 December 1969 the builder Girolamo Moncada was holding a late meeting in his office in viale Lazio, the centre of a spate of new development, on the western side of the city. It was attended by, among others, his sons, the firm's accountant and the Mafia capo Michele Cavataio. Not unusually, all the men were armed.

Cavataio, described as 'a cunning killer with a face like a gorilla and a turbulent past', was suspected of inciting the Mafia war, setting families against each other and creating suspicion and trouble. Finding himself pushed aside by the new generation, he had built a powerful, if unofficial, group of older capos around him and orchestrated a series of murders.

After the war was over, tensions were still running high in Palermo, and Cavataio represented a common enemy. He attempted to blackmail his way out of trouble by boasting that he had drawn a map of the Palermo Mafia families, including the names of all the members. The police had no knowledge of the Mafia groupings or the identity of the various families – even making such a map was dangerous. While the boss of Catania went through the motions of negotiating with him, Salvatore Greco, whose villa had been partly destroyed by the bomb at Ciaculli, put together a group of hit men, with Bernardo Provenzano at the head.[5]

At 7.30 on that December evening two police cars stopped outside Moncada's office. While Totò Riina stayed in one of the cars to direct operations, six men in police uniform ran towards the building. Bernardo Provenzano and his friend Calogero Bagarella were in the lead, followed by Damiano Caruso, from the Riesi family. They burst into Moncada's office, pointing machine guns and shouting 'Freeze!' Before anyone could think about moving, Caruso opened fire – destroying the advantage of surprise. One man was shot in the chest and fell. The accountant managed to fire a shot but was hit in the stomach. Moncada's sons were hit several times. Cavataio ducked behind a table and returned fire, shooting Bagarella full in the chest. He caught Provenzano in the hand, then dived under the desk, playing dead.

The order was to set fire to the office. The men looked around at the corpses and at the wounded groaning on the floor. Provenzano wanted that map. He'd heard that Cavataio kept it hidden in his sock, so he grabbed his ankles and started pulling. As he heaved, he felt some resistance and realized that Cavataio was still alive. As they struggled, Cavataio, who had his gun in his hand, tried to shoot Provenzano in the face, but he had run out of bullets. Provenzano was trying to shoot him with his machine gun, but it jammed, so he clubbed him unconscious with the butt. When he got a hand free, he drew his own handgun and shot him point-blank.

The shoot-out had lasted just a few minutes and left five men dead. Provenzano, covered in blood, carried his friend's body out to the waiting cars and heaved him into the boot. They buried him secretly on top of another body in the Corleone cemetery.

The viale Lazio massacre became one of the most notorious events in the history of Cosa Nostra, and nearly forty years later the trial of its alleged protagonists, now old men, is still ongoing. Although there were initially protests against the high-handed way the assassination of Cavataio had been decided and executed by the Palermo families, the other clans no longer had the stomach for a fight, and the Grecos, with their ambitious allies the Corleonesi, consolidated their power.

There were lessons for Provenzano from viale Lazio too, as the historian Salvatore Lupo explains: 'A frontal attack such as that is a highly unusual event in Mafia history. Usually the adversaries circle each other, one of them falls into a trap and is disappeared, or there's a set-up and someone tries to shoot him.

'The Mafia is not made up of gangs who shoot at each other. The horror of that attack brought down the full weight of law enforcement. The Mafia manages to operate undisturbed when it doesn't hurt anyone. Any mafioso who understands that, tries to do business and settle disputes without creating a massive disturbance.'

A disturbance had most definitely been made, and yet the shoot-out prepared the ground for Provenzano's promotion. His reputation for tenacity was affirmed, as was his nickname, *u' tratturi* ('the Tractor'), because, as one collaborator expressed it, 'where he passed, the grass no longer grew'. He was unstoppable, dogged and fiercely determined. The country boys from Corleone were discovering that, wherever you are from, violence is power.

After his acquittal in Bari, Liggio spent most of his time being treated in clinics in northern Italy. In December 1970 the court of appeal sentenced him to life for the double murder of Dr Navarra and his colleague. But by this time he was nowhere to be found.

In Liggio's absence Totò Riina represented him on the ruling commission of Cosa Nostra, making up the triumvirate with Gaetano Badalamenti, the boss of Cinisi, and Stefano Bontate, the 'prince of Villagrazia'. Riina was ambitious and steely, sarcastic and intolerant of mistakes. It would not be long before the Corleone cuckoo shoved his fellow commission members out of the nest.

One Palermo mafioso voiced the alarm of many Palermitani, who knew the Corleonesi had their sights on the city: 'What's Riina going to do in Palermo, if we're all united? We'll give him a kick up the arse and send him back to Corleone to grow corn.'[6] Going back to the rural Mafia was the last thing on Riina and Provenzano's agenda, and everybody knew it.

The new bosses of Corleone were an unknown entity. They had started out as rustic bandits, thugs and killers, and made careers for themselves in Cosa Nostra – not the usual trajectory for a Mafia boss, points out Salvatore Lupo. 'Liggio was defined as a gangster and a killer, which does not correspond to the usual model of capomafia.'

Until that point Mafia bosses had come from dynasties raised on organized crime. These Corleonesi had no such pedigree.

Riina was bitter about men of honour like Bontate, who came from middle-class, old-money families. 'He was crazed with jealousy and envy', said Francesco Di Carlo. 'He was drunk with power.

'I said to him once, "You've got it in for these people because they come from a big dynasty that goes back hundreds of years, great-great-grandfathers who got rich in Cosa Nostra, and you had no one before you, not even your father. . . ." His family were poor, some of them had been in prison, they were dirt poor. I remember doing a whip-round and giving him money for the Corleone family's legal expenses.'

Riina never lost that instinctive need to overcome the poverty of his roots: when he made millions later in his career, he bought land – the peasant's dream – land of his own. Provenzano would return to the countryside when he had to, holding meetings in farm buildings and sleeping in sheep sheds, but he didn't have the same need to possess land. But for now the two friends' ambitions centred on the city.

Circumstances were in their favour. In 1972 Badalamenti and Bontate were arrested, and while the older bosses were in prison, Riina continued his relentless rise. Even though kidnapping had been outlawed, the Corleonesi snatched prisoners on other families' territory, causing huge embarrassment and making large amounts of ransom money.

Nino Calderone, whose brother was the boss of Catania, like others on both sides of the law, regarded the Corleonesi as a new breed, unlike any mafiosi they had dealt with before. 'The heads of the Corleonesi were incredibly ignorant, but they were cunning, like devils, and at the same time they were smart and ferocious, which is a rare combination in Cosa Nostra.

'Toto Riina had intuition and intelligence and was difficult to fathom and very hard to predict. At the same time he was savage. His philosophy was that if someone's finger hurt, it was better to cut off his whole arm just to make sure.

'Binnu Provenzano was nicknamed*u viddanu,* "the lout", because of his fine manners. My brother called him *u tratturi,* "the Tractor", after his skill as a murderer, and after the effect he had on any problems, or people, he had to deal with.'

Riina and Provenzano had built on their different strengths and respected their differences; as their reputations grew, few others felt comfortable around them, and they never needed to justify their actions to each other. They knew where they came from and what they wanted to achieve. Riina, backed by Provenzano, had taken Liggio's place. As the situation required, Provenzano would transform himself from a ruthless killer into a political operator.

In 1970 the court of appeal in Bari found Bernardo Provenzano and Salvatore Riina guilty of conspiracy and banned them for life from holding public office. Fortunately for them, they didn't need to occupy any public office in person. They had someone to do it for them. Their key political contact was Vito Ciancimino, the son of a Corleone barber and one of the most corrupt and malign influences on the Palermo political scene.

Ambitious, greedy and self-obsessed, Ciancimino would take the Corleonesi a long way.

2

Palermo ambitions

AT THE END of the 1950s the landscape of Palermo began to change rapidly. The price of property soared as land became available for development and people left the countryside and moved into the city for work. Beautiful Liberty villas, with elaborate brickwork and elegant balconies, were pulled down. One famously lovely villa on via Libertà was bulldozed in the middle of the night, just before a protection order came into force. The nineteenth-century villas surrounded by lovely gardens were swept away, replaced by multi-storey apartment blocks, ugly cement and glass constructions jammed close to each other.

Restoring the crumbling palazzi in the heart of the city was considered too expensive, so the carved stone balconies were left to collapse, windows buckled and cracked, and parts of the roofs fell in. The old gardens, untended, were parched and rubbish-strewn. Residents of the old palazzi would have their water and electricity cut off in a bid to force them out of the old quarters and into the new flats on the edge of town. The families who moved in, often penniless immigrants, lived in conditions worse than anything they had left behind.

The commissioner for public works at this time was Vito Ciancimino, the son of a barber from Corleone, whose relentless ambition was visible in his sharp expression and aggressive manner. His curly hair was greased back, and he wore a Hitler moustache and affected a cigarette holder. Like Riina and Provenzano, he was in a hurry to make his fortune in the city.

The Christian Democrat mayor of Palermo, Salvo Lima, was a slick operator who built political connections across the country and was a member of the inner circle of the Prime Minister, Giulio Andreotti, rising to finance minister and MEP. He was persistently accused of having Mafia connections, to which he responded that in Sicily you simply couldn't avoid them. He had close ties with the La Barbera brothers, powerful bosses in Palermo, and the multimillionaire Salvo cousins, who collected taxes for the whole of Sicily, thanks to their links with the Mafia. The alliance of Ciancimino and Lima brought corruption and degradation to the city for decades.

Under Cianimino corruption exploded in the city: over half of the four thousand building licences issued over the course of four years (1959 to 1963) went to the same three people, none of whom had any development or building experience (one was a janitor, one was retired) – all of them front men for developers who were paying substantial kickbacks to the Mafia. While these massive developments swallowed up the green spaces and citrus groves to the west of the city, Cosa Nostra laundered millions in drug money through the builders' books.

Ciancimino was raking in kickbacks from overpriced contracts for public services and giving the Mafia a large cut. In a city that frequently endured temperatures in excess of 30° C in summer, 40 per cent of water leaked from rusty old pipes. In the poorer quarters, where bomb damage from the Allied attack during the Second World War had not been repaired, old tenement buildings had been opened like dolls' houses and left exposed to the elements. Many areas had no running water: residents had to queue at standpipes with jerry cans.

The old system of patronage in Sicilian politics was as strong as ever. Ciancimino was described as a 'puppeteer' manoeuvring the city council, but he in his turn was controlled by the Corleone Mafia. During the boom years in Palermo, Ciancimino was 'in the hands of the Corleonesi, Riina and Provenzano', according to the Palermo boss turned supergrass Tommaso Buscetta. One collaborator, a politician and mafioso, revealed: 'Ciancimino was very close to Bernardo Provenzano, who steered his political evolution.'[7]

'There's nothing in Corleone', explains the historian Salvatore Lupo. 'It's only once they arrive in Palermo that the Corleonesi make a career for themselves. The fact that this close-knit group comes from the same home town reinforces their ties. Ciancimino is one of them. Clearly, the fact that he's their *paesano* strengthens the unit.'

'Riina and Provenzano are fugitives, and they don't have the where-withal to range across the horizons of politics and business', Giuffré later told magistrates. 'They have a limited education and, living in hiding, it's difficult for them to keep up direct contact with people in these fields. Provenzano surrounds himself with advisers, people who see how things are going to go, who help Provenzano reinvent himself. . . . There's Vito Ciancimino, one of the former mayors of Palermo, who helped his fellow Corleonesi climb the ladder of power.'

His close ties with Ciancimino reinforced Provenzano's position within the organization, and he guarded the contact jealously. Ciancimino would remain an indispensable contact behind the polit-ical scenes throughout Provenzano's rise to power. Even when he had been thrown out of the Christian Democrats for Mafia connections, Ciancimino continued to wield extraordinary influence, since he could still deliver the Mafia vote.

Provenzano had the phlegmatic character and diplomatic skill to manage a man of Ciancimino's arrogant and abrasive manner. Ambitious and unscrupulous, with a sharp tongue and a ready put-down, Ciancimino intimidated people. He could also be utterly ruth-less. When an old friend and company manager who had been paying Ciancimino millions of lire in kickbacks for contracts came to see him with a problem, the old weasel told him, '*sono cazzi tuoi, stai molto attento*' ('It's not my fucking problem, just watch yourself').

Riina, perhaps recognizing Ciancimino's aggressive manner as close to his own, couldn't stand him, and the feeling was mutual. 'Provenzano is all right', Ciancimino told Giovanni Brusca, an ally of the Corleonesi. 'I can't be doing with Riina.'

Provenzano had to nurture and manage the relationship not only between Riina and Ciancimino but also between the supposed polit-ical allies Ciancimino and Lima. The two politicians were a couple of prima donnas, always falling out, and it was Provenzano's job to smooth things over and find a way to keep both of them happy. Riina became increasingly exasperated with their constant demands and competitive bickering, and eventually lost patience with Ciancimino altogether. Brusca recalled: 'Riina said he couldn't take any more, he would have to fight his *paesano,* this fellow Corleonese, he needed to teach him a good lesson. He had been put on the spot so many times when Ciancimino failed to deliver on his commitments, and he couldn't stand the way Provenzano was always defending him.'

But Provenzano's patient approach paid off. During the 1970s Ciancimino was doing more for his Mafia friends than signing thousands of illegal building licences. It later emerged he was laundering money for the Corleonesi on a grand scale in Canada.

When Ciancimino became mayor of Palermo in 1970, since his Mafia connections were well known, it caused such a scandal that he was obliged to resign after a few months. After that, Ciancimino remained a more discreet presence behind the scenes, building up his portfolio and maintaining a patronage system that meant people's jobs in public office were held for them while they served time in prison. He also kept his position in Provenzano's inner circle, advising him on political matters.

During this period the increase of Cosa Nostra's power, fuelled by drug money, was astonishing. One heroin trafficker was described by historian Pino Arlacchi as a 'travelling milk salesman in the 1950s, a small-scale building contractor in the mid-'60s, and during the '70s, until his arrest for drug trafficking in March 1980, one of the leading financiers and industrialists in Sicily'. The Corleonesi were determined to tap into this well of opportunity.

Liggio was finally arrested in 1974, at the flat in Milan where he was living under an assumed name with his companion and their two-year-old son. After years of evading arrest and fixing trials, he would not leave prison alive again. He had already handed over executive power to his deputies, Riina and Provenzano, but continued to instruct them from prison. He made them joint leaders of the Corleone family, and they were to alternate as boss every two years. Riina, his ambition on fire, took the first turn as leader and never stepped down.

This arrangement seems to have suited Provenzano. The differences between the joint leaders were emerging: Provenzano liked to move behind the scenes, quietly building his empire; Riina displayed

Liggio's uncontrollable violence, his leadership characterized by cunning, ferocity and ruthlessness. Riina's joint rulers on the commission, Badalamenti and Bontate, were entirely unprepared for his tactics. In 1975 he kidnapped and murdered the father-in-law of one of Bontate's most valuable and prestigious contacts, the tax collector Nino Salvo. It was a breathtaking act of disrespect, and Riina piled on the humiliation by refusing to give up the body, denying any knowledge of the crime.

Provenzano stayed in the background, studying how to make his political contacts work for him, refining his skills as a mediator. His quiet, questioning approach failed to impress those mafiosi who preferred a more direct, even aggressive style. While Riina was making millions through the drug trade, Provenzano was focused on more prosaic sources of income: sewage and garbage. Rather than go for the highest margin, he saw public contracts as a less risky way of making money, useful for laundering profits and consolidating territorial control.

Badalamenti, the wealthy boss of Cinisi and head of the commission, had got rich on drug trafficking and kickbacks from the construction of a new airport sited at Punta Raisi, an alarmingly narrow strip between the mountains and the sea. The Corleonesi pronounced that his hoarded drug millions were sufficient pretext to expel him from Cosa Nostra, removing one of their most formidable rivals at a stroke.

One contemporary figure who has shed light on the dynamics of the Corleonesi's race to power is Gioacchino Pennino, a doctor of good standing, a respected member of the upper middle class and a mafioso, who had been involved in politics in Palermo. Many years later Pennino, faced with criminal charges, revealed the relationship between Ciancimino and Provenzano.

'From what I can gather,' Pennino recalled, 'the cultural level of my associates was very low, apart from Bernardo Provenzano, who clearly had a good level of knowledge and followed politics very closely. He spoke intelligently, and with enough depth to give me the impression that he ran the political life of the Palermo area.'

He would soon discover the reality of Provenzano's influence. When Pennino, who was a member of Ciancimino's parliamentary group, had had enough of Ciancimino's high-handedness, he decided to leave, but he couldn't make a move without permission.

'I went to see Michele Greco [another respectable middle-class mafioso who later became the boss], explained the situation to him, and said I didn't feel I could go on like this, at the mercy of Ciancimino.'

The following day Pennino received a visitor, who told him he had an appointment, but didn't say with whom. The doctor was driven to the meeting in a small Fiat, belting along country lanes towards Bagheria. He was dropped off at a bar, where he was told to wait for his next escort.

'I was taken to a farmhouse that was used as both a store for vegetables and an office. There I met a man I'd never seen before, who was introduced to me as Bernardo Provenzano, while the other man called him Binnu.'

The meeting did not pan out as Pennino expected. He was barely allowed to speak. 'I hadn't even had time to explain what the problem was, when he turned on me. Clearly he knew everything about the situation, and he verbally attacked me. He told me to stay where I was, that things were just fine as they were.

'At the end of the meeting, which I found utterly mortifying, Provenzano told me I needed to keep quiet and not stir up any rebellious feeling in the Ciancimino camp.'

On a subsequent occasion Pennino was startled to meet Provenzano as he came out of Ciancimino's villa in Mondello, a palm-lined marina near Palermo and the favourite seaside residence of Palermo's rich. Pennino was leaving by the main gate when he saw Provenzano going in. 'It was a few months after our stormy encounter. We nodded in greeting but didn't stop to talk.' Pennino related other occasions when he had caught sight of Provenzano strolling openly along the streets of central Palermo, in spite of being officially wanted by the police, clearly with no sense of danger.

As Ciancimino's fortunes declined, Pennino tried once again to be released from his group and went to see Provenzano at his favoured meeting place, another mafioso doctor's surgery. Pennino was extremely apprehensive, but this time Provenzano didn't get furious with him. He merely wanted to know how many people were planning to desert Ciancimino, and whether there was any way of repairing the damage. He was still apparently hoping to exert his influence and save Ciancimino's political career.

'Greco had warned me to be careful, as Provenzano was considered extremely dangerous', the doctor reported. He was naturally anxious after their last encounter, but to his surprise, he found Provenzano quite civil. The doctor said he had no intention of taking anyone else with him, and Provenzano, satisfied with his reply, said nothing more.

Pennino made it clear that Provenzano exercised power behind the scenes. He also revealed for the first time Provenzano's nickname, *u ragioniere* ('the Accountant'). 'He has infiltrated everywhere,' he explained, 'and quite honestly I'm worried about what he might be able to do.'

Ciancimino was thrown out of the Christian Democrats in 1983, after a sustained campaign by his fellow politicians, and was finally indicted in 1984, following revelations about his links with Provenzano and Riina. He was eventually convicted of Mafia association, and the authorities seized assets worth $12 million, which they believed to be a small percentage of his illegal profits. Police found deposit boxes stuffed with notes – and this, the court was reminded, was a man who had never held a job.

Twenty years on, he had still not paid the Palermo city council, which had been a complainant in his trial, a penny of the restitution ordered by the court.

When a reporter from Rai TV news contacted him by phone to ask whether he was going to pay the moneys the council was demanding, he crowed: 'I've got it all in loose change. They can send a railway car for it, and I'll fill it up with coins, like a piggy bank!' Though he disappeared from front-line politics, Ciancimino remained one of the most important members of Provenzano's entourage.

The mutually beneficial relationship between the minister of works and Provenzano did not go unnoticed. An investigative journalist, Mario Francese, had understood that the Corleonesi were controlling public contracts through politicians and businessmen, and published some explosive stories in the *Giornale di Sicilia*. He described a 'third level' of the Mafia: the bosses who sit behind their desks in public buildings, pursuing their interests through government office.

Before he could dig any deeper, Francese was shot near his home on a chilly January morning in 1979, and his death was recorded as a 'crime of passion'. Decades would pass before the crime was laid at the Corleonesi's door.

The Mafia's code of honour is a shadowy sort of constitution, generally invoked to provide a pretext for murder. If there was ever a rule about not murdering public figures, the Corleonesi defied it. Ugo Triolo, a magistrate in Prizzi, just south of Corleone, would have no truck with the overbearing attitude of mafiosi and, instead of listening to their demands, threw them out of his waiting-room. Riina and Provenzano, schooled by Liggio in the art of terror and intimidation, wouldn't stand for it. It was the first time they had killed a servant of the state: they gunned him down brazenly in the middle of Corleone, and dumped his body in the street outside his house.

Riina and Provenzano's strategy unfolded over a number of months. Towards the end of the 1970s they installed as head of the commission Michele Greco, who, according to the supergrass Tommaso Buscetta, was too ineffectual to be anything but a cover for the Corleonesi's rise to power. They moved insidiously, committing murders that could be blamed on others, exposing the prominent Palermo bosses to police investigation while they remained in the shadows, wreaking havoc.

At a meeting of mafiosi in Palermo, Provenzano and Riina announced their plan to murder the retired police colonel Giuseppe Russo, a tireless investigator who had made life difficult for them. The plan was immediately opposed by the more moderate faction, led by Giuseppe di Cristina, boss of Riesi, in central Sicily. He believed in Cosa Nostra's policy of not harming representatives of the state. Stung by their humiliating defeat, Riina and Provenzano reported Di Cristina's opposition back to Liggio, who promptly sentenced him to death.

During the years of Riina and Provenzano's rise to power, investigators were warned about the two men's savage reputation. In 1978 Di Cristina contacted the carabinieri and told them he wanted to talk. He had already survived one attempt to kill him, and he knew the Corleonesi were planning to try again. There was no protection system for informants in place at that time, but he wanted the authorities to know what they were dealing with.

'Salvatore Riina and Bernardo Provenzano, nicknamed *le belve*, ['the Beasts'] because of their ferocity, are the most dangerous men Luciano Liggio has at his disposal. They have both committed about forty murders each.' Di Cristina told the police about the Corleonesi's tactics of taking over the commission by intimidation and violence, kidnapping and murdering their way to power. He described a situation in which the 'old-style' Mafia, the traditional heads of families who lived openly as figures of great respect in their neighbourhoods, were being swept away by the new breed of outlaw, who lived on the run and set their enemies against each other. 'The Corleonesi are invisible targets because they are almost all fugitives and run few serious risks with regard to their rivals or from the police.'

He tried to steer the police towards capturing Provenzano, who had been seen, Di Cristina said, in Bagheria, a leafy suburb of Palermo, on a Sunday, being driven in a white Mercedes by the young Giovanni Brusca. Bernardo Brusca, the driver's father, was boss of San Giuseppe Iato and one of Riina's staunchest allies, an 'untouchable', according to Di Cristina. It was a significant tip-off, but Provenzano had several bolt-holes at that time, and the carabinieri didn't find him.

Di Cristina told police he would shortly be taking delivery of an expensive bulletproof car, as he knew the Corleonesi were trying to kill him. He never received the car. Within a few days of his secret meeting with the police Di Cristina was shot dead in a busy Palermo street. There were no arrest warrants for Riina or Provenzano. Instead, police charged Di Cristina's friend Totuccio Inzerillo, because he had been murdered on Inzerillo's territory. Exactly as the Corleonesi had planned it.

Any investigator who got close to the Corleonesi's drug operations was cut down: the brilliant police captain Boris Giuliano, who was following drug money between Italy and the USA, was shot dead at a bar close to his home one July morning in 1979. The agent who took over his investigation, Emanuele Basile, was shot in the back while carrying his four-year-old daughter in his arms. Senior members of the Mafia commission were enraged: they had not been consulted or informed about these assassinations. The Corleonesi were doing as they pleased, and it seemed there was nothing anyone could do to stop them.

One early morning in September 1979 three killers shot down judge Terranova and his bodyguard right outside his home in a quiet Palermo back street. Terranova had returned to Palermo after his attempts to prosecute Mafia crimes in the 1960s had met defeat, and he was about to take over as chief investigating magistrate. The murder appears to have been a settling of old scores on several fronts: he had recognized the scale of the Corleonesi's operations and had dared to prosecute Liggio.

More experienced mafiosi tried to warn the Corleonesi that attacking the representatives of the state was too risky. Years later, investigators would record the rueful musings of an old-school mafioso: 'You don't touch the state . . . you can say what you like, but no one touches the state. The state, if it wants to, can crush you.'[8] Many believed that if you waged war on the state you risked alienating public support, and also exposing Cosa Nostra to retaliation. But the Corleonesi, in their rush for power, simply didn't believe the state would react against them.

Piersanti Mattarella, president of the region of Sicily and a Christian Democrat known for his refusal to adopt the Mafia's agenda, had tried to put a stop to the corrupt distribution of government contracts. This sort of interference would not be tolerated by Cosa Nostra, and Mattarella was murdered in January 1980 on the orders of Riina and Michele Greco, backed by their allies on the commission, including Provenzano, Bernardo Brusca and Ciccio Madonia.

As they demonstrated their impunity, and their defiance of the commission, with this frontal attack on the state, Riina and Provenzano's main intention was to strike fear into their rival Mafia families in Palermo. They were just warming up.

The rise of the Corleonesi began as an insidious, creeping terror and culminated in their takeover of Palermo and domination of the international drug trade. Their leader and mentor, Liggio, had infiltrated other Mafia families with his own men, insinuating his killers into the heart of Mafia clans all over the country. The principal tactic, which Provenzano later deployed to his own ends, was to turn old friends and families against each other. In the confusion that followed, the Corleonesi killed with a ruthless abandon that became known as the *mattanza*, after the annual slaughter of captive tuna fish that turns the sea red with blood.

One mafioso later recalled the apparent warmth and camaraderie among mafiosi at Christmas 1980, just before the slaughter started: 'We all kissed each other, we celebrated together and wished each other Happy Christmas. You'd never have known there was so much hate burning under the surface.'[9]

The first Mafia boss to fall was Stefano Bontate, the most powerful man of honour in Palermo, gunned down at the wheel of his car. Two weeks later Totuccio Inzerillo, the drug baron, was shot dead getting into his bulletproof Alfa-Romeo after a tryst with his mistress. It wasn't enough to kill the heads of the Palermo families: Riina went after every last man loyal to them. The Corleonesi's anonymous killers emerged out of nowhere to strike. In the panic that ensued, terrified men tried to pledge their loyalty to their new masters by killing their own family members. But Riina trusted no one: over 200 men he suspected of having had links to the losing factions were 'disappeared', strangled or shot.

So many men were murdered in Palermo over the terrible months of 1981 that police could do little but pick up corpses. On one day twelve men were found shot dead in different parts of the city. 'It was not a battle between rival families,' said Tommaso Buscetta a few years later, 'it was a manhunt.'

The entire Inzerillo family was murdered or driven into exile: many fled to the USA, where they took refuge with their relations the Gambino family. The Corleonesi's vengeance pursued them: Inzerillo's brother was found dead in the USA, a bundle of dollars in his mouth and another stuffed in his underpants.

The Corleonesi's aim was to eradicate their enemies, and they nearly succeeded – but not entirely. Riina eventually issued an edict that those who left Sicily would be allowed to live but could never return. However, members of the Inzerillo family who had fled their assassins would begin to drift back to Palermo twenty years later. The return of Palermo's banished mafiosi was to cause acute difficulties for Provenzano and threatened to cause another war.

Such bloodshed on a massive scale required a robust response from the state. For years the courts had run into trouble when they tried to prosecute individual crimes: the law needed a more precise instrument to tackle the mafia. Pio La Torre, head of the Communist Party in Sicily and a member of the parliamentary anti-Mafia commission, insisted it should become a crime to belong to the organization. He also believed the state should seize the Mafia's assets if it could be proven that they were acquired with profits from criminal activity. This represented a major threat to the Mafia, whose accumulation of secret wealth was its chief *raison d'être* and had never been seriously challenged before.

When General Dalla Chiesa was invited to return to Palermo in 1982 as prefect, La Torre represented a prospective ally in an extremely difficult situation, a beacon of energy and clarity in the war against the Mafia. But as Dalla Chiesa took up office, in April 1982, Cosa Nostra prepared his welcome: Pio La Torre was murdered as he drove to work.

It was a devastating blow for Dalla Chiesa, who was already in a difficult position: he had been promised extra powers to take on the Mafia but was beginning to realize that these were never going to materialize. Although his earlier reports had given the anti-Mafia commission essential intelligence on the Corleone clan's business activities, he was treated on his return to Palermo as a semi-retired soldier who knew nothing of the 'modern' Mafia.

He had been lauded for successfully taking on Italy's left-wing terrorist groups, but many claimed that his tactics against terrorism would not work against the Mafia. Over a few tense and difficult months, while Dalla Chiesa investigated links between the Palermo Mafia and captains of industry in Catania on the other side of the island, he was increasingly isolated and vulnerable. In September, just a few months after arriving in Sicily, General Dalla Chiesa and his wife were gunned down in their car, blasted with shots from Kalashnikov rifles.

The murder of Dalla Chiesa was 'an act of arrogance by the Corleonesi', commented Badalamenti, watching news of the assassination on television; 'they planned this in response to the general's challenge to the Mafia.'

The assassination of a national hero, who had been deserted and isolated by the state, provoked an outcry from the people and a response, finally, from the government. The measures that Pio La Torre had tried so hard to push through parliament, making it a crime to belong to the Mafia and allowing the state to confiscate property acquired with the proceeds of organized crime, became law.

For once the outrageous killing of a public official had not cowed the authorities but had provoked the first major set-back for Cosa Nostra in years. It was the first serious challenge to the Corleonesi's policy of frontal attack on the state, and sowed controversy within the organization that rumbled on for years.

The magistrate who had taken over from Terranova, Rocco Chinnici, was determined to continue his predecessor's hard line against the Mafia. He was ambitious and energetic and began a thorough investigation into the Mafia's financial dealings. Unflinchingly, Chinnici signed arrest warrants against Palermo boss Michele Greco, Riina and Provenzano for the murder of Dalla Chiesa.

As soon as the warrants were issued, the Greco family, backed by their allies the Corleonesi, planned their retaliation and Chinnici was assassinated. One insider later confided that the strategy of war held them to an inexorable course of violence. 'They told me it had been a mistake to kill Dalla Chiesa because it stirred up a lot of trouble, but having started, it was necessary to continue with these actions against anyone who stuck their nose in the Mafia's business.'[10]

This reference to a 'mistake' was repeated some years later by Dalla Chiesa's killer, Pino Greco, in a conversation recorded by police. Pino *scarpuzzedda* ('Little Shoe') Greco was one of the Corleonesi's most ruthless and prolific killers, but he was troubled by the general's assassination. 'This Dalla Chiesa murder – we really didn't need it',

Greco told a trusted associate. 'It'll take at least ten years to steady the ship.'

He indicated clearly that Provenzano was behind the assassination. 'This business has been a joke at my expense, and it was the Accountant who played that joke on me. This is the work of the Accountant – you know who I mean, the one who gives the orders.'

Greco had been given guarantees for his part in a murder that brought the Corleonesi a sharp increase in prestige – but, he complained, whatever he had been promised had failed to materialize. Besides which, with the advent of the La Torre law, the killing had caused Cosa Nostra more problems than it solved.

The echoes of this brutal phase reverberated for years. In 1984 *scarpuzzedda* Greco disappeared at the hands of his own men. Many within Cosa Nostra considered the murder of Dalla Chiesa a pointless crime – they didn't believe the general had the power to do them any real harm, since he had been isolated and abandoned by the state – but Greco may have been the only one to say it.

Once he had dispatched his rivals and demonstrated what Cosa Nostra would do to any obstruction from the state, Riina completed his bloody revolution. He made Provenzano *capo mandamento* of Corleone and built himself a majority on the commission. He changed the boundaries of the remaining families (Cosa Nostra's territory is divided into sectors, or *mandamenti*, each comprising three families; each *mandamento* has a representative on the commission) so that his most loyal allies gained control of their area. In some places he changed the borders; in others he elevated families to control *mandamenti* – to put his men in positions of power.

'Riina was – what do you call it, the little beastie that burrows away underneath you and you don't even know it's there? Woodworm.' The boss of Altofonte, Francesco Di Carlo, had a healthy mistrust of Riina; he accused him of making Cosa Nostra fragmented and secretive. 'He wanted a piece of every other *mandamento* – and most of the time he got his way.'

'Riina didn't have a very great trust of the Greco family,' explained Alfonso Sabella, who was assistant prosecutor in Palermo during the 1990s, 'so he moved their *mandamento*, Ciaculli, to Brancaccio, to the east of Palermo, and put his faithful soldiers, the Graviano family, in charge. Where a family was particularly loyal to him, the family was promoted to *mandamento*.'

The Corleonesi's rise to power shocked many mafiosi by its sheer arrogance and its violence. Later Provenzano would be among those who played down their role in the bloodshed, portraying Riina as the sole author of the slaughter. This may not be entirely accurate. Riina did not take kindly to being countermanded. If Provenzano had opposed him, it seems unlikely he would have survived this terrible phase of Cosa Nostra's history. He not only survived, but he remained Riina's joint leader. Giovanni Brusca claims Provenzano was constantly offering arguments against acts of violence, but that his objections were simply brushed aside. Others remain convinced he backed the policy.

'There's no doubt that Provenzano took a full part in the Mafia war against Bontate and Inzerillo', cautions chief prosecutor Pietro Grasso. 'He was involved in the planning stage because he was with Riina: they were jointly lieutenants and regents of Luciano Liggio. Provenzano has a case to answer.'

The Corleonesi's excessive use of force had already brought new anti-Mafia laws into play, but their sustained war against the state would sow the seeds of their destruction.

3

Love and title deeds

SAVERIA BENEDETTA PALAZZOLO lived in a narrow street in Cinisi, west of Palermo, with her parents, two brothers, Paolo and Salvatore, and three sisters. At twenty-seven she was an unaffected young woman working as a seamstress in a local shirt factory. She had no trace of vanity, made all her own clothes and did her own hair – she pinned her thick curls back and never wore make-up. She divided her time between working and keeping house for an elderly aunt, who had a little money and a more comfortable lifestyle than Saveria's own parents. She would talk to her aunt about her ambition to have her own dressmaking business. She could not see herself like the other women she knew, who got married and spent the rest of their lives keeping house. She was clever and industrious, and she was bored.

Cinisi was a small town on a promontory, a prosperous and peaceful place, under the ever-watchful eye of the local Mafia. Nothing escaped the notice of their gossips and spies. The Mafia boss was the self-appointed moral guardian, who could give permission for a marriage or stop the couple from seeing each other, offer advice and guidance on all matters and resolve disputes.

Provenzano was thirty-seven, on the run from enemies within the Mafia and from the police. He had been living in different towns all over western Sicily, travelling with his friends from Corleone, protected by mafiosi who knew him as Liggio's man. In Cinisi he was the guest of the boss, don Tano Badalamenti, who had taken in many fugitives over the years, including Liggio. Giovanni Impastato grew up in Cinisi in an embattled family: his father was a mafioso, and his brother was thrown out of the house, and subsequently murdered, as a result of his outspoken campaign against the Mafia. As a boy, Giovanni would go with his father to take food and run errands for Liggio. He recalls Provenzano's arrival created quite a stir. 'People were fascinated by him', he says. 'Here was this young Corleonese who they believed was unjustly persecuted by the law; he was seen as a courageous outlaw on the run. It wouldn't be hard to be drawn to a mafioso like him; he had charisma, a certain fascination.'

Saveria found herself irresistibly attracted to the outlaw, who was always well dressed but never showy, and seemed much older than her. He came from outside Cinisi and had seen something of the world. She had cousins who had been forced to give up their *fidanzati* because they came from the next village. She wanted more than Cinisi had to offer. According to his reputation, this bold young man was not afraid of anything, and yet he seemed the quiet type. He was drawn to her direct, unaffected manner, her intelligence and resourcefulness. She seemed to understand that he didn't want to talk all the time, that he liked solitude and needed time to think. She didn't ask him questions or demand that he visit her constantly. At last he had found a woman who seemed implicitly to understand his life. He courted her in secret, but before long their relationship attracted attention.

Giovanni Impastato, who has carried on his brother's anti-Mafia campaign, remembers the Palazzolo family, not wealthy nor explicitly connected to the Mafia, but moving in the right circles: 'Saveria would have understood what kind of man he was', he says. 'You can see what those men are like. Women like my poor mother still believed the Mafia was a force for good. Saveria's family will not have done badly through that connection.

'They lived in that semi-legal environment; the father didn't have an active role in the Mafia, but they were very close to [Gaetano] Badalamenti's family. Anyone with ambition had aspirations to be part of that world – it was the dominant culture. If you could worm your way into Mafia circles, you would never lack for anything.'

If his courtship of Saveria was initially approved, Provenzano's precarious situation made it difficult for them to marry. It would be hard to find a priest willing to risk prosecution for aiding and abetting a fugitive. And Saveria's family did not want her to leave Cinisi. So the couple, no longer in the first flush of youth, were *fidanzati* for a few years, during which time he would disappear for weeks on end, and she never knew whether she would see him alive again. But she always had the sense not to ask him what he had been doing.

She wasn't seen much around town; since everyone knew each other's business, she took care to avoid the hairdressers and the shops where women exchanged news. He wasn't the jealous type, but the last thing she wanted was for Binnu to hear anything about her from gossips.

At last he asked Saveria to run away with him. This was customary practice in those parts when a formal marriage was impossible because the families disapproved, or the couple were too young, or because there wasn't money for a big church wedding. Often a family member would secretly lend them a room to help out. Once they had spent a night together, the family might bewail their dishonour, but the couple were officially engaged. Saveria and Bernardo stayed with one of her cousins. By now everyone knew they were living together as an unmarried couple.

'It was a scandal', the local priest recalled in an interview with Sicilian journalist Salvo Palazzolo. 'A girl from such a good family . . . how did she end up involved with that sort, everyone wondered. How was it possible? Her mother always came to Mass.'

The local police were embarrassed. When they questioned Saveria about her boyfriend's whereabouts, she claimed not to know. Then she appeared in town, visibly pregnant and proud. 'When the police saw I was expecting, they sent for me', she reportedly told the local priest. 'They asked me, "How can you tell us you don't know where Provenzano is hiding, given your condition?" And I said, "Wait a minute, can't a woman have a baby with anyone other than her husband?"'

Not when her husband is a mafioso, as she knew, and the police knew perfectly well. Cosa Nostra takes a strong line on women's moral conduct. Saveria was apparently enjoying the mystique of her relationship with an outlaw, and unafraid of moral condemnation. She no longer belonged in this small town, and it seemed she didn't care what anyone thought.

When the rumour reached Badalamenti that Saveria was expecting a baby, he was furious. A young mafioso in his charge, seducing a local girl! It was very bad for Cosa Nostra's image. As the local boss, he was the people's moral guardian, and men were to treat women with respect at all times and protect the ideal of the family. (If a wife discovered her husband was having an affair, she'd take the children and go back to her mother's. The boss would take it upon himself to pay her a visit and persuade her to come back.) Badalamenti couldn't allow any sort of public immoral behaviour: 'He told Bernardo Provenzano he had to formalize his relationship with her', recalls Giovanni Impastato. 'Even if they couldn't get married in church, he wanted the situation sorted out.'

Provenzano did as Badalamenti instructed and started looking for a suitable plot of land to build his new family a home. On the outskirts of Cinisi in the stony, sloping countryside Provenzano chose a plot of land to build a home for himself and his beloved. According to investigations by the carabinieri, the deeds were signed and registered by Saveria's brother Salvatore, and Bernardo had plans drawn up showing a spacious villa for a young family to grow into.

However, once work was under way, the builders received an unexpected visit from the carabinieri, wanting to know who owned the place. Before any further investigations could ensue, the plot was sold, with its unfinished structure, stalled and rusting, still in place. Bernardo and Saveria, who now had a healthy baby boy, named Angelo after Bernardo's father, would have to find somewhere else to build their first home.

This was Saveria's first taste of the rootlessness of her life ahead: she could no longer run back to her parents in Cinisi, but she and her new family had no place to call home. She could, however, draw on the intelligence and resourcefulness that Binnu had so admired in her; she had some understanding of the Mafia's rules and its *raison d'être*. Over the years she spent with Binnu, Saveria, coming from a legitimate family, would need all her personal resources to withstand the pressures of life in the Mafia. She had to renounce any personal ambition and throw in her lot with a man who lived in constant danger. She was fortunate in that Binnu's nature made him more disposed to spending time with her and their son than with his Mafia associates, but he was often forced to move around, for security reasons or for meetings, and she would never know where he was going or for how long. She had to accept anything from him, on faith.

'A woman who comes from a Mafia background doesn't ask for explanations for the things she sees', said the *pentito* Leonardo Messina. 'The true wealth of a man of honour is a wife who understands his role.'

Ninetta Bagarella, who married Totò Riina, grew up immersed in the Corleone Mafia: her two brothers, Calogero and Leoluca, were Provenzano and Riina's running mates. (Calogero was killed at the viale Lazio massacre in 1969.) At twenty-one, when her *fidanzato* was already on the run from the police, Ninetta earned the dubious honour of being the first woman to be arraigned for aiding and abetting the Mafia, by taking messages between her fiancé and his associates. Young as she was, she had shown an acute understanding of how Cosa Nostra operates within Sicilian society. The attractive young woman wore a light floral dress, and her dark hair long, to make a dramatic appearance in a Palermo court.

'You say I am guilty, but I am only guilty of falling in love', she cried. 'You cannot judge me for loving a man, it's my natural right. You ask how I could have chosen a man like Riina, about whom people say such terrible things. Is it against the law to love a man like Salvatore Riina? I love him and I know he is innocent.'

She was, inevitably, released without charge and three years later married her man in a church wedding. (The priest who conducted the service was later questioned by police, who accepted his defence that he could not condone two souls living in sin.)

Both Ninetta and Saveria, once they had committed themselves to these two outlaws, glamorous as they may have been, were destined to live their married lives as fugitives. Saveria and Binnu's passion grew as they stood together against the 'unjust persecution' of the state, and the drama of their lives unfolded within its constrictions. There was money – though not always – and there were gifts. (Ninetta acquired enough fur coats to need a whole refrigerated room to store them, and serious jewels. Saveria was not interested in a fancy wardrobe or furs, but she and Binnu were undoubtedly comfortable.) Ninetta couldn't take the children and run home to mamma if her husband strayed, but then the Mafia has its particular code of honour in these matters: 'You can do what you want,' Riina reportedly said to a young mafioso who had been caught with his mistress, 'but you must never disrespect your wife publicly.' Binnu just wasn't the type to indulge. While his Mafia friends enjoyed celebratory feasts and wild parties, he preferred to be alone, at home.

By going on the run, Provenzano had (albeit temporarily) cut off his route back to Corleone and his family, and he needed an alternative support structure. Saveria, with her family in Cinisi and her unquestioning acceptance of his chosen career, provided him with the security he needed. He recruited her relations to be his business associates and representatives. Her brother Paolo was a front man for many of Binnu's enterprises, including the lease of a substantial tract of land. A police report described him as 'particularly closed. A man of few words, extremely withdrawn and retiring, who never talked on the phone, and never met anyone.' An extremely difficult subject for surveillance, in other words, and a most welcome addition to Bernardo Provenzano's family circle.

Provenzano continued to register shares in his wife's name. The young mafioso Giovanni Brusca later recalled that he and his associates had been told to favour a construction company with which Provenzano's wife was associated. 'We wondered, is he crazy, to put his wife in as a partner? We knew that sooner or later he was bound to have problems if his wife was mixed up in it.'

Saveria and Bernardo made their base in Bagheria, aided by his contacts in law enforcement and local government and by a culture that protected the Mafia. During this period they lived a quiet life, with no fear of arrest. When their son was seven, Saveria became pregnant again, and they had another baby, another boy, whom they named Francesco Paolo. In a culture where the customary greeting for newly-weds is *auguri e figli maschi* ('congratulations, may you have sons') Provenzano was doubly blessed.

'I know Bernardo Provenzano has an immense property in Bagheria, in the grounds of a grand villa', one *pentito* later testified. 'I've never known exactly where it was, but from what people told me it was a beautiful place, in classical style . . . Provenzano lived here undisturbed with his family.'[11]

In the mid-1980s a series of high-profile Mafia crimes turned up the heat on Riina and Provenzano and led to a series of arrests. Binnu and his family decamped to Trapani, where the boys attended school under an assumed name.

When Provenzano began to receive substantial kickbacks from waste management and other public contracts, he needed to start investing his profits. He bought businesses and properties, which he registered to members of his *fidanzata*'s family. A tenacious investigator managed to uncover the extent of Provenzano's property investments.

Colonel Angiolo Pellegrini arrived in Palermo in early 1981, just as the Mafia war was breaking out. It was a frenzied time: while the Corleonesi were murdering their rivals on their own territory, Cosa Nostra's influence was spreading.

Pellegrini was working with Giovanni Falcone, who had begun his painstaking paper trail, following drug money through international banks. Rotund, moustachioed and every inch the no-nonsense army investigator, Pellegrini liked to work the same way: investigations based on diligent, detailed detective work.

'We asked for a computer, to log the data we were collecting, and were told it was not essential', he says jovially. Now retired from the army, it's unlikely he has let a day go by without buttoning himself into his suit and trimming his tidy goatee. 'Now it's easily done with a database, but we wrote everything by hand in old ledgers and created a massive index. It was essential for us to be able to make the links.'

A particular case had come to Pellegrini's notice, in which a modest family from Cinisi had made some spectacular property acquisitions. The family name was Palazzolo. They had no criminal record, although it emerged during the course of the investigation that the daughter, Saveria Benedetta, had left home and was living with the fugitive Bernardo Provenzano. It was the first time investigators had heard that the outlaw from Corleone had a woman living with him. They were also surprised to discover that he had two children. Pellegrini entered the Palazzolo family in his ledger and proceeded to track them through title deeds and company registers.

Saveria Palazzolo's name began to show up again and again. In a very short space of time she had acquired substantial shares in a building company, Italcostruzione, 12 hectares of land near Castellammare and an apartment in Palermo. The carabinieri found her name on two further properties and two plots of land in the suburbs, as well as a vacant lot in Palermo's fast-developing viale Strasburgo.

By the time the carabinieri went looking for Saveria, she had already left Cinisi. 'She had disappeared', recalls Pellegrini. 'We set up investigations into the family and in the area, to see if we could find any leads that would take us to her, and to Provenzano. We didn't find her.'

His report read: 'La Palazzolo, officially spinster and housewife, possessing no assets prior to 1972, in the course of five months, from December '72 to April '73, acquired property for the considerable sum of 26 million lire [£13,000]. Her investments were managed by the well-known mafia accountant Giuseppe Mandalari.'

Four months after the carabinieri demanded to see the deeds of the plot where they were building, the report went on, 'La Palazzolo hurriedly sold all her properties to the company Simaiz s.p.a., a company set up for the purpose and administered by Mandalari. This sale is without doubt directly related to the discovery of building works which were intended to construct a safe house (far from prying eyes) for Bernardo Provenzano.'

Saveria Palazzolo was charged with money-laundering in November 1983. Provenzano was charged with Mafia association, and a business associate was arrested for money-laundering. The latter went to prison, leaving a wife and two children to fend for themselves, while the lovers were nowhere to be found.

The case against Saveria Palazzolo came to court in 1990, and she was required to explain where she had got the money to acquire properties and shares. Her reply, sent by post and delivered to the court in her absence, revealed her own profound double standards. The letter appealed to the court's belief in the virtue of women – she mentions a maiden aunt and her own role in caring for her. She also portrays herself as a dutiful daughter, and a woman who understands little of the difficult world of business, merely signing complicated documents as required. Her acquisition of a small fortune was not only legitimate, she maintained, but the result of considerable personal sacrifice.

Most illustrious Signor Presidente

The assets that are alleged to be the profits of illegal activity are in fact monies earned by the undersigned in her own right. In point of fact, the undersigned has always earned her own money from legal employment first as an embroiderer working from home, subsequently as a seamstress.

In between times, the undersigned assisted her paternal aunt Benedetta Palazzolo in her activity as a dressmaker, without receiving any financial recompense, because of the special relationship between herself and this particular aunt. And in fact, the undersigned also took on the duty of caring for her and assisting her in all matters until the end of her life.

According to family tradition, since the young woman had taken particular responsibility for looking after her aunt, the aunt took care of her niece's future. She and another relative bought the young woman a piece of land worth 13 million lire.

One day the undersigned met the Cavaliere Sebastiano Provenzano, and recalling that her father had spoken well of him, decided to ask him for advice about her investments.

The Cavaliere replied that if a good opportunity turned up, he would let her know. Years went by, and when she was least expecting it, the Cavaliere contacted her with a proposal that she buy two plots in Latomie district, in Castelvetrano.

The undersigned admitted she lacked sufficient funds to make the acquisition, but the Cavaliere told her not to worry, since the deal would require a small initial investment, while the rest could be covered by a complex network of loans and bank cheques guaranteed personally by himself, to be repaid with the profits of agricultural production (olives and vines).

The down payment was arranged by the Cavaliere via mutual funds and complex bank processes which the undersigned is not technically capable of accurately describing.

Conveyancing and all other matters concerning the transaction, as well as investment of the remaining funds, were handled by the Cavaliere, leaving the undersigned merely to add her signature as required.

From the above information it is clear that the funds are all from legitimate sources.
Signed
Saveria Benedetta Palazzolo

The letter aimed for the right note of virtuous industry: here was an enterprising young woman doing her family duty, with ambitions to run her own business. She had a clear idea of what she wanted but needed legal advisers to sort out the complicated financial stuff. If they had done anything underhand, she implied, it was nothing to do with her.

The judges did not go for the story about the humble seamstress and the elderly aunt. Neither were they at all convinced by the apparently coincidental meeting between Saveria Palazzolo and the cavaliere Provenzano (no relation to her husband), who was suspected of being a front for another of Bernardo Provenzano's investments. They wanted to demonstrate that, if the Mafia was going to use women to conceal their illegal business dealings, then the women were no longer off-limits.

In 1990 Saveria was given two years and six months for receiving stolen goods, later commuted to aiding and abetting. She was given a reduced sentence under house arrest, which, since she was already living 'at home', whereabouts unknown, was conveniently unenforceable. It did mean that she was no longer free to live as a legitimate citizen, should she decide to do so, and that she and the boys, now aged seven and fourteen, were condemned to life on the run. Binnu had relied on the justice system's blind belief in the goodness of women and had exposed his wife to prosecution. Now they were tied together in an inexorable bond, united against the law.

4

Bagheria's feudal lord

THE ROAD INTO Bagheria, once thick with lemon groves, is a jumble of small streets built up with no kind of planning or regulation: most of the houses are plastered but not painted; many are unfinished, clad in scaffolding. This is urban sprawl at its most chaotic and unattractive. A lovely eighteenth-century villa, the towering Villa Cattolica, resting place of the celebrated Sicilian painter Renato Guttuso, appears at the bend of a road on the edge of town. Right next to it, standing in what should be parkland, loom the ugly industrial silos of a concrete plant.

A short distance off the main road stands a warehouse, a rough concrete building with imposing steel doors fastened by an iron pole. There are houses around it now, but once it was isolated, out in the lemon groves. You go up a couple of steps and walk across what was once a small office, where the manager would sit with his paper and his phone. The hangar, now empty, was an ironworks which traded under the name ICRE, making nails and wire fencing, owned by Leonardo Greco. Greco was the main contact for the heroin trade: morphine arrived from Turkey and was turned into heroin in a secret lab in Bagheria, before being exported to New York.

Greco's warehouse was the reference point and meeting place for mafiosi in the area; it was also known as the 'death chamber'. Condemned men would be brought to the nail factory to be interrogated and beaten, then strangled, and their bodies dissolved in acid. The acid bath, beneath a grating in the floor, would have been ready for them when they were brought in, its acrid stink filling the airless space. The place is empty now, but the damp greenish concrete, the pitiless, windowless walls, every stain and metal staple preserve its horrible memories. In one corner is another grating over a cistern, where the victim of a Mafia feud was buried beneath the stones. Two years later, when the feud had been resolved, his remains were given back to the family.

It was here that Bernardo Provenzano first met Nino Giuffré, or *Manuzza* ('Little Hand'), so called because one of his arms is deformed. Giuffré, tall and reserved, was a striking figure. At this point he was Caccamo boss Ciccio Intile's driver, a teacher at the technical institute in Caccamo and newly initiated into Cosa Nostra. He would become Provenzano's most important ally, and ultimately the author of his downfall.

'Every time we went to Bagheria of a morning, Provenzano was there', recalled Giuffré years later. 'This ironworks was one of the most important places in which Provenzano used to make appointments, apart from being where the Corleonesi murdered their enemies. People were given appointments here, people who were perhaps no longer considered trustworthy, and once inside the door, they'd never leave. Provenzano used this place for two purposes: as a death chamber and for meetings with his closest allies.' The two, as Giuffré of course knew, are not mutually exclusive.

A short way from the warehouse, at the turning off the main road to Messina, on a sharp bend, is a bar, the Diva, painted bright pink, where Giuffré and Intile stopped for coffee when they were in the area. It didn't matter that there was a police road-block just yards away and they were both wanted men; no one made any attempt to stop them.

On one occasion, after knocking back their sugary espressos from scalding white cups, the two men headed over to the ironworks. A car parked outside aroused their suspicion, but while they watched and waited, a 'friend' came over. 'We've got a couple of tuna fish in the boot', he explained. 'We're just waiting to unload them. There's been some problem on the road, and we're waiting for the all-clear.' The 'tuna fish' in the boot were two corpses, victims of the Mafia war, destined to disappear into an acid bath.

The Corleonesi's attack on the Palermo families had begun in earnest, with a bewildering ferocity that left mafiosi and investigators wondering who could be behind it. After the violent deaths of the supreme Palermo boss Stefano Bontate and his ally Totuccio Inzerillo, Greco called a meeting at the ironworks. Giuffré recalls: 'Leonardo Greco stood up and announced that the Corleonesi's rise to power had begun, and that he and his family had pretty much made their choice of leader. So it was his advice to the assembled company that the various *mandamenti* should align themselves with Bernardo Provenzano. And that's what happened.'

But while Riina was fighting his war in Palermo, Provenzano was attending to business. 'The Mafia's money had to be kept moving, it had to be invested, and Provenzano was in charge of that side of things', says Angiolo Pellegrini. 'While Riina was being the great warrior, Provenzano was managing his companies through front men. Riina was making Cosa Nostra's military decisions, while Provenzano was running the economy.'

In the early 1980s the carabinieri's chief investigative tool was the phone tap. With about fifteen men drawn from the companies at Partinico and Corleone, Colonel Pellegrini worked out of the cramped operations room at the Palermo prosecutor's office, listening to calls and tracing Provenzano's ever-expanding network. Fortunately for the agents listening in, the mafiosi had not yet learned to exercise discretion while using the phone.

'Our targets were not as sophisticated as they are now', recalls Pellegrini. 'They had basic codes, but weren't generally as cautious as they subsequently became.'

One day an agent heard the following exchange, picked up on a phone tap:

'Nardo!'

'Carmelino!'

'How's everything? . . . Could you tell the accountant to get the invoices ready, I've got the cheques here for him to sign.'

'Nardo' – Leonardo Greco – and Carmelo Colletti, Mafia boss of Agrigento, chatted about business before arranging a meeting at Greco's HQ, to exchange sums of money. At that point the police listening in to the phone calls did not know the identity of 'the Accountant'.

Pellegrini discovered companies registered to various blameless individuals, which turned out to share the same electricity account or were connected to the same answerphone. If you phoned the construction company to order cement, you might get through to a supplier of radiography machines. Pellegrini started mapping these curious connections. On one big sprawling graphic of the health suppliers, all the meandering pen lines led to Provenzano's favourite nephew, Carmelo Gariffo; another showed all the companies connected to Leonardo Greco. And connected, somehow, to all of them, was the mysterious 'Accountant'.

A few years later the developer Angelo Siino revealed that 'the Accountant' was the fugitive Provenzano. Siino also revealed that the investigators' failure to figure out 'the Accountant's identity was a source of great amusement: 'It was unbelievable, we were all on those tapes, we · were talking about "the Hunter" . . . that was Nitto Santapaola [boss of Catania], he was identified; and people were talking about me, using my nickname, "the Builder" . . . We were always talking about this man "the Accountant", but he was never identified, neither was I . . . and we had such a laugh about the fact that everyone was looking for an accountant . . .'

The carabinieri had also, unknowingly, recorded Provenzano's phone conversations. After Siino's revelations, fifteen years after the event, someone was dispatched to look in the archives. But the tapes were no longer there. Provenzano had apparently covered his tracks.

Provenzano made Bagheria his base. He and other capos occupied splendid villas in the town's lush parkland, beyond the gaze of inquiring eyes. According to one insider, Provenzano lived 'on the edge of Bagheria in a large villa, full of stucco and frescos, surrounded by high walls which enclose a wonderful garden, full of shrubs and flower beds'.[12]

Whenever there was trouble, Provenzano would be spirited away to another of his safe houses in the area – Palermo, Monreale, Ciminna. During this period he used his contacts in the health sector to provide him with the perfect transportation to meetings: an ambulance. He was also sighted in a white Mercedes chauffered by the young Giovanni Brusca. He held meetings in private homes, in his friends' villas, in offices and businesses. He met his capos in furniture shops, perched on plastic-coated sofas, to settle disputes and nominate debt enforcers.

In Mafia terms the boss's territory is all-important: he can never go far from his power base and must show his strength in his feudal home. If he has his territory under control, he will always have people to protect him. Riina seldom moved house in twenty-three years 'on the run', and enjoyed an existence untroubled by the knock at the door. For several years Provenzano lived comfortably in Bagheria, master of all he surveyed.

'The Bagheria Mafia was Bernardo Provenzano's Mafia', Giuffré explained.

Bagheria was once the playground of the rich, a place where the wealthy of Palermo built themselves grand summer residences. The Villa dei Mostri, in the centre of town, features eccentric gargoyles at the gates, mocking the passers-by on their Sunday *passeggiata*. Recent development has been so haphazard and careless that imposing stone gateposts are left stranded between new apartment buildings. Parts of ancient walls have been incorporated into traffic islands. The town hall in Bagheria is an ugly modern building on the wide main street, flanked by upmarket shops. Its smoked-glass windows conceal a dreary past of graft and greed. For years planning and development in the town were blighted by Mafia interference. Showrooms, villas and blocks of flats sprang up on protected ground, cement foundations paving over the last green spaces. Provenzano's associates built themselves villas in the centre of Bagheria, even within the parkland of the historic Villa Valguarnera.

'Everything in Bagheria was run by the Mafia', said the *pentito* Angelo Siino years later. 'Nothing moved without the Mafia's say-so, because the nerve centre of life in Bagheria was in the Mafia's control.'

To consolidate his power base Provenzano made an unusual alliance. At a time when Cosa Nostra enjoyed close links with some Christian Democrats he nurtured contacts within the Communist Party, which enjoyed a majority on the council. It has since been claimed by collaborators that some councillors signing off development contracts colluded actively with the Mafia, and that whole departments were completely under the control of Cosa Nostra. A number of building contracts were awarded to the same group of companies, none of them local concerns: behind them were international connections linked to drug trafficking. Party members who raised the alarm were silenced, intimidated or expelled.

On the witness stand Giuffré painted a graphic picture of what he claimed was Cosa Nostra's grip on a whole town.

'All roads lead to Provenzano', he said.

'What does that mean, exactly?' asked the prosecutor.

'It means', the witness replied, 'that in Bagheria you are dealing with the not inconsiderable power of Provenzano. It wasn't just the planning office that was in the Mafia's hands. The political side was just the same. If a candidate for mayor didn't get the go-ahead from Provenzano and his people, you can rest assured he would never get elected.

'If he wanted to canvass votes in Bagheria, if he didn't have the go-ahead from the family and from Provenzano himself, a candidate could drive past on the A13, but he'd better not stop.

'I'll give you an example of how it worked. One local businessman had a brother. I think I met him: I can't remember his name, but I do remember he had a beard. He was a radical member of the Communist Party, had been for years. As soon as this businessman started dealing with us, his brother was forced out of the Communist Party and made to join the Christian Democrats. There was no room for someone like him on the Bagheria council. If you wanted to get anything done, it had to be with the full knowledge and consent of Cosa Nostra, otherwise forget it.'

Political corruption was not confined to Bagheria by any means. In the neighbouring satellite town of Villabate, the most prominent of Provenzano's contacts was Nino Fontana, known as 'Mister Millionaire'. Fontana was the deputy mayor and a front man for Simone Castello, one of Provenzano's most resourceful allies. Fontana and Castello were old friends and business partners. Fontana was leader of the socialist co-operatives behind the building contracts, but he also ran a scam to get EEC compensation, in which the fruit and vegetable growers' associations were ordering their members to destroy large quantities of their citrus crops to qualify for EEC grants.

In this environment of corruption and greed, Pio La Torre, recently appointed regional secretary of the Communist Party, made a preliminary effort to clean up the party and expose links with Cosa Nostra, but his demands for an investigation met with ferocious resistance.

Bagheria was still the playground of the rich – not the old aristocracy but the new moneyed criminal class. At the opposite end of town from the death chamber, along the shoreline at Mongerbino ad Aspra, mafiosi built themselves luxurious villas where their friends and families came to spend the summer holidays. On the winding coast road, high above the waves, is the walled entrance to Pino 'the Shoe' Greco's villa – tiered apartments descending to sea-level, among the pine trees. The villa boasts thirty-six rooms in different apartments, where high-ranking fugitives would bring their families to stay, occupying separate floors, each with its own living quarters. From their white-tiled balconies they looked out from the rocky promontory at Mongerbino and drank champagne with their host, the hit man.

To tour the little winding roads along the shore is to trace a map of Mafia country: in Aspra, Brancaccio boss Giuseppe Guttadauro had an elegant house by the shore, with a glassed-in terrace overlooking the water. Along the coast is a pretty fishing village with blue- and red-striped boats pulled up on the sand; a couple of streets back is the seaside hideout used by Trapani capo Matteo Messina Denaro. Police identified it by following Messina Denaro's girlfriend. Inside they found unmistakable clues to his presence: cigarette butts of his favourite brand and his greatest passion, a Playstation.

At the end of a narrow sandy path, right on the beach, is the villa belonging to Ciccio Pastoia – long-time friend, driver and 'alter ego' of Bernardo Provenzano. The villa is a masterpiece of 1970s' modernism: a two-tiered curving glass and cement structure covered, on the outside, with blue glass swimming-pool tiles.

While the Riina family drank cocktails with the Grecos overlooking the sea at sunset, and Ciccio Pastoia clinked glasses with his friends on the sheltered balcony of his villa, not far away men in industrial gloves were dissolving their erstwhile friends in acid baths.

As the capos relaxed and celebrated their latest victories, a young police captain, Beppe Montana, took his little boat out and nosed about the coves and bays along this stretch of coastline. He suspected that several mafiosi living in hiding had properties along the shore, and he spent his Sundays posing as a holidaymaker, peering into walled gardens and discreet terraces.

Back at the prosecutor's office, following their paper trail, investigators were pursing links between the various companies connected to Provenzano. Tracing connections between board members or investors, they arrived at a number of companies all located in the same Palermo street. Many of the trails led to Pino Lipari, a former surveyor and consultant for ANAS, the national road transport corporation. He had no criminal record and no apparent connection to Cosa Nostra, but Lipari emerged as one of Provenzano's most faithful associates and senior manager of his business interests.

Lipari was a busy, clever little man in his mid-forties. He had worked for the Cinisi boss Gaetano Badalamenti and had excellent contacts in local administration. Provenzano had met Lipari while he was in hiding as Badalamenti's guest. His faith was rewarded when Lipari came up with a system for milking the health system of billions. Together they would cream off a fortune from state funds, putting the Mafia on a new financial footing.

The Sicilian public health system was overstretched and crumbling after years of chronic underinvestment. Lipari had contacts in the local administration who would ask no questions about the inflated prices demanded by Provenzano's health companies. If hospital suppliers leased them expensive, cutting-edge machines that staff didn't know how to work, no one objected. Apparently legitimate companies appeared, with proper-sounding names and board members who were almost all relations or girlfriends of Bernardo Provenzano or his consultant Pino Lipari.

These companies were repeatedly awarded contracts for supplying the major hospitals in the region. The success of Lipari's system showed how much money there was to be made from health supplies if you had the right contacts in the administration – and there was no reason the system couldn't be rolled out across other areas, even on the mainland.

'When we tapped their phone lines, we discovered that there were meetings held in advance to agree who would win the contracts', says Pellegrini.

'We discovered a monopoly of health supplies,' Pellegrini wrote in his report, 'a cartel of companies which was grabbing bigger and bigger slices of a highly profitable market, given the high cost of scientific equipment used in hospitals.'

Provenzano's business activities signalled a new departure for Cosa Nostra: 'It was something completely new to us,' says Pellegrini, 'that a clan could be waging war on one front, while at the same time it was dedicated to developing the health supplies business. This is what became known, famously, as *la mafia imprenditrice*, "Mafia enterprise", whose methods are largely non-violent and whose front men have no previous convictions.

'There were some who underestimated what we were dealing with at that time. But not us. We never thought of these people as *viddani* or ignorant peasants, I've always liked the Sicilian saying "big boots, smart brain". Peasants' boots they may wear, but they've got good minds. I have always regarded them as extremely dangerous and extremely shrewd. I always thought of Provenzano as "the Accountant", because he made calculations. The work he was doing required a good brain.'

Pellegrini's 1984 report explained Cosa Nostra's qualitative leap: 'The mafioso, once his authority is secure, no longer needs to resort to violence or threats to impose his will; his presence and his word are enough for him to be involved in any business on his own terms and conditions.

'Businessmen have grasped this reality, recognizing the Mafia's authority: considering that, if they do not submit to the Mafia, they could not pursue their business activity, they have preferred and prefer to deal preventively with organized crime, thus avoiding the high cost of damage and personal harm.'

Since no local businesses could risk reporting Mafia extortion to the police, Pellegrini continued his assiduous tracking of suspects. The most difficult task faced by investigators was conducting surveillance on foot. 'If we sent anyone to follow a target, they would find themselves being followed. We'd be spotted in minutes. If they saw a vehicle they didn't know, they'd send out men in cars to block us in. We did manage to take photographs from inside a van or a truck, while we were pretending to set up road works.'

It came to the team's attention that the Bagheria Mafia was investing in a new diagnostic health centre, a project of particular interest to Provenzano. Riina used to tease Provenzano about his predilection for investments in health, but he was not the only one to spot a personal interest. Pellegrini has strong suspicions that the health business provided cover for Provenzano while he was on the run. He and his family needed health care over the years, and he also needed access to money, offices, bank accounts and so forth. The various health supply companies provided him with this infrastructure. Pellegrini suspects they also became channels for something else.

'We had our suspicions that there was drug trafficking going on. We picked up a conversation between two men – it may have been Lipari or Carmelo Gariffo – and one of them said, "Come and meet me, I've got something for you."

'It was a very intense moment for us, as we were convinced that one of these men would lead us to Provenzano.'

Carabinieri followed Carmelo Gariffo's car down corso Calatafimi, a long, tree-lined avenue on the outskirts of Palermo where exclusive villas are concealed by high walls, and watched him turn into a courtyard. They waited for him to come out but soon realized, when there was no sign of anyone coming or going, that there must be another exit. Sure enough, two hours later, Gariffo arrived from the other direction in a different car. After his driver searched the street for any suspicious vehicles, Gariffo, carrying a suitcase, got into his own car. The carabinieri gave chase but quickly realized they were being followed by the other driver and turned off.

'We don't know whether that suitcase contained drugs or money,' says Pellegrini ruefully, 'because we decided not to intervene, as it would have alerted the organization that we were watching them.'

Some years later he learned that Provenzano was staying just 50 metres from that courtyard, in an elegant villa with its own lush garden, surrounded by palm trees and purple bougainvillaea.

Pino Lipari was arrested in November 1983 and charged, along with seventeen others (some of them, including Provenzano and his companion Saveria Palazzolo, *in absentia*), with money-laundering. When Lipari left prison five years later, he was summoned by Uncle Binnu, who valued his business acumen and networking skills enough to risk re-employing a man with a criminal record.

After the success of his inroads into the health system, Provenzano was determined to achieve the same thing with other public contracts. Riina had a head start in this field through his man Angelo Siino, known as the Mafia's minister of public works, who controlled the awarding of contracts. Siino was a wealthy man, an exuberant type with a handlebar moustache and a passion for expensive watches, with a house in central Palermo, just off the fashionable via Libertà. He was exceptionally well connected, since he was the reference point for every major contract awarded throughout Sicily. But Provenzano took a dislike to him (he was Riina's man, and competition between the two was already heating up) and unceremoniously replaced him at the Mafia's 'ministry of works' with his own faithful business manager, Pino Lipari.

Siino, for all his powerful connections, had made a tactical error (probably on instructions from Riina) by blocking one of Provenzano's favoured Communist-backed construction companies from a lucrative contract to build aqueducts. He may have underestimated Riina's mild-mannered friend, but in any case he was swiftly punished for it – locked out of any future contracts in Bagheria. Giuffré recounted: 'It was war'. 'Not with guns, perhaps, but it was definitely war – on the political front, with Siino trying by any means, fair or foul, to crack open this protectionist fortress.'

Siino got his revenge: after his arrest he became the first state witness who had had close contact with Bernardo Provenzano and revealed how the Accountant managed his empire.

Lipari, as the new 'minister of works', operated a cartel to divide up contracts between a small, hand-picked group of companies known as the Tavolino or Round Table. These companies agreed among themselves whose turn it was to get the contract, so there was no need for them to discount their prices to underbid the others.

Quite the reverse: when a company was 'awarded' a contract, it paid 'tax' to the Mafia, which was reflected in its fee – and the fee, of course, came out of the public purse. People in Palermo were paying more for their water, waste disposal and street lighting than the inhabitants of any other city in Italy.

Lipari directed the Round Table from behind the scenes, closely monitored by Nino Giuffré and others, who were called in to 'keep order' if any of the companies failed to come up with the kickback. If any companies who were not members of the cartel made the mistake of thinking they could bid for a contract, Giuffré made sure they were 'strongly discouraged'. A bottle of petrol and a suggestive box of matches would usually do the trick, but sometimes he had to smash up a digger or set fire to a car.

'This cartel operated in the name of Provenzano', Giuffré explained. As a result, most of the time things went very smoothly.

This quantum leap in the Mafia's economic power had been foreseen, and might have been prevented. Sadly, the carabinieri's 1984 report on Provenzano's stranglehold on public administration was shelved. 'There was so much going on at the time', says Pellegrini, 'it sort of got lost.'

Pellegrini feels some satisfaction that his investigation was eventually proved right in almost every regard but inevitably also disappointment that the report, based on many months of assiduous police work, was overlooked. Actually it was swept aside by the events of what became known as *l'estate caldo*, the 'hot summer' of 1985.

On a Sunday afternoon in July, Beppe Montana, the young officer in charge of the squad hunting down fugitives, was shot dead as he got out of his little boat. The resourceful Montana had tried to make a virtue of his lack of official protection: running around on a scooter and snooping along the coast in his boat on his days off, looking for Mafia hideouts. Just over a week later his friend and colleague Ninni Cassarà, an idealistic, hard-working officer, was gunned down outside his home. Cassarà's murder was set up by several members of the Mafia commission, who had a personal investment in seeing his brilliant career brought to a premature end. Afterwards, according to insiders, there was a celebration.

Anti-Mafia prosecutors Falcone and Borsellino, who had spent the summer of 1985 incarcerated for their own safety on the prison island of Asinara (an irony not lost on them, considering the lovely seaside villas where the mafiosi would be spending the holidays), finally delivered their massive compilation of evidence for the biggest Mafia trial in history, known simply as the 'maxi'. An underground bunker had been built, lined with cages where over 400 defendants stood and watched proceedings, intimidating witnesses, sometimes heckling, even throwing food. The accusations were based on Buscetta's description of Cosa Nostra as a unified organization, with a hierarchical structure, and a central part of the prosecution focused on the rise of the Corleonesi to dominate this hierarchy. The trial opened in February 1986, although a third of the defendants were still at large. The most important of these were Bernardo Provenzano and Totò Riina.

Their boss, Luciano Liggio, had lost none of his attitude after a decade behind bars. He was an undoubted star of the proceedings, strutting and posturing from his cell overlooking the court, wielding a Cuban cigar as a gangsterish prop, demanding that his rights be respected. He insisted at one point that the defendants couldn't concentrate on the proceedings with the police guards watching them. In between court appearances Liggio painted: landscapes, seascapes, bunches of flowers – the career criminal's artistic soul burst out of him in splashes of colour. His lawyer encouraged the press to see this outpouring as the sign of a profound and sensitive humanity.

After his arrest in 1974 Liggio had directed Cosa Nostra from prison, but as the months passed, power devolved on to his joint lieutenants, Riina and Provenzano. They continued to shelter behind the figure of a nominal head of the commission: Michele Greco.

Greco was arrested ten days into the proceedings, tracked down to a deserted farm building in the mountains, and took his place alongside the caged mafiosi. In a statement delivered to his lawyer he emphasized his religious credentials: 'They call me The Pope, but I can't compare myself to any pope, not even the current one, except that my clear conscience and my profound faith make me, if not their superior, certainly their equal . . . I have always worked the land, which I inherited from my parents. I read a great deal, mostly the Bible.'

Once Greco was behind bars, there was no one to stand in Riina and Provenzano's way.

When the supergrass Tommaso Buscetta took the stand, the audience in the bunker was electrified – none more so than his former friends and allies in their cages. Never before had such a frank exposé of Cosa Nostra been heard in open court. Liggio was allowed to question him directly, but faced with Liggio's arrogant, strutting figure, Buscetta denied even knowing him. Liggio's vanity got the better of him, and he puffed up his own role, insisting he was on intimate terms with the most prominent Mafia bosses of the century.

While this drama played out in the concrete bunker, Riina and Provenzano were never far away.

5

The split

LIKE ALL THE best partnerships, Riina and Provenzano polarized
people.

'Signor Provenzano's sophisticated mind' was appreciated by Cosa
Nostra's minister of public works, the developer Angelo Siino. Riina
was 'a clod, a goatherd', despised for his failure to think strategically.

Riina's godson Giovanni Brusca preferred Riina's directness.
'When there was a problem, Riina would confront it, deal with it. He
would give his response – good or bad – but at least he gave it. Not
Provenzano. He is a slippery one. I call him the Philosopher, because
he never takes a stand about anything.'

When Liggio appointed his two trusty lieutenants joint leaders in
his absence, he knew they had different qualities. By the time their
mentor was arrested, the two men had a long history together. They
shared a home town, Corleone. 'The fact of having a common origin
strengthens their bond, it makes them a tighter group', says historian
Salvatore Lupo. They called each other *paesano* even when they
weren't on the best of terms: it was how they knew each other.

Both men played to their strengths: Riina was not particularly interested in contracts; Provenzano considered drug trafficking too risky.
Riina had a caustic sense of humour – as Provenzano began to suffer
with prostate trouble, Riina liked to tease him about his health problems
– but he could also throw a good celebratory banquet (particularly if
there was an execution to be toasted with champagne). Provenzano was
more private, a family man, affectionate to those who sought him out.

Few could see it from the outside, but they worked as a team. When
a difficult step had to be taken, they bought time by deferring to each
other.

'My friend and I don't always agree on everything,' Riina confided to Giuffré, 'but we never get up from the table until we've come to an agreement.'

To Giuffré this was a significant statement: it showed Riina, the hot-headed dictator, in a different light, forced to negotiate with his counterpart. Provenzano was always conscious that the leadership should appear to be harmonious. 'If there were disagreements, they sorted them out,' says the anti-Mafia prosecutor Pietro Grasso, 'so whatever happened was their joint responsibility. Even if they disagreed, they made a public show of being united.'

When the two leaders attended meetings together, Provenzano tended to say little or nothing during the discussions. On occasion he let it be known that he would give his view at the following meeting. This fuelled suspicions (which he carefully nurtured) that he had to consult an important contact. 'You have to remember that, according to the rules,' said Tommaso Buscetta, 'only one representative from the Corleonesi should have been allowed to attend commission meetings. Provenzano and Riina came as a couple. And the thing that made everyone furious was that Provenzano would never agree to anything. Even Riina was uncomfortable with the way he acted. All this proves to me that, at least in this particular phase, Provenzano was the boss, while Riina was champing at the bit.'

'When the commission held a meeting, Riina would go one time, the next time he'd send Bernardo Provenzano, or else they'd both cancel at the last minute and rearrange the whole thing', Brusca recalled.

Both were masters of the art of *tragedie* – a concept peculiar to Mafia culture, meaning pretending to be something you're not or manipulating others to believe what you want them to believe. In terms of a secret society like the Mafia, the ability to manipulate information (or disseminate rumours beneficial to you or detrimental to your adversaries) is essential. They would set brothers against each other, send rumours flying that old friends were plotting against each other. In the confusion their target would end up dead, killed by his own side. Riina could make a person believe he was in danger from a certain quarter, when in fact the danger came from Riina himself. Provenzano would feign ignorance about a murder when he had already given his consent. They played their parts: Provenzano may have seemed more avuncular, and Riino more dynamic, and men would gravitate towards one or the other; when they met in private, each would learn who had confided in the other.

The differences between the two men were not always so stark and clear. Provenzano was not just the man of peace: he put down a rebellion by a splinter group of gangsters in Gela, on Sicily's industrial south coast. The armed gangs, or *stiddari*, caused havoc in the town, stealing and shooting in the streets. Provenzano crushed the rebels in a violent war in which over 300 died.

Riina may not always have been the man of war. Lupo points out that we only have the *pentiti*'s accounts of Riina's leadership qualities – and they were all, by definition, his enemies. We don't have Riina's words of advice, his encouragement. 'Maybe Riina was a good mediator too.'

Maybe. On the other hand, Riina liked people to know that he didn't care how many he had to kill as long as he got his way. When he met the woman he loved, a teacher from Corleone, he told a friend, 'If they won't let me marry her, I'm going to have to kill some people.'

The man they called *u curtu* ('Shorty') spread fear. He had no problem condemning his allies to death. On the least suspicion of betrayal, or a notion that someone else had more charisma and might outshine him, he would order an execution. Riina had inherited from Liggio a small private army of killers, who were not all based in Corleone, or even Palermo, but planted in the different families in other parts of Italy. The secretive manner of his infiltration made him greatly feared.

We assume that Riina had taken the commanding role. 'Put simply', says assistant prosecutor Alfonso Sabella, 'in Cosa Nostra, whoever has military force has the power. Provenzano had political contacts, but that never held sway in the Mafia.'

But the balance of power between them was very complex. There is some disagreement about whether the two men's mentor and boss, Luciano Liggio, favoured Riina or Provenzano. He reportedly stood up in court and said, pointing to Riina, 'He is close to my heart.' When asked about Provenzano, he said: 'I know he's from my home town, but I don't know him.'

Buscetta suggested that this was deliberately misleading: that Provenzano was keeping out of the limelight, operating as Liggio's deputy while allowing Riina to attract all the attention. He portrayed Provenzano as an inscrutable loner who increased his power and charisma by being elusive. 'Provenzano would give people the run-around', he recalled. 'He was quite capable of giving someone an appointment at the top of a mountain. After walking for a whole day, the man would get to the appointed place – and find no one there. While he was walking back down, the fellow would meet one of Provenzano's men coming the other way, who informed him that the appointment would be postponed for a few weeks. And he'd tell him where to meet – somewhere completely different, maybe even a different province. The man would get there at last – and again no Provenzano. This would happen three or four times. Months would pass in which no one would see Provenzano, then suddenly he'd pop up when people were least expecting it. He has always liked to keep people guessing.'

In their judgement in 1992 on the murder of senior police investigator Emanuele Basile, who was shot in the back while he carried his four-year-old daughter in his arms, magistrates had already identified Riina's role as the executioner, the man of action, as distinct from Provenzano, the business brain.

'Cosa Nostra has a financial empire run by extremely competent individuals', said judge Antonino Caponetto. 'It's unthinkable that Riina could be running the whole thing. Riina is in charge of the armed wing of Cosa Nostra, while the organization, the powerful economic side, is run most successfully by others, with profits running into millions of billions of lire.'

Provenzano was acquitted of Basile's murder on the grounds that he would have been too busy running Cosa Nostra's financial affairs to have been bothered with messy matters like this. 'We only have to consider', reads the sentence, 'all the acquisitions made by various companies owned by the Corleonesi to understand how, in a convenient division of labour, it's Provenzano who represents the reference point for all the clans' investments.'

Provenzano had an important part to play, the judges concluded, but Riina was the 'true architect of the new bloody terror strategy'. While Provenzano looked after contacts with politicians and industrialists, Riina took care of territorial control.

'There's no reason he shouldn't have done it without my knowing,' Brusca later told investigators, 'but as far as I'm concerned Riina never got involved in contract management. He never had companies involved in handing out contracts; he was principally interested in collecting protection money on his territory.'

'When these great contract managers burst on to the scene, like Brusca, Siino . . . and undoubtedly Provenzano,' explains Sabella, 'Riina took a step back, partly because he didn't consider contracts sufficiently lucrative.'

Provenzano dealt with bankers, politicians and company directors, who found him easier to talk to; Riina dealt with hit men and enforcers.

After the Mafia war Riina and Provenzano's Corleonesi reigned supreme. However, the difference in their leadership styles and ideals was now becoming more polarized. Riina, who had never stepped aside to let Provenzano take his two-year turn as leader, as Liggio had instructed, became increasingly intolerant of dissent. When Provenzano disagreed with him, it took all his skill and cunning to say so without incurring Riina's wrath.

Giovanni Brusca described an episode that illustrated the difference between the two men. 'Two characters had to be eliminated. They were called to a meeting to discuss the problem, and Riina wanted them killed there and then. But Provenzano said they should let them go, and then see about what should be done. Salvatore Riina said he was boss and they had to do as he said.'

The two bosses had always appeared side by side at meetings through the 1970s, but after the war Riina usually attended commission meetings alone. The *pentito* Salvatore Cancemi explained: 'Provenzano attended all the commission meetings in the '80s, but Salvatore Riina didn't agree with the way he conducted meetings; he didn't agree with his terms, the arrangements he made, or even the subjects he raised for discussion. As a result, Riina and Provenzano made a deal. They would meet on equal terms and come to an agreement acceptable to both of them, then Riina would present their joint viewpoint to the commission.'

Buscetta didn't believe for a moment that Provenzano had been pushed aside: rather, he thought that he had a secret hold over Riina. Buscetta suspected he had access to a high-level contact on whom Cosa Nostra depended. 'If Provenzano managed to survive the Mafia war in spite of being out of favour with Riina, he must have had a guardian angel.'

Provenzano's tendency to prevaricate had been useful once, but Riina was finding it increasingly infuriating. Giovanni Brusca, the Corleonesi's executioner, would be waiting, shotgun at the ready, for his orders – while Binnu delayed. Brusca preferred his godfather's more direct style: 'If Riina said, "Falcone must be killed in Palermo", Provenzano would come out with some objection, like, "I think it's better to do it in Rome." He would always play for time.'

Provenzano knew better than to disagree openly with a murder sentence. Giuseppe di Cristina had tried that, when he and Riina were planning to kill the carabiniere Colonel Russo – and paid for it. 'Provenzano claimed he wanted Stefano Bontate dead as much as anyone, but he never got round to giving Aglieri the order to do it', Brusca complained. 'Provenzano has always been the same: he waits for others to take the initiative.'

Months later, long after Bontate was shot dead, Riina joked with his godson: 'I'm still waiting for my *paesano* to give Aglieri the order.'

Another sign of division between the leaders, however outwardly united they might seem, was that both men kept their business and political contacts to themselves. Giuffré observed that Provenzano's contacts with professionals included lawyers and politicians, 'many of whom I don't even know, because Provenzano has always been very guarded and kept his contacts to himself. He has a part of Cosa Nostra which is just *cosa sua*, "his thing", his own private business.'

'After the war Riina and Provenzano had the whole of Sicily in their hands', Giuffré later said. 'For a time they were in perfect synchrony. Then there were some nasty disagreements between them, made worse by the people around Provenzano, who did not see Riina in a good light. The more time passed, the worse the arguments between them became, and if they hadn't arrested Riina, I think we would have seen some fireworks.'

Within the constraints of the joint leadership, perhaps Provenzano was already mapping out the future of the organization.

The two leaders also had different approaches when it came to politics, and it was this that eventually led to a definitive rift between them. By the time the maxi-trial was half-way through, Cosa Nostra's cosy relationship with some members of the ruling Christian Democratic Party, which had provided mutual benefits for over a decade, was coming apart.

Falcone's sustained pressure on Cosa Nostra was making things difficult for the Corleonesi. He was attacking them where it hurt: seizing assets and property that had previously remained beyond reach, and making sure that sentences stuck instead of being overturned within months. Young mafiosi swept along with the excitement of getting rich by violence were suddenly looking at long gaol sentences. As the maxi-trial progressed, those Christian Democrats who had previously exerted their influence on behalf of the Mafia sent word that there was nothing they could do to rig the outcome.

The risk represented by the young bloods stuck in gaol was clear: many of them would do anything to get their sentences reduced – even talk. Riina, a master of violent, stirring rhetoric, described collaborators, or penitents, as the worst evil ever to afflict Cosa Nostra and ordered his men to 'hunt down' members of the penitents' families and kill them. He made it sound like a new sport.

That spring the political crisis was the burning topic of commission meetings. Parliament had been dissolved, and a general election was scheduled for June. Riina was frustrated and enraged that he could no longer force 'tame' politicians such as Salvo Lima to do his bidding.

The commission was summoned to a meeting. Each member was collected by a trusted driver with instructions from Riina and delivered to a group of buildings out in the country. The cars drove into a garage, where the heads of the Mafia families could get out without

73

being seen and were shown through a door into the building. They entered a large, formal meeting room at the centre of which stood a long table, with chairs all the way down – at least ten comfortably each side, and one at the head. According to Giuffré's account, they greeted each other as old friends, grasping each other by the shoulders and planting a kiss on both cheeks: Matteo Messina Denaro, the young, fast-living boss of Trapani, who took his customary place on Riina's right; the violent, ambitious Graviano brothers from Brancaccio; the implacable hit man Pieruccio Lo Bianco, who would himself be murdered. But for now they were all friends.

Some faces were new: a few of the commission members were unable to attend, owing to their unfortunate arrest, and were represented by a brother or a son. Once the bosses were all seated, smoking cigarettes or taking sips of water, Riina strode in and took his position at the head of the table.

'Everyone knows each other?' Riina asked peremptorily.

One capo got to his feet. 'Uncle Totuccio,' he addressed Riina, 'I don't know this gentleman here', pointing to Giuffré. Riina formally introduced Giuffré to Nino Madonia, the eldest son of the powerful Madonia clan, as they could not otherwise speak freely in each other's presence, and the meeting got under way.

Riina announced that he was planning to dump any politicians who had shown themselves to be untrustworthy. To punish their contacts within the Christian Democrats for failing Cosa Nostra, Riina announced that the organization would be backing the Socialist Party, the PSI, and their allies the Radical Party in the forthcoming elections. The switch was intended to send a clear message, a classic Mafia threat: 'We made you, and we can destroy you.'

The capos were somewhat alarmed by this news: many of them had contacts in the Christian Democrats who had served them well over the years. The discussion was long and heated. Provenzano wasn't there, by arrangement with Riina. The joint leaders had made this decision on security grounds – in case Riina should be arrested or (God forbid!) murdered at the meeting, Provenzano would remain at large – but it suited Riina to control the information that reached Provenzano. The two leaders held regular face-to-face meetings where they discussed policy. But Provenzano had other friends on the commission who would quietly report back to him: Carlo Greco from Bagheria and Pietro Aglieri, boss of Santa Maria di Gesù. They, among others, wanted to know what the PSI would do in return for votes. 'It's all in hand', Riina assured them. 'I have been given guarantees.'

The Socialists, under Bettino Craxi, in whom Riina had invested great hopes for a fruitful collaboration, were campaigning for a limit to the magistrates' power. This was intended to protect their own activities from investigation, but it also clearly served the Mafia's purposes. But Riina had another reason to back the Socialists. He had not just 'woken up one morning and decided to vote PSI', he explained: he had been in negotiations with a prominent industrialist. One of his companies had been awarded a series of development contracts; in return, he had promised to talk to his political contacts about fixing trials.

At the end of the meeting the decision was toasted with strong local wine, and the bosses were served an enormous lunch: local dried sausage with fennel seed and veal on the bone with bread and black olives; a mountain of fragrant pasta with tuna and capers; thick slices of tomato in a pool of olive oil and scattered with salt. After exchanging jokes and catching up with news of other *mandamenti*, the bosses dispersed, as they had come, through the hidden garage door, each with his driver, back to their secret hideaways.

Provenzano's representatives reported the decision back to him. He heard the news with many misgivings. Provenzano has been described as a Christian Democrat loyalist, true to the old guard, but his concerns were more pragmatic: Cosa Nostra's most useful and long-standing contacts were members of the Christian Democrats, and he saw no good reason for alienating them. At the same time, he didn't believe the Socialists would deliver.

He arranged to meet Riina to discuss the ruling. They talked cordially enough but quickly ran into difficulties. Riina was infuriated by Binnu's dogged reasoning and his endless objections. He stormed about the room and slammed his fist on the table, his voice piercing and relentless. Provenzano, as always, sat quite still, smiling and looking down, giving no ground. Eventually, Riina persuaded Provenzano there was nothing he could say to change his mind. 'I accepted the decision to vote for the Socialists,' Provenzano later told Giuffré, 'but that doesn't mean I agreed with it.'

Once the decision had been taken to support the PSI, the capos received their orders. Fax machines beeped into life, spewing out pages with the names of the new candidates they were to support. Giuffré rushed round to the local representatives, who were putting the finishing touches to their own campaign to support their old friends and allies from the Christian Democrats. Many of the campaigns had been funded out of their own pockets: leaflets had been printed, jamborees and outdoor banquets planned. Speeches were prepared, with posters and coloured lights. When Giuffré turned up and told them, in his lugubrious manner, that they had a new candidate, they were not best pleased.

'It was a real problem, particularly in areas where they'd supported the same party for years, and some of them were hostile to the new policy. The capos told me they were finding it extremely difficult to persuade their people, as we were changing a long tradition. But those were the orders, and we had to obey.'

The Mafia's support for the PSI was scarcely a secret. An election poster appeared in the window of a bar in Brancaccio belonging to a local mafioso. The bar had been closed down because of the owner's criminal association, and the door was sealed by the authorities, but the owner's defiant message was clear.

At the June elections the Socialists made significant gains. Furious claims that they were backed by the Mafia were dismissed as sour grapes. A few months later the Socialists pushed through a referendum to limit magistrates' powers.

But any advantage the Mafia gained in the elections was lost when the maxi-trial verdicts were announced in December 1987. After a record-breaking five weeks' seclusion, eating and sleeping in their Spartan quarters in the concrete bunker, the jury finally returned its verdicts.

On a December evening the prisoners listened in silence to the verdicts being read in the judge's high, tremulous voice, for well over an hour. They inflicted heavy blows on Cosa Nostra, with guilty verdicts for 344 defendants and a total of 2,665 years in prison. Liggio was acquitted of running the organization from prison, but life sentences were pronounced for nineteen mafiosi, including Totò Riina and Bernardo Provenzano. It was an unprecedented defeat for the Mafia – previous trials had almost all resulted in acquittals for lack of evidence. Riina had failed to fix the verdict.

Provenzano maintained that Riina's decision to support the PSI was a disaster. Giuffré remembers that election as the beginning of a major dispute between the two leaders. 'I'd have to say that at this precise moment the rift between Riina and Provenzano got wider, a rift that most people had not really noticed before this point. But Provenzano didn't agree with this experiment in supporting the Socialists and the Radical Party, and I think I'd have to say that events have proved him right.

'Unfortunately the strategy misfired and the rift opened up between the Mafia and politics, because there was an inevitable reaction from both the Christian Democrats and the Socialist party, so that by the '90s we had both [justice Minister Claudio] Martelli and [Giulio] Andreotti against us.' Instead of heeding their 'warning' and making concessions to the Mafia, the Christian Democrats supported a raft of anti-Mafia measures.

The division between the two men became more marked; although they maintained the peace in public, the façade was becoming increasingly thin. The two men who had hatched so many clever plots against their enemies were getting close to hatching similar plots against each other.

The next few years were some of the most turbulent in Cosa Nostra's history. Sensitive to any threat to his charismatic leadership, Riina turned on the star players in his own ranks. Even better: he would get the man's closest allies to do it – convinced, by Riina's skilful manipulation, that their lives depended on it. The hit man Pino 'the Shoe' Greco had been the Corleonesi's most reliable killer and Riina's host at his elegant villa until his brilliant career went to his head, and Riina had him murdered by his own men. Another reliable hit man for the Corleonesi, Agostino Marino Mannoia, who had been part of so many of Riina's execution squads, suddenly vanished. Filippo Marchese, the enthusiastic strangler of Palermo's notorious chamber of death, disappeared in a vat of acid, just as he had dispatched so many of Riina's enemies. While Riina was reinventing the savagery of organized crime, his killers buried the bodies on a rubbish dump.

During this time Riina allegedly hatched a plot to murder Provenzano. With the full knowledge that his words would be taken as a threat, he inquired: 'Does Binnu go out in the morning or the evening?' Anyone hearing that innocent-sounding question would know that he would be doing Uncle Totò a favour by dispatching his irksome joint leader. Provenzano began to see less of his friends and made plans to tighten his security.

Falcone and Borsellino gained the confidence of men of honour who were appalled by the way the organization was going and wanted to take their revenge against the Corleonesi by revealing the secrets of Cosa Nostra. Nino Calderone, whose brother Pippo, capo of Catania, had been murdered, agreed to collaborate with Falcone in the spring of 1987. He revealed a great deal about the Mafia's political patronage and its protection rackets. He also trespassed on the holy ground of Provenzano's contracts, giving investigators a detailed picture of the relationship between Cosa Nostra, captains of industry and politicians. When Francesco Marino Mannoia revealed the Corleonesi's *modus operandi*, Riina killed his mother, his aunt and his sister. And there were more.

Falcone's tremendous progress in his investigations irked many of his colleagues, who were jealous of his success and hostile to his methods. Cosa Nostra took advantage of confusion and infighting in the Palermo prosecutors' office (known as the Poison Palace) and unleashed a new round of violence and intimidation. Two senior judges, who were due to hear the appeals against the maxi-trial verdicts, were murdered.

While the prosecutors argued, sinister forces were at work, threatening Falcone's use of 'penitent' mafiosi. In May 1989 Salvatore Contorno, who had been in hiding in the USA after giving important testimony in the maxi-trial, suddenly turned up in Sicily. Police arrested him in a hideout stacked with guns of every size and calibre.

He had apparently returned to wreak his revenge on the Corleonesi. As conspiracy theories abounded, Falcone was accused of letting Contorno come back to kill off the mafiosi he couldn't catch.

A rebellion began to foment against Riina's leadership among capos and soldiers who felt his iron rule too harsh. Even his brother-in-law Leoluca Bagarella was angry enough to talk about a rebellion: he had been told he couldn't marry his fiancée because her uncle (the strangler) had been murdered, which would have lowered his status.

By 1991 the situation had got so bad that finally government ministers realized they could not turn a blind eye to organized crime any longer. After a government reshuffle Claudio Martelli, the justice minister, saw an opportunity to make his mark. Never mind that just a few years earlier, he had been campaigning against the magistrature. He invited Falcone to become director of penal affairs in the Ministry of Justice, and Falcone, exhausted by the jostling and back-biting, the poison and rumour-mongering in Palermo, accepted. Against all the odds it was the beginning of a serious fightback against Cosa Nostra.

Falcone initiated a review of organized crime cases across the whole country, which resulted in the rearrest of bosses just released from prison, including Michele Greco. Magistrates suspected of leniency towards Mafia defendants were scratched off any lists for new positions. A super-prosecutor's office was planned, to co-ordinate organized crime investigations across the country, while specialist local anti-Mafia pools were created. Finally the government accepted the importance of a co-ordinated anti-Mafia strategy.

Corrupt councils were dissolved in towns, including Bagheria, across the south, wherever the Mafia had infiltrated local government and drained funds. As the maxi-trial sentences came up for review, the judge who had overturned several sentences against mafiosi, Corrado 'sentence killer' Carnevale, was transferred.[13]

After years of complacency the anti-Mafia crusade finally became a vote-winner, and political parties came under pressure to root out Mafia candidates in Sicily and elsewhere. Riina's violent regime had provoked a devastating response. The capos, weary and disoriented by so much violence, were disaffected.

The difference in approach between Riina and his joint leader had become more marked than ever. The capos closest to the highest echelons of Cosa Nostra gravitated to one side or the other as they tended towards the policy of violence or of industry.

'Ordinary people supported him [Provenzano]', said one mafioso, not knowing the police were listening to his every word. 'They didn't support that other one [Riina], who was serving the interests of a handful of crazy maniacs. I gave these people my life. I am honest enough to admit it, Riina is a complete madman. The other one is more moderate, let's face it. I've talked to the old man [Provenzano], I've eaten meals with him. He is a completely different proposition. Wise.'[14]

Brusca, 'the Executioner', remained loyal to his godfather, Riina, who was a man after his own heart. He admired him, and he feared him. He liked the fact that he could joke around with Riina in a way he never could with his own father, but he retained a healthy respect for his anger. 'If anyone needed money, Riina would be the first to put his hand in his pocket. But if any of us tried to trick or short-change him, he went berserk. He's generous in his own way. In general, if there was a problem that needed sorting out, he would give his answer, yes or no. You knew where you stood. But with Provenzano – never.'

Some felt judged by Provenzano's clean-living, pious style. Matteo Messina Denaro, an ambitious, womanizing young blood from the west coast, Playstation junkie and chain smoker, was no great fan of Uncle Binnu either; according to Brusca, 'he was Riina's man, and never got on with Provenzano.'

Provenzano gathered around him a loyal band of moderates: the developer Pino Lipari, who had been convicted of Mafia association in the maxi-trial but continued to serve; his great friend Piddu Madonia, scion of a Mafia dynasty and loyal deputy; and the young, charismatic boss of Santa Maria di Gesù, Pietro Aglieri. Nino Giuffré, coolly detached, quietly building up his own empire around Caccamo, remained on the sidelines for now.

Onofrio Morreale was a trusted member of the upcoming generation, particularly favoured by Provenzano. If he was known at all to the Bagheria Mafia, it was as a common armed robber. But Provenzano chose him personally as his 'pupil', according to Giuffré: Provenzano presented him for initiation to Cosa Nostra in a ceremony kept secret from all but a handful of insiders. While the situation in Bagheria was somewhat volatile, Morreale's privileged position was kept quiet. Later he was engaged to Nicolò Eucaliptus's daughter and considered the natural heir to Provenzano in Bagheria.

In the organization at large there was a motion to split from the Corleonesi, but you didn't divorce a violent abusive boss like Riina with impunity. The only way out seemed to be to annihilate Cosa Nostra itself. A group of bosses held a meeting to discuss dissolving the organization, laying down their arms and splitting up the families. 'We were talking about breaking up the whole thing, before 1990', said Nino Giuffré. 'In the '60s Cosa Nostra had been dissolved and gone underground, so there was a line of thought, particularly amongst the older members, that we could close the whole thing down and start up again once things had calmed down. If we had, we would have avoided so much evil. But the Corleonesi wouldn't do it.'

Provenzano, for all that he disagreed with Riina's methods, was one of those Corleonesi. Throughout this phase of mounting disaffection within Cosa Nostra he bided his time, plotting his own strategy. Plotting, perhaps, how to remove Riina and take his place.

In the meantime Provenzano and Riina met regularly on Saturday afternoons, to discuss business and settle up payments. Provenzano would be dropped off by his regular driver, Ciccio Pastoia, at the Città Mercato, the biggest shopping centre on the outskirts of Palermo, and picked up by Riina's driver. He'd be taken to the nearby house of a trusted intermediary, where Riina would be waiting. These meetings were almost always in private, just the two of them. They would never talk on the telephone, so these meetings were the forum for all their planning and accounting. If they were at times explosive, their hosts were too discreet to hear it.

While the storm gathered about them, towards the end of summer 1991 many of the most powerful Corleonesi were living in hiding in and around Trapani, on the western tip of the island. They lived as though the apocalypse they had created was far away, in a dream. Trapani is an ancient port, with a picturesque historic centre within ancient stone walls. The cobbled streets twist and turn around the fixed point of the cathedral. The modern city spreads out from the city walls, its traffic-choked streets sprawling along the coast and up the hills behind.

Along these streets the fugitive boss Bernardo Provenzano buzzed on his moped, hopping between Trapani and the Mafia fiefdom of Mazara del Vallo. Provenzano lived like a normal citizen during this turbulent period. And not just him but the other Corleonesi as well: Riina, Bagarella and Brusca. It was quite an undertaking for the boss of the local Mafia family responsible for their safety and hospitality. Each one had a villa for himself and his family to live in, a bodyguard and driver assigned to him, and a trusted messenger.

The mafiosi had money, and they had style: Armani and Rolex watches. Provenzano favoured cashmere suits and silk shirts. One young mafioso was most impressed when he met 'the Accountant' (he would never dare to call him Uncle Binnu, and certainly never heard him called 'the Tractor'). He described 'a very distinguished gentleman, about sixty, very well kept. He was wearing a yellow polo shirt, buttoned up to the neck, and a checked jacket. What made the greatest impression on me were his shoes: they were beautifully made, in brown leather, with an oval painted on, and a flying duck.'[15]

Provenzano would receive such extravagant items as gifts, but he wore them as curiosities: they meant very little to him. What gave him the most pleasure was a set of clothes that would help him blend into the background – wherever he found himself.

Life among the fugitive bosses was congenial; they were like a big happy family, as Giovanni Brusca describes it, 'before the poison set in, before the betrayals, the confessions'.

Banquets had always been an important part of the Corleonesi's style: after a major victory, a summit or a ceremony to initiate new members they would have a great feast. They were important bonding occasions, to consolidate a feeling that the men were all working

Bernardo Provenzano after his arrest on 11 April 2006, after forty-three years on the run. 'You don't know what you're doing', he told police.

The sheep farm near Corleone where Provenzano lived for a year before he was finally arrested. The two men are by the door to his hideout. The owner had put up a TV arial for him, and built on a new bathroom.

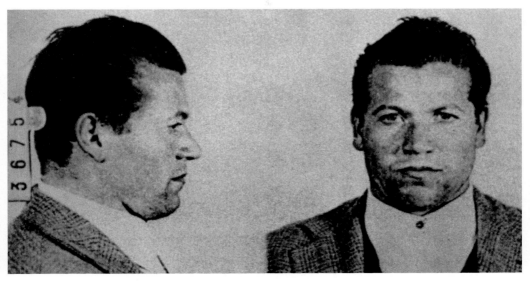

Bernardo Provenzano (known as 'the Tractor'): police mugshot after his arrest for stealing cheese and cattle rustling in 1958, aged twenty-five. During his four decades as a fugitive this was the only image the police had to go on.

Bernardo Provenzano (by now known as 'the Accountant'): police mugshot, 2006, aged seventy-three. He had been convicted in his absence of twenty-one murders and been given three life sentences.

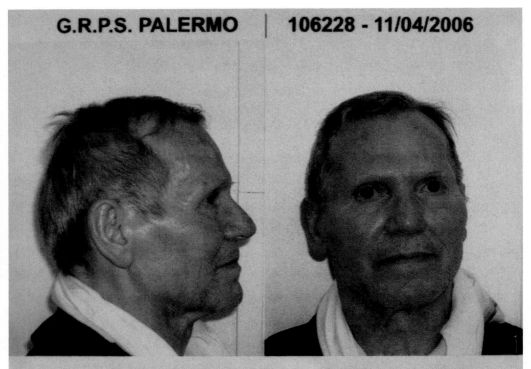

G.R.P.S. PALERMO | 106228 - 11/04/2006

Provenzano before leaving for his brief military service in the air force, 1954. He was dismissed after only six months on grounds of ill health, with a record of good conduct.

Totò Riina as a young man, pictured on his ID card. He and Provenzano grew up in Luciano Liggio's gang of cattle rustlers and became his joint lieutenants in the Corleone mafia.

Totò Riina, already a wanted criminal, in Venice in the 1970s. Riina and his family lived in hiding for decades as he and Provenzano built their empire, straying from home only on exceptional occasions and, apparently, holidays.

Saveria Benedetta Palazzolo, Provenzano's companion of thirty-seven years and the mother of his two sons. She lived with him on the run until 1992, when he sent her and the boys to live in Corleone.

Luciano Liggio, boss of the Corleonesi and Provenzano's mentor, in court, 1987. He was a man of extreme violence and intense rages, changeable and moody as a child.

Vito Ciancimino, son of a Corleone barber, during his brief term as mayor of Palermo, 1970. Provenzano steered Ciancimino's political career and protected him.

and fighting together, on the same side. They were ostentatious occasions: everyone would bring something – everyone *had to* bring something, and the arrival at the banquet would look like the journey of the magi, as twenty or thirty gangsters arrived bearing gift-wrapped boxes.

Serious gastronomy is a manly concern in Sicily; every Sunday men drive many miles to get the best beef cuts or the freshest cheese. The guests would outdo each other to bring something particularly good. They would bring pasta al forno, with ragù and tomatoes, and mozzarella cheese that melted into long strings; some would bring packages of meat that the barbecue king, the bearded murderer Calogero Ganci, would sear expertly on his home-built grill. They'd bring fish, or seafood, to be grilled and spruzzed with lemon and olive oil. On one occasion Giovanni Brusca brought prawns and scoffed the lot while the other guests were distracted by the beefsteaks and involtini of minced veal and melting caciocavallo cheese. The rest would bring puddings: cannoli from Piana degli Albanesi, the little mountain town isolated from the world, where the sheep's-milk ricotta makes the perfect sweet creamy filling. There would be the best local wines to drink, and cases of champagne.

These men-only banquets were exuberant occasions where this happy band of murderers could let off steam, releasing some of the tension that had built up between them and the continual stress under which they lived from day to day. Totò Riina, who was naturally sociable, would be ready with witty put-downs; even the normally grim-faced Leoluca Bagarella would lighten up. The banquets would last six or seven hours and would usually end with a food fight or a dousing with buckets of water. Once, Brusca recalled, the Trapani boss was trapped on a table, screaming for mercy, surrounded by murderers trying to tickle him.

The festive scene was very different from another Christmas banquet, some years before, when the Corleonesi were rising to power. In 1982 Riina had invited Rosario Riccobono, boss of Partanna Mondello, to the west of Palermo, and his men, to a friendly barbecue. Riccobono had tried to prove his loyalty to the ambitious Riina by betraying members of his own family, but he underestimated

Riina's notion of loyalty. After a congenial barbecue, sated on grilled spicy salsiccia and beefsteak, Riccobono dropped off in his chair. He was woken by his host's executioners, tightening a rope around his neck. None of his men survived that festive celebration.

The Christmas banquet in 1991 was celebrated in Mazara del Vallo in style: the Corleonesi wanted to show they were riding high. The major capos were all there, and Riina presided, becoming his jovial self as such occasions demanded, teasing and wisecracking with his men. The Christmas feast was a welcome occasion to laugh and joke with each other and, for the time being, forget what loomed on the horizon. But there was one boss who wasn't present on that Christmas Day.

Provenzano spent the day riding around Mazara del Vallo on his moped. He explained that it was for security reasons, so that he and Riina could not be taken together – in the past both police and Cosa Nostra had used the quiet days of Christmas to strike. The ostentatious banqueting culture was not to his taste, it smacked of decadence. This was to be the last of the great formal Mafia feasts: under Provenzano's rule only a trusted few were ever invited to sit down with the boss, and no one went to restaurants any more. Such extravagance, such risky effusion, was no longer the order of the day.

By staying away, Provenzano also put a further distance between himself and Riina's bloody dictatorship. He had seen what was coming, and he didn't like it.

6

Family matters

O N A BRIGHT sunday morning in Corleone on 5 April 1992 the carabiniere barracks were abuzz. It was election day, and the armed forces were on the alert throughout Italy, but this local anticipation had less to do with politics than with a highly unusual visitor.

The imposing yellow barracks dominated the wide central square of Corleone, set back behind a high wall. Its courtyard, bristling with palm trees, echoed with the sound of striding boots. Cars parked under the trees outside the gate were showered with blossom. Across the square a few tables were arranged on the pavement outside the bar, but the locals drank their coffee inside, talking earnestly about the impostors from the north who claimed to represent their interests. A huge hoarding advertised 'Don Corleone's aperitif'. In front of the barracks, behind a cast-iron fence, a garden stood closed and locked, its fountains dry, its plants withering among the rubbish left by night-time trespassers.

A few days earlier the carabinieri had received a visit from Bernardo Provenzano's lawyer announcing that his long-time companion, Saveria Benedetta Palazzolo, would be coming to live in Corleone, bringing her sons with her.

The former seamstress had disappeared from view more than fifteen years earlier, after a brief courtship with the outlaw from Corleone, and was presumed to have been living with him as a fugitive all these years. The lawyer had insisted on total secrecy, to avoid a press scrum.

Saveria arrived promptly at the station with her lawyer and her sons in tow. She hurried in through the tall gates, her heels clicking over the flagstones. She wore a dark suit and pearl ear-rings – an ageing look for her forty-seven years. Her greying hair was swept back from her face, which had an intelligent, if guarded, look. Her eyes were pale blue and penetrating, with sharp, expressive eyebrows and high cheekbones. If she was nervous about voluntarily entering a carabiniere station after years of avoiding the police, she certainly didn't let it show.

'Signora Palazzolo here has come to see the captain', her lawyer announced to a young officer on the desk.

'Well, he's extremely busy, you know there's an election . . .'

'I don't think you understand. Signora Palazzolo *Provenzano* is here to see the captain', the lawyer explained.

The young officer blanched and leaped into action, fairly running off to inform his senior officer that the distinguished visitor had arrived.

Signora Palazzolo was ushered into the captain's office, anxious to get the formalities over with, and drew on all her reserves of dignity to confirm her personal details: 'Born in Cinisi, in Palermo district, on 13 July 1945, permanent address via Generale Artale 48, Cinisi.' She announced, for the official record, her boys' names and ages, and their paternity. The two boys, aged nine and sixteen, acutely uncomfortable and sensing themselves observed, listened in silent humiliation. Years later they described that fateful day in an interview with the BBC.

'At the police station that day they asked us a lot of questions', said Angelo. 'It was a very strange thing for me, I'd never been in that situation before. I felt like a fish out of water. I was sixteen, and he [Paolo] was only nine, he didn't even understand what was going on, they just stood him in the corner.'

'I was just watching what was going on and not really understanding, as usual', added Paolo, laughing.

'They asked all the usual questions that have been asked of us endlessly – where had we been, who had been protecting us . . . but these are questions I will never answer.'

What had life been like for them on the run, before they and their mother came out of hiding to live in Corleone?

'I'll give you a short answer, but I'm not going to explain it', Angelo replied. 'It was like being under house arrest.'

The captain was longing for answers to his questions, but he could not insist: he remained congenial and respectful, hoping, perhaps, to build a good rapport with the Boss's wife. The wife of one of Italy's most wanted was sitting in front of him, and there was nothing the captain could do to make her tell him where he was. He ventured: 'I hope your husband will follow your excellent example . . .' Every time he mentioned her husband, she raised her eyes heavenwards, with exasperation, or possibly hinting that he was no longer on this earth.

The warrant for Palazzolo's arrest had been revoked some months previously, after her three-year sentence for money-laundering had been commuted to aiding and abetting, which for family members was not a crime (Italian law has always favoured the principle of keeping the family sacred, a principle that the Mafia has always successfully exploited). There had been frenzied preparation for this apparently spontaneous appearance: her lawyer had been working for months to make sure that there was no risk of her being arrested. Tommaso Cannella, one of her husband's closest allies and his strategist, had smoothed the way for her return by obtaining guarantees from local politicians that there would be no trouble.

'I have no outstanding debt to the law', announced the Boss's wife. 'I wish to reside in Corleone undisturbed, I intend to bring up my boys here, and I will be living with my brother-in-law Salvatore.'

With that announcement she had clearly said all she intended to, and her manner left no opening for further questions. The carabinieri had, for the first time in over two decades, a living link to one of their most wanted criminals, within their grasp – but they could find no pretext to detain her. Instead, they politely gave her a lift up the hill to her brother-in-law's house, a large but unpretentious ochre town house on the corner of via Colletti, a narrow cul-de-sac in the old part of town.

The door opened to admit the small party, then closed again, firmly shutting out the officers who had delivered them. From that moment on, the carabinieri kept a close watch on her movements, in a surveillance operation that would continue for the next fourteen years. The locals, old couples who had lived in the same narrow cobbled streets all their lives, would have noted the arrival and said nothing. Washing hung from every floor, sheets and shirts would have drifted in the breeze, as they do to this day, half-hiding white-haired grand-mothers sitting on their balconies. In the dusty streets at the edge of town, between tractors and woodstacks, boys would play in the dust, shouting and chasing each other, just as Binnu used to play with his friends.

Angelo and Paolo followed their uncle up three flights of stairs and put their bags down in their new bedroom. They could step out on to the balcony, with its corrugated plastic roof: from here they could see across the rooftops to the mountain ridge and down onto the tiny courtyard below. This town would have been at once so familiar to them from family stories and so strange. Their father talked to them often about his childhood, the beatings and hardship – and here they were, in his family home. Paolo, as he later recalled, was sullen and brooding about having to make another move. Angelo had to cheer up his little brother and take care of his mother.

As soon as the local police heard about the notorious family's arrival, they knocked smartly at Salvatore Provenzano's door and, refusing to be outdone, requested that Palazzolo accompany them to the station to make a statement. 'I will only come in the presence of the carabinieri', she told them. The subsequent procession to the local police station, and more fruitless questioning, observed by an officer of the carabinieri, was an uncomfortable ritual for all concerned and did nothing for relations between the two security forces.

Provenzano's wife's appearance in Corleone, homeland of the ruling clan of Cosa Nostra, electrified the island, sparking a frenzy of rumour and speculation. Nothing in Cosa Nostra is done without consideration of the signals it will send out; the membership, spread across the island and often unreachable by all the usual means, must rely on the correct interpretation of signals, hints and symbolic actions. Investigators contacted their informers for any inside gossip, trying to grasp the meaning of Provenzano's wife and children sud-denly materializing with no explanation.

In the feverish debate that followed, a consensus emerged: if the boss's wife and sons were coming out in the open, claiming their right to live as legitimate citizens in Corleone, it could only mean that her companion of over twenty years was dead.

Where had Palazzolo and her sons spent the years as fugitives from justice? It was said that the boys spoke English and German fluently; how perfect for the sons of an international gangster. Since their father's younger brother Simone lived in Germany, it was widely assumed they had been living with him. Uncle Simone, who had left Sicily in 1969 after he was charged with attempted murder and conspiracy (of which he was later acquitted), was tracked down in 2000 by a reporter at his modest suburban apartment block in Nordrhein-Westfalen, and asserted that the family had indeed been living with him. Asked about his brother's millions, he replied: 'Are you having me on? You have got to be joking. I was the one who supported Bernardo's boys. Until a few years ago I paid for the house they rented in Corleone. But then they inherited some money.'

Simone was aggrieved by the carabinieri, who had made sudden appearances to search the apartment and once accused him of being his brother. 'You don't know what it's like to endure what I have been through', he lamented. 'To be considered a certain way because you're supposed to be part of something that actually does a lot of good.'[16]

Saveria's principal income, after she moved to Corleone, was wired to her from Germany, but although they lived modestly, it seems unlikely that Binnu's wife and two children were supported solely on Simone's factory wages.

These days the family's exile in Westfalen is considered an urban myth. Paolo speaks German because he's a language student. Provenzano never strayed far from home: he regularly attended commission meetings, which would have been impractical if he had been living abroad. But he was always extremely secretive about where he was living: he didn't tell even his closest advisers, and would usually change drivers *en route* to meetings. Police secretly recorded conversations in the Provenzano home and gave tapes of the boys' conversations to a dialect analyst, who detected a slight Trapani accent. They took photos of Angelo and Paolo to schools in Trapani, where a few schoolchildren positively identified them.

Some of the years in hiding the Provenzano family had apparently lived comfortably in a luxurious Palermo apartment. For a long period Provenzano was living with his family in his private fiefdom of Bagheria. Gino Ilardo, himself a member of a powerful Mafia dynasty, remembered: 'Provenzano was always very attached to his family and spent the major feast days at home with them, at the beautiful villa where they lived.' It seems safe to assume the family lived together until their formal parting in 1992, as guests of various well-wishers in western Sicily; since they weren't being actively sought, they could do as they liked.

They were leading peaceful private lives undisturbed by the police, so what was behind the decision to send them away to live publicly in Corleone? Binnu and Saveria had been together for twenty years, and she was a rock for him, an intelligent, wise companion; losing her was a terrible wrench. The boys were affectionate and bright, Angelo was fair, like his father, respectful and eager to please. Binnu had created space for them at the heart of his existence – while other bosses sacrificed family life to serve the organization day and night, and used their money and power to entertain mistresses, Provenzano's family life was sacrosanct. It must have taken an immense effort of will to give that up and resign himself to a solitary existence. Binnu was security-conscious: he would have known that from now on meeting up with his companion would be a rare and high-risk event.

Provenzano was a fond family man: he wrote to his old friend and business associate Pino Lipari: 'Kisses for the children, who must be getting big by now, kisses for the children and their mum and dad, wishing you a world of good.' When he was not in prison, Lipari took a paternal role in the boys' life: he gave them advice and sought guidance on their education.

According to the correspondence between Lipari and his old friend, Provenzano sent his sons to live in Corleone because they needed to become legitimate citizens, get identity cards and access to secondary school. Other Mafia bosses have sent their children to college and educated them outside the criminal underworld, to raise them in civil society. Provenzano had discussed this burning issue with some of his closest associates, who were facing the same dilemma. His friend Pino Lipari had insisted it was the only right thing to do. Provenzano mentions in one letter to a friend his concern about a young man too inexperienced and green for 'this evil life we lead'. He didn't think it a safe or nurturing environment for his own young sons.

The boys' 'legitimate' life back in Corleone, however, was not untroubled. Saveria tried to live quietly, lodging with her brother-in-law until she found an apartment to rent. They moved into a third-floor flat in a modern block set back from the road, with discreet glazed balconies. She was elegant but never showy, drove a Fiat Tipo, not a Mercedes, and left the house infrequently, usually with Angelo, to visit family members or for meetings with her lawyers. Salvatore would call in, driving his eccentric off-road buggy (he didn't have a licence). She wore her thick curly hair cut short and never went to the hairdressers unless strictly necessary: she washed and dried her hair herself, let it go grey and never spent time on her make-up. There was no room for pampering in Saveria's life.

In spite of her efforts to blend into the background, the police didn't forget about her. They frequently raided the flat, trying to surprise Provenzano on a secret visit to his family and putting his wife under intense pressure. They would bang on the door at 5 a.m. and burst in, guns in hand, turning the place over and rousing the children out of bed. The neighbours, who had had no trouble with the family, complained bitterly about the dawn raids. Other relations felt the pressure too: Saveria had no female friends but visited her sister in Cinisi now and again. The police raided her sister's house as well – turning out kitchen drawers and emptying cupboards on the floor, terrifying the children and wrecking the place.

At nine and sixteen years of age the Provenzano boys were traumatized to find themselves catapulted into the public eye. On their first day at high school in Bisacquino, a short bus ride south of Corleone, reporters staked out the playground to take the first pictures of the Boss's sons. Some of the journalists sent in hastily handwritten notes via Angelo's classmates, asking for a couple of words on how he felt about his new school. At lunchtime, when all the children went home, Angelo walked out of the gate into a baying mob of reporters and quickly took refuge back inside the school. Photographers glimpsed a fair-haired, broad-shouldered lad, bewildered and frightened. Over an hour later the press pack showed no signs of losing interest. Angelo finally walked out with a friend, wearing dark glasses and holding an exercise book up to his face. Besieged by pleas for a photo and a few words, trapped in the schoolyard, finally he faced the photographers and challenged them tearfully to go ahead and take his picture.

'Some gentlemen you are. So you've got me. *Bravi.*'

They snapped away for a few minutes, then he walked out of the gate and fled for home.

After he had gone, the photographers' triumphant scoop was overshadowed by shame that they could treat a child that way. After some discussion, pity for the boy outweighed the value of the photos, and they all agreed it would be wrong to publish them. The pictures – which show a tall, blond, open-faced boy in a red polo shirt battling to compose his emotions – have never appeared in any newspaper. (Such journalistic scruples did not last, however. When Paolo later graduated, in 2005, the ceremony was invaded by journalists, who outnumbered guests of the students.)

It quickly became apparent that Provenzano's boys were not violent thugs; they had no apparent need to prove their criminal pedigree. The shocking truth of it was that Francesco Paolo and his older brother, Angelo, were good students, quiet and conscientious. Teachers observed they kept themselves to themselves.

Angelo eventually got a surveyor's diploma at the Di Vincenti Institute, near Bisacquino, and signed up for an engineering degree at Palermo University – near enough to commute from home. It was his father's wish that he should get a degree (Provenzano had left school at seven and fervently wished better for his son), but Angelo didn't finish the course. He was needed at home to look after his mother and manage the family's affairs.

He abandoned his ambitions to be a surveyor, although his father tried to convince him that continuing his studies would be the best course, and it became a source of conflict between them. Binnu had discussed with his old friend Lipari the merits of study versus work: Lipari, a white-collar financial manager for the Mafia, was convinced that Angelo would need a decent degree, since it was going to be pretty difficult for him to set up in business. He wrote to Provenzano:

> I don't need to tell you this, but it would be useful if the boy put a bit of effort into finishing his studies, even if it involves some sacrifice. Having a degree will be more use to him than inheriting a fortune, and he'll be able to take a different approach to life. You know any commercial or business enterprise will always be subject to extreme scrutiny, and he'll need serious capital.
>
> There are tax concessions for new businesses, and you can get financing from the state. In the main, the laws are set up for people who need this kind of help, and in my opinion your son is not in quite the same position, so it would be better for him to concentrate on his studies – that will give him a much better chance of making something of himself, using his intelligence and his talents.[17]

The son of a Mafia boss enjoys tremendous privileges: through his father's contacts he can exploit connections in academia, business or politics. Being forced to make his way in the straight world presents far greater challenges.

Provenzano, like many a good bourgeois Sicilian son of a peasant farmer, tried to get his sons work in an insurance company and urged his friend Nino Giuffré, also the father of two boys, to do the same. Giuffré recalls: 'He said we owed it to our sons to give them a legitimate future.'

Unfortunately the firm in question began to attract investigators' interest and media inquiries, and eventually, with all the negative publicity, went into receivership. Angelo got a job in insurance, but when his bosses realized they risked getting bad PR just for employing the son of the fugitive boss, they did not renew his contract.

Saveria and the boys moved to a villa on the edge of Corleone, just round the corner from Binnu's favourite nephew, Carmelo Gariffo (unfortunately, he was in prison for much of this time and thus unavailable to keep her company). It was a big place for three, built with money allegedly sent by Provenzano's brother Simone out of his German wages. Discreetly positioned, the villa overlooked the fields below the town. A high fence in front obscured the curious gaze of passing journalists or of visitors to the local restaurant, the Leon d'Oro. The villa was large but not particularly showy; a long feature window, sandblasted glass with heavy black frames, gave it a modern ecclesiastical look. The shutters were kept closed.

In 1994 Angelo opened a launderette, the Splendor, in the same street. It was a good choice of business: nice clean work offering minimal and civil contact with the local community. Humble too: it was important for Provenzano's family not to display any of the wealth accumulated over a long career of illegal activities. Since so much care had been taken to conceal it, better to live on charity from their uncle, who had established himself successfully abroad. Investigators tried unsuccessfully to discover whether the capital used to open the launderette came from the profits of crime or whether the family were laundering anything more lucrative than trousers.

Provenzano's friend Lipari was unimpressed with the family's choice of business. In a conversation with a retired local teacher he insisted opening the launderette was a mistake. While police investigators listened in, Lipari said, 'It's shameful, it's undignified for the Boss's wife to be washing underpants for the Corleonesi. What sort of work is this for a family in their position?' He repeated his view that Angelo would have done better to stay at university instead of lowering himself to this sort of activity.

Provenzano's boys struggled with their legacy, both within the family and outside it. In their position it seemed all roads were closed to them. Mafiosi regard civilians as non-persons, according to one *pentito*, inferior in every way and unworthy of consideration. The interests of a made member are paramount in every case. In such a discriminatory set-up, why would a high-ranking mafioso decide to keep his sons out of the organization?

Ask the wife, investigators say. As the one responsible for instilling Mafia culture in the young and raising them to understand and accept the code of honour, she holds a powerful veto over the children's future. Police listening to her private conversations gathered that Saveria made the decisions that affected the family. How the sons were brought up must have been largely her decision. Bernardo is smart, but Saveria no less so; she is described as spectacularly intelligent – a woman with the strength to raise her sons outside the organization.

Saveria Palazzolo, upright and taciturn, had always distanced herself and her sons from the Mafia life. She and her husband had protected their privacy, insisting on family time while other men of honour ate and celebrated major festivals and major crimes together. By raising her boys as civilians, Saveria tried to keep them clear of what their father called 'this evil life we lead'. It can't have been an easy decision. They would never be offered the respect their father enjoyed. She had to raise them to value a different kind of respect. They would need to observe the rule of law. (Indeed, when Angelo's Fiat 500 was stolen in Palermo, he reported the crime to the police – which shows what a different world he lived in from his father – and his father's friends. When Riina's son, by contrast, got an upset stomach from eating too many arancine, greasy fried rice balls, he plotted to murder the barman who had sold them to him.)

Bernardo Provenzano had been a criminal since he was seventeen. He had made the leap from peasant culture to exalted circles of business and politics – but he was still a career criminal. Saveria clearly loved her man and has stuck by him. But this life is not for her sons. Without making the dramatic choice that some turncoats have chosen in order to remove their children from the culture and lifestyle of organized crime (enjoying state protection, making a clean break), she has done all she can to keep them out of it.

Lipari counselled his friends to raise his sons outside the organization but failed to follow his own advice. When he was arrested for Mafia association, he drew his family into the business to help him. His son Arturo became a messenger, visiting him in prison, taking messages and receiving instructions, carrying out his orders with filial zeal. His wife took home his dirty laundry and cut the little folded notes out from the hem of his trousers for Arturo to copy out and deliver. His daughter Cinzia trained as a lawyer and, although it may not have been his original intention, when he needed her help, she became his representative.

Provenzano's choice of a legitimate path for his sons is remarkable, because the Mafia boss traditionally fulfils his duty by passing on the culture and power accumulated in Cosa Nostra to his heirs. Giovanni Brusca, serial killer and proud father of little Davide, revealed that Mafia bosses are obsessed with their inheritance. The mafioso, as Brusca described him, has one ambition: to pass his power and wealth on to his sons. If he can't do that, his whole career has been wasted. He explained the confidence with which he and his associates mapped out their sons' futures: 'We never thought we would lose. We thought we were invincible. We never realized we were running down a blind alley. Do you see why it is significant that Provenzano, a fugitive for forty years, has kept his sons in school all this time?'

According to Brusca's analysis, the great symbolic return to the family home in Corleone was principally so that his sons could stay in school without having to make up stories and fake IDs. It had already become extremely complicated, keeping their identities a secret: girlfriends asked questions, teachers needed information. Brusca was clear: Provenzano's philosophy was different from Riina's. He wanted his sons to study and did not want them involved in any way in Cosa Nostra.

It has not been easy for them. Their father made the decision that they should leave him, and the life they were used to, and go to Corleone, a place they had never lived – where not even their mother had lived. They knew no one, but everybody knew them. In a private conversation recorded by police years after their appearance in Corleone, they recalled their outrage at the way their mother had meekly submitted to their father's order to leave. They felt she had been overlooked and ignored: 'She went along with every decision, she never had the courage to say, "I want to do this, I don't want to do that, let's do it this way, let's do it the other way." '[18] While everyone knew what was good for them, no one seemed to be paying any attention to their needs.

Provenzano continually pointed out to his sons that his own childhood had been full of misery and deprivation, while his sons had lacked for nothing. Paolo bitterly resented his father for this view. He could tell them all he liked that they were privileged, but the boys' lives in Corleone were not easy, and they'd never been given the opportunity to express that.

'[He thinks he's done] everything for us. He's always saying, "Let me tell you about when your uncles and I were small . . ." He says his father beat him, and that at nine years old he went out selling stuff, whereas we've had everything on a plate. You know he's always asking, "Have you ever lacked for anything?" He's never given us the chance to say, "Actually, yes." Why does he do it, why does he look for reassurance all the time? Well I'm sorry, I'm sorry.'

Family life was never simple, and the trio was never allowed to forget that their movements were always under observation. Before the Christmas holidays in 1999, police bugs picked up whisperings about a secret family trip to Germany. They would be staying with Bernardo's brother Simone, and no one was to say a word about the arrangements outside the immediate family. Bernardo's sister made a vast quantity of buccellati, Christmas biscuits filled with dried fruit and almonds. And another brother bought hams and salamis, claiming they were a gift for his doctor. Such was the whispered urgency of these preparations that the police were convinced that the family was preparing a festive reunion with Bernardo.

German law does not allow extensive surveillance except in cases of suspected terrorism, and it took several days for the Italian police to get permission to install cameras on every angle of Simone's apartment building. On Christmas eve Saveria and the boys arrived, and the apartment door closed swiftly behind them. In the following days no one entered or left the apartment, not even to go to Mass on Christmas day. The police were getting jumpy. Finally, they made a last, desperate request to the German authorities for permission to search the flat.

The small family party had spent days inside the apartment building, staying in a borrowed flat down the hall. They had made every attempt to arrange the trip in secret, but they were used to intense police surveillance, so it was no surprise when Simone opened the door to half a dozen Italian agents, who poured in and searched the flat thoroughly. Hours later, after dark, they had to concede that there was no sign of the Mafia boss. Whether Simone's brother had just escaped through a secret passage or was not even intending to visit, the police never managed to figure out. For the family it was a depressing rerun of so many previous occasions and impossible to recreate the festive mood after they had gone.

After her move to Corleone the couple were able to meet only seldom: she was too closely observed to be able to risk it. They knew this would be the case when they took the decision for her and the boys to come out of hiding. For such a close couple it must have been a painful separation, made worse by worries about each other's security and health problems, with only intermittent letters for reassurance. She put up a brave front. But her house was watched by cameras and eavesdroppers twenty-four hours a day. Sometimes the police agents monitoring their listening devices could hear her crying.

There was another explanation for the family's mysterious return to Corleone. Perhaps Provenzano was running out of options. In his home town he had family, people loyal to him and dependable, to whom he could entrust his wife and sons. He didn't have the means to support himself and his family in exile: it would have been an expensive business, especially with Binnu's medical and legal bills to pay. 'His family never had the same disposable income that Riina had', said Brusca.

At that moment Provenzano could not count on enough manpower to protect his family outside Corleone. In Corleone he still had contacts – his brothers, his wife's sisters and his nephew.

Supergrass Tommaso Buscetta maintained Provenzano had another, more powerful reason for sending his family back to his home town at that time: the deterioration of relations with Totò Riina. Pressure was mounting in the leaders' increasingly difficult relationship: Riina was becoming more unpredictable, more determined and easily enraged. Riina and Provenzano had done a deal, under which both their families would be safe in their home town. Provenzano had sent his family to Corleone to protect them from Riina.

'With that gesture Provenzano makes his official break with the past', said Buscetta. 'From that day on he is playing his own game, he is no longer in partnership with Riina. He must increase his security to a new level, in which there is no room for his family. From now on, he works alone.'

In the early months of 1992 the atmosphere within Cosa Nostra was tense. Falcone's new measures had caused a crisis within the ranks of mafiosi in prison: they could no longer expect to be released from prison within months, nor could they be guaranteed to find their fortunes intact on their release. Riina had raised the stakes by waging all-out war on the state, and his associates knew he would not back down, not now. He was locked into an escalation of violence that many men of honour no longer supported. As one *pentito* recalled: 'The phrase you heard was *ora ci rumpemu i corna a tutti*: "Now we're going to break all their heads." '

Provenzano's plan was to distance himself from the terrible events ahead. He had deep misgivings about Riina's strategy and intended to disappear from view during what he knew would be a disastrous period for Cosa Nostra. He had kept such a low profile that on most of the lists of defendants for many of the crimes committed by Cosa Nostra during this period his name did not even appear. By the time his family appeared in Corleone, without him, the general conviction among magistrates in Palermo was that he must be dead.

7

Goodbye Totò

'INSIDE THE COMMISSION there was a heavy atmosphere, a chill that turned icy', recalled Giuffré. 'We were getting close to the day of reckoning. A lot of people, most of them politicians, had made themselves scarce after the Mafia war, but when you're dealing with Cosa Nostra, once you've begun something, you can't back out. A number of politicians had eaten from the same plate as Cosa Nostra, and then they spat on us. Salvo Lima was one of the ones who had done a runner. But running away didn't help him because his time had come.'

Lima, the Christian Democrat politician and MEP, one of Giulio Andreotti's closest allies, had been a powerful friend to Cosa Nostra. When he was no longer prepared to use his influence in Cosa Nostra's favour, his time, as Giuffré put it, ran out.

On 31 January 1992 Italy's Supreme Court upheld the sentences handed out at the maxi-trial. It was a historic defeat for the Mafia. And yet, for Falcone's team at the ministry of justice, triumph was tempered by their knowledge of the enemy: while the victors in this round celebrated with champagne, they knew they would pay for it before too long.[19]

Riina, who had been fully expecting his influence to prevail, was incandescent. 'He had become unrecognizable from his former self', said Giuffré. 'There was a ferocity in his eyes that was frightening. Before, he had kept everything on a tight rein, now he started losing control.

'Once the decision had been taken to kill politicians, Riina, who knew many of us had contacts and friends in that world, told us not to ask him any favours.'

The verdict was a devastating indictment of Riina's leadership: he had failed to exert his influence in Rome. He needed to make a swift and decisive response to this outrage, and he had plans.

He had been holding a series of extraordinary meetings to plot the organization's reaction to its political troubles. In late December the regional commission had gathered, as they did every year, to exchange Christmas greetings and gifts, and drink a toast to their success in the New Year. They met at a secluded farmhouse in the forest near Valguarnera, in the mountainous province of Enna. On the surrounding slopes lay the remains of abandoned sulphur mines; in the town the visible scars of poverty remained: old men hauling at mules, women in headscarves and black widows' dresses wheezing home with their little bit of shopping.

Up at the farmhouse the 'new rich' were gathering – sons of peasants in cashmere sweaters, members of the Mafia commission, settling themselves around a long table. 'Shorty' Riina at the head, with hard black eyes and jowly face, smiled and joked with the men one minute and threw an icy glare around the room when he wanted silence. Provenzano, 'the Accountant', sat near by, his half-moons on a string round his neck. He hardly ever attended these meetings and seemed uneasy.

Riina announced to the assembled company that they were going to war with the state. He explained that the representatives of the state with whom they had always enjoyed fruitful relationships were no longer to be trusted. 'If we want peace,' he announced, 'first we must have war.'

The meeting lasted several hours, with much discussion, in a mixture of Italian and dialect, about launching a separatist movement – a theme to which Cosa Nostra returned, whenever its 'tame' politicians started ignoring orders. A frontal assault on the state, Riina insisted, was inevitable. Provenzano, with his customary attention to detail, raised numerous questions about how this was to be achieved, and whether it would not be better to see how the next phase turned out, with the election in the coming months. Riina snapped at his old adversary's objections with weary irritation, mocking Provenzano's clerical style. The discussion churned on, over platters piled with bloody grilled steaks and bottles of red wine; they agreed that nothing would be achieved without a higher body count. When the men finally rose from the table, they were resolved. They raised their glasses in a toast to war.

In the following weeks Provenzano, more circumspect than his associates, took soundings among his contacts in politics and industry to gauge likely reactions to another high-level assassination. Giuffré attended a midwinter meeting of Provenzano's faithful, where each of his capos was given a sector from which to report back: the contracts man Pino Lipari was asked to talk to industrialists; Provenzano's childhood neighbour Vito Ciancimino, the former mayor and minister of works, was asked to take soundings among his political contacts; others were to talk to masons and businessmen. Between them they were to listen to opinion formers in every sector.

'At that time Provenzano had a series of faithful friends and advisers who were not necessarily men of honour, but politicians, businessmen, doctors', says assistant prosecutor Nino Di Matteo. 'He primed these contacts of his, who were sufficiently well connected that they could test the mood in the corridors of power, to understand, if they were to kill Falcone and Borsellino, what sort of reaction there would be. Would the judiciary hit back hard, or would most of them (sadly) be secretly pleased? Through his high-level contacts Provenzano was able to take the pulse of power in the country at that time – this was undoubtedly his major strength.'

Although Provenzano would later decry the bombings as a disaster for Cosa Nostra, at the time his information indicated there would be a positive response from certain quarters. His contacts in the north were deeply alarmed about the corruption scandal threatening to engulf them. He, like everyone else, went along with Riina's grand plan.

'I don't believe Provenzano would have stood by and let Riina have his way if he didn't agree with the policy', says Di Matteo. 'If he wanted to stop the bombings, he could have done it. He was in full agreement with the politics of a violent attack on the state by Cosa Nostra. There was a well-founded fear within the organization that new investigations were in progress that would go a lot further than any previous initiatives. Provenzano, whose business dealings, in particular his lucrative contracts, would be vulnerable to any serious investigation, had as much stake in the assassinations of Falcone and Borsellino as anyone else.'

The organization would become increasingly embattled as its access to power was denied. In the middle of February a Socialist politician was accused of taking bribes, and the scandal quickly spread to the prime minister, Bettino Craxi, threatening to expose the whole intricate system of bribery and corruption at the highest levels of all the political parties.

While Cosa Nostra's response to these outrages was under discussion, a power struggle was developing behind the scenes. A meeting took place near Palermo in February 1992, unusual in that both Riina and Provenzano were present but particularly memorable because Provenzano turned up wearing a bishop's robes, complete with mitre and sash. The whole scene was witnessed by a nineteen-year-old woman, who later became a collaborator. Giusy Vitale gave her mafioso brother a lift to the meeting and remembered being astonished to see a senior cleric alighting from a chauffeured car to attend a meeting of Cosa Nostra – until her brother explained it was Provenzano in disguise. Riina was reported to find the whole scene very distasteful and told Binnu not to pull any similar stunts again.

At this meeting, held in a farmhouse in the countryside near Palermo, there was a bid to push aside some of the older figures in the commission, in favour of young bloods, a movement spurred on by the ambitious Vitale brothers, Leonardo and Vito, and supported by the young Trapani boss, Matteo Messina Denaro. These young guns were all for the use of violence and self-styled followers of Totò Riina. At this meeting he rewarded the Vitale brothers by giving them control of Partinico. It was a clear message to anyone thinking of opposing him in future.

Towards the end of February another summit took place. The commission met again at the farmhouse in Enna, and here Cosa Nostra's top representatives – Riina and Provenzano, Nitto 'the Hunter' Santapaola, boss of Catania, and Piddu Madonia, capo of Caltanissetta – agreed the strategy for a series of top-level assassinations.

The Corleonesi already had the blood of many on their hands: about a thousand people had died during their bid for total control in the early 1980s. Eminent representatives of the state had been shot down in broad daylight, in busy streets. Now they were planning the most devastating bomb attack ever attempted – on a moving target in an armoured car. Giovanni Falcone was not going to be allowed to destroy years of empire-building.

The supergrass Nino Calderone saw this decision as an act of desperation. 'A spectacular public bombing is never in the interest of the Mafia . . . it is a sign of weakness.' It was a response to a series of defeats, which the Mafia no longer knew how to tackle. 'The Corleonesi and the other dominant Mafia families lost their heads.'

It's tempting to imagine Provenzano trying to dissuade his *paesano* from such a risky strategy, particularly in the light of his later peaceful regime. Tempting, but wrong.

'The leaders of Cosa Nostra were in full agreement over the decision to murder Falcone and Borsellino', says Di Matteo. 'So much so, that Provenzano put forward his own men in Palermo for the via d'Amelio bombing [which killed Borsellino]. Those two attacks involved men of honour from both factions: those close to Provenzano, like Aglieri, and those close to Riina, like Brusca.

'Provenzano may not have attended every commission meeting, because of the rule that he and Riina alternated, but according to the *pentiti* who were in a position to know, he took a full and active part. It was not until he understood the reaction to the bombings that he changed his strategy.'

Riina's godson Giovanni Brusca, who had killed many times for the organization, was outraged that Provenzano later distanced himself from the decision to wage open war on the state. He was deeply mistrustful of the Accountant's background manoeuvres.

'I noticed that throughout the whole preparatory phase Bernardo Provenzano and Pietro Aglieri were never to be seen. They were just like a bucket and mop: wherever one went, the other followed. They had a perfect understanding. It's no secret that I could never stand them, because they're the kind who let everyone else do the dirty work and think they can keep their hands clean.

'Provenzano never came out with his opinion,' Brusca said, 'but before you jump to any conclusions, this doesn't mean he was against the bombings. He just wanted someone else to do the job. I never once heard him say he was opposed to a murder.'

In private Brusca vented his frustration to his godfather that Provenzano had held back during the planning phase. Riina merely laughed, and said, 'I tied up the dogs. They can't say they didn't agree to it.'

According to Brusca, there was some discussion between Provenzano and Riina about whether to kill Falcone in Rome or in Palermo. Matteo Messina Denaro, the ambitious and dedicated young capo from Trapani, was detailed to follow their target everywhere in Rome, note his movements, watch when he was alone, when he walked, when he took the car. But then there was a change of plan: Riina brought Messina Denaro back to Sicily and told him the assassination had to happen in Palermo.

Pietro Grasso, chief anti-Mafia prosecutor, believes Riina had a motive for killing Falcone in Sicily: 'Riina's neither ingenuous nor mad, and nor are the other bosses who made that decision with him. We can only surmise that someone gave them a guarantee: kill him by all means, but do it in Palermo. Don't worry about the state's reaction. There won't be any major consequences.'

Provenzano had learned from his soundings in the corridors of power that some would not be unhappy if judge Falcone was removed. It seems improbable, to anyone who witnessed the outcry after Falcone's death, but he was getting perilously close to a major corruption scandal, and several prominent figures were risking exposure and disgrace.

'Falcone had turned his attention to the Mafia's involvement in contracting', Giuffré recalls. 'That was too hot. But after he had completed his investigation and delivered the files, he was transferred. We breathed a sigh of relief: if he wasn't there to see the investigation through, it was bound to stall. But we'd got it wrong: it wasn't like other times, when people were promoted and you never heard of them again. It was much worse.'

Falcone's files contained 990 pages of closely researched figures, payments and bank transfers, details of every named company that had dealings with Cosa Nostra, including several run by Provenzano and his consiglieri Masino Cannella and Pino Lipari.

'The situation got dangerous because we were afraid', Giuffré recalled. 'But not just us. The whole Italian machine, political and economic, was afraid. They started talking about Falcone becoming president of a new national anti-Mafia organization, and that was too much. That was the straw that broke the camel's back.'

Falcone's death sentence had been uttered years earlier, when he persuaded Tommaso Buscetta to talk: now it was time for action. Cosa Nostra's cosy relationship with power was under threat of exposure. If members of Cosa Nostra were afraid, how much more terrifying for the politicians and industrialists who had been dishonestly lining their pockets for years. The symbiotic bond between certain Christian Democrats and Cosa Nostra had existed for decades but had changed in tenor. From agreeing to support candidates in exchange for fixing contracts, Cosa Nostra became dictatorial and threatening. Riina's link to the party, the MEP Salvo Lima, was told to fix the maxi-trial verdicts. He was warned: 'Stick to your promise or we'll kill you and your whole family.'

According to one *pentito*, in 1980 Prime Minister Andreotti had flown to Sicily to meet the boss Stefano Bontate, and to protest in person against the murder of the Christian Democrat president of Sicily, Piersanti Mattarella. The boss reportedly told the prime minister to back off: 'We're in charge here,' he told the Italian premier, 'and if you don't want to destroy the [Christian Democrats], you do what we say, otherwise we'll take away your votes.'

The confirmation of the maxi-trial verdicts was clear evidence that their contacts in the Christian Democrats were no longer any use to Cosa Nostra. After the verdicts Riina had to show his political friends that this wasn't good enough. Provenzano claimed that he tried, in his paternal way, to protect Lima: 'I put my hands up to stop him banging his head', he told Giuffré. But it wasn't enough.

Lima had a villa in the elegant beach resort of Mondello, Palermo's marina, with excellent restaurants and palm-lined streets. On 12 March 1992 Lima was driving away from his house when he noticed two men on a motor bike in full-faced helmets heading towards him.

He scrambled out of his car and started to run, but they shot him as they drove past, leaving him wounded on the pavement. They turned and came back for him, shot him several more times and roared off. It was Riina's personal valediction to a long and fruitful relationship with the Christian Democrats.

Falcone, meanwhile, was embroiled in a row with the magistrates' ruling body over the nomination for the new 'super-prosecutor' position. While he struggled to continue with his work, Cosa Nostra was preparing its revenge. In May, when Falcone flew home to Palermo for the weekend, as he did every Friday, a series of security breaches were scarcely noticed – the police failed to check the route he was to drive into the city. A group of men in overalls had been laying a pipe under the motorway, but no one had noticed anything unusual about them. Up in the hills above, a trio sat and watched, smoking cigarettes and waiting for a signal. As judge Falcone's motorcade swept into view, Giovanni Brusca, peering through binoculars, pressed a button on his remote control. Far below them the road, and three bulletproof limousines, erupted in a massive explosion that tore up the ground for 100 metres around. The three bodyguards in the front car were killed instantly. Falcone and his wife, Francesca Morvillo, barely regained consciousness and died later in hospital.

As news of the massacre spread, cheering erupted in Palermo's Ucciardone prison. An old enemy of Cosa Nostra had finally got his reward. The team behind the bombing met at a house belonging to Salvatore Cancemi, a mafioso who had been involved in planning the massacre. As they drank champagne and toasted their enemy's violent end, Cancemi knew they had created a disaster. 'This bastard will destroy us all', he muttered to another member of the team.

Cancemi had sensed the reaction to Falcone's murder: it was, as he surmised, an outrage that would come close to destroying Cosa Nostra. Ordinary people turned out in their thousands to pay their respects to the dead and scream abuse at the politicians who had let them down.

With a heavy heart Falcone's friend and close colleague in the anti-Mafia pool Paolo Borsellino took his place at the prosecutor's office in Palermo. Borsellino was marked by the Mafia as a dangerous man – he was known for his moral rectitude and seemed to inspire trust: he had persuaded several key Mafia figures to collaborate and was accumulating vast files of incriminating evidence. He was also trespassing on Cosa Nostra's prized public contracts.

'The acceleration of events that led to Borsellino's death', said the *pentito* Angelo Siino, once the Mafia's minister of public works, 'was due to the fact that he was about to broach the issue of the major contracts, the management of £60 billion spent by Sicilian politicians with the Mafia's agreement.'

As Borsellino worked night and day on his huge and rapidly increasing caseload, Cosa Nostra plotted to prevent him exposing their precious contracts. On a Sunday afternoon, outside his mother's flat, on 19 July, he and five bodyguards were killed by a massive car bomb.

This time the city came out *en masse* to express its rage and disgust at the Mafia's violence and the state's failure to protect its own. Women went on hunger strike in the central square of Palermo to demand government action. A small group of ordinary citizens organized a mass protest in which people hung sheets over their balconies, bearing anti-Mafia slogans. The Mafia had been thrown out of the beds where it had lain, cosy and undisturbed, for so long. The Corleonesi had finally gone too far.

The government's response, at last, was swift: in an operation named Sicilian Vespers thousands of soldiers were transferred from the north to do guard duty, protecting magistrates and other public figures and institutions, and freeing up local police and carabinieri to hunt for the killers. Young servicemen in Alpine uniform, complete with pheasant tail feather in their hats, stood guard nervously behind bulletproof glass cabins. It felt like a city at war. 'Invite a soldier for coffee!' said leaflets posted along the walls and on lamp posts. 'Show them we're not all mafiosi.'

Several collaborators have hinted that there were forces beyond Cosa Nostra at work in the massacres at Capaci and via d'Amelio. Elements of the state, allegedly, wanted Borsellino dead. On this part of the story the case has not yet closed.

Giancarlo Caselli, a distinguished, white-haired judge from Turin, had volunteered to step into the post of Palermo's chief prosecutor, a cause for celebration among anti-Mafia campaigners – whose numbers had swelled in recent months to include most of the city. Within weeks of his arrival dozens of mafiosi were behind bars. For once there was back-up from the government: eight years after Buscetta risked his life by agreeing to talk to Giovanni Falcone a law was passed to give collaborators proper protection and to help them assume new identities.

Another sign that all was not well within Cosa Nostra was the number of prisoners turning state's evidence. Mafiosi who opposed Riina's strategy and had witnessed the massacre of the 'losing side' in the war of the early '80s turned themselves in rather than face his wrath. Many who had enjoyed the high life under his leadership, accumulating wealth and relishing their power, could not see the point of 'this life' from the inside of a prison cell. After the bombings the number of *pentiti*, already higher than ever before, rose to over 400.

Salvatore Cancemi, who had been involved in the bombing at Capaci, walked into a carabiniere station and announced that he wanted to talk. He encouraged other mafiosi to take the same step 'because Riina is a dog, a demon, a devil who has destroyed Cosa Nostra'.

Mafiosi who had worked for Riina, murdered for him and then found themselves despised and outcast, were savage in their criticism. The supergrass Nino Calderone said, 'He's got cunning eyes and a peasant's face. The man's crazy about money – he would do anything to get his hands on a kickback or get rid of a rival. To him, we were just dead meat.'

After the bombings, satisfied that he had got the government's attention, Riina tried to force them to come to terms. He wrote a list of demands, and his intention was that if they were not met, the bombing would continue. His sense of his own power had become exalted.

'I met up with Totò Riina some time after the assassination of Falcone and Borsellino', his godson Brusca 'the Pig' later recalled. 'I asked him how it was going, and he said, "They've given in." Out of respect and good manners, I didn't ask what he meant. I was used to seeing Riina as someone who acted in the interests of the organization.

He added: "I've made my request. I have given them my list of demands. I've given them a list this long." And he held up his hands to show how huge it was.'

Riina's demands were typically uncompromising: overturn the maxi-trial verdicts, abolish harsh prison conditions for convicted mafiosi, reverse the confiscation of assets and repeal the law protecting *pentiti*.

'It was understood', Brusca said, 'that if Riina's demands had been met, we would have stopped the bombs.'

To concentrate minds, Riina decided to give the state one more shake, a *colpetto*, to be sure he had made his point. His target this time was Pietro Grasso, one of the judges from the maxi-trial, who had been working with Falcone in Rome. Grasso had been coming home every weekend to visit his sick mother-in-law on Saturday afternoons. She lived in Mondello, the lovely Norman cathedral town above Palermo, and Grasso's habitual visits had been noted.

'There was a manhole in the street outside her house,' Grasso recalls, 'and they were going to park a van over the top of it and fill it with explosives. A van had been procured for this purpose, and the floor cut out. They'd got the key to open the manhole cover. But then they noticed there was a bank near by, whose burglar alarm could have interfered with the signal from a remote-control detonator.' They had already sourced a different sort of remote in Catania that wouldn't have caused interference, when the would-be assassins were arrested in a round-up of mafiosi. In the meantime the poor lady died.

Grasso had the uncomfortable experience of interviewing his would-be killer, the collaborator Gioacchino La Barbera, about the plans for his execution. 'He was ashamed, and afraid to find himself face to face with his intended victim,' Grasso recalls, 'but I had the disturbing sensation of having narrowly escaped death, and I needed to know every detail.'

Riina's list of demands has never been found. It seems improbable now that the state would have engaged in talks with Cosa Nostra, in the aftermath of a savage attack on its eminent representatives. But those who were in Palermo at the time do not find it surprising. Police and magistrates alike were so traumatized by the events of 1992 that they were willing to try anything to stop the bloodshed.

A senior carabiniere, Colonel Mario Mori, has revealed that a deal was in progress during the turbulent late summer of 1992, but it was not about whether to accept Riina's high-handed list of demands. In fact, it was a deal to try to bring about Riina's capture.

Colonel Mori revealed that a meeting took place in July 1992 between Ciancimino's son Massimo and another senior carabiniere, Colonel DeDonno. 'We wanted to get Riina and put an end to the bombings', Mori later explained to magistrates. 'We were looking for contacts within the organization . . . and DeDonno told me he had a good relationship with Massimo Ciancimino. We thought we could try to sort out a meeting with a member of Cosa Nostra through him.

'A further meeting was arranged in Rome, at Ciancimino's house near the Spanish Steps. Present were myself, Colonel DeDonno and Vito Ciancimino. I asked Ciancimino if he had any contact with Cosa Nostra that would enable us to try to come to an agreement to stop the bombing. He said he might be able to set something up through an intermediary.

'He proposed a meeting abroad. I said, "I want Riina's head." He jumped out of his seat and shouted, "You want to get me killed!"

'A few weeks later we met again. He asked for a map of the district where Riina was eventually found. I personally believe he knew where Riina was hiding.'

The deal Mori wanted to offer Cosa Nostra's leadership was this: you give yourselves up, and we will respect your families. A man of honour must be able to protect his family, it's one of the basic tenets of his position. But this simple formula was more complicated than it seemed: these families would need somewhere to live. So not only the mafiosi's families but also their homes would have to be respected – those luxurious villas and cars, their income, perhaps, and even their bank accounts. This was the objection some Palermo magistrates raised. In the climate of anger after the bombings at Capaci and via d'Amelio any such deal, they pointed out, would have quickly unravelled.

One mafioso who sought protection from the law was Balduccio Di Maggio, who had become embroiled in a power struggle in the Mafia fiefdom of San Giuseppe Iato and was in fear of his life. Brusca, the boss of San Giuseppe Iato, was hunting Di Maggio at this time and had several men on the case in different parts of Italy. Di Maggio's time was running out. But he had key information, which might save him. The police believed they had identified where Riina was living and showed Di Maggio hours of surveillance video, from which he was able to point out Riina and his family members coming and going from their grand Palermo villa. For the carabinieri, who had only one ancient photo of Riina from 1958, with Brylcreemed curls and a pencil moustache, the identification was a major breakthrough.

At 8.15 on 15 January 1993 an unremarkable beige Citroën was stopped in a traffic jam in a Palermo street. The little man who was bundled out into the street looked stricken, then relaxed when he realized his assailants were officers of the state, not Mafia assassins. He was taken into custody and photographed in handcuffs. The full-length police shot was circulated to the news media worldwide: Salvatore Riina, godfather of Corleone, 'la Belva', the savage killer driven mad by power, and wealthy beyond the dreams of avarice, had been caught. His physical reality was a shock to all those who had followed his murderous career: he was extremely short, square-headed, with a jowly peasant look and an expensive suit. He spoke softly, addressed investigators respectfully and stood up when magistrates entered the room. (This mild demeanour did not last: during his court appearances he could no longer contain his rage and scorn. He accused Caselli of being a communist agitator and insulted the witnesses, accusing them of moral turpitide and lying.)

Conspiracy theories crowded in. 'There was supposed to be a meeting on 15 January to discuss the progress of the negotiations', Brusca recalled. 'I don't believe it's any coincidence that Riina was arrested that day.'

Riina had been betrayed by Balduccio Di Maggio. At least, that was the story. But evidence began to emerge that someone else was moving behind the scenes, and that someone may have been his long-term partner in crime, his rival for Luciano Liggio's favour and competitor for power, Bernardo Provenzano. Provenzano was always close to Ciancimino: perhaps he was the person Ciancimino had contacted to negotiate with the carabinieri behind the scenes. After all, it was in his interest to get rid of Riina. The deal on the table was simple, according to one theory: if Provenzano could stop the bombing, his freedom, and that of his closest associates, would be guaranteed. Colonel Mori has always denied that anyone offered Provenzano protection, at any price.

The first suspicions that Riina's arrest had been part of a deal were raised when the Mafia managed to clear out his luxurious villa in via Bernini, Palermo, after the arrest.

After their leader was carted off, Brusca and Riina's brother-in-law Leoluca Bagarella took charge, starting with the immediate evacuation of Riina's wife and four children to safety and privacy in Corleone. Riina's men watched the villa, waiting for the carabinieri to seal it off. But to Brusca's amazement nothing happened. Eventually he sent his man Angelo La Barbera into the villa to remove the most inflammatory documents, hidden in a safe built into the wall; documents relating to contracting, as well as money, letters, accounts and legal files. La Barbera removed the whole safe with a pickaxe.

Again they waited for the police to arrive. When no one came, Brusca sent in a trusted contact who went through the place clearing out carpets, silver, jewellery, pictures – anything of value. Riina's villa attested to his extremely expensive tastes. He had collected gold ingots and designer watches, ceramics and art. Brusca's man took what he could and stored it all until he was himself arrested some time later (Riina's son Giovanni reportedly confronted him in prison, saying that when the stuff had been cleared out of his warehouse, there were some pictures missing).

When the villa had been stripped of everything that looked important, La Barbera took a few men with him, chucked out everything they found and made a bonfire in the garden. The flames consumed several of la signora's fur coats, some personal letters and photos, and her trousseau. She was furious, but La Barbera protested that those were his orders.

As soon as Riina was arrested, Caselli had ordered an immediate search of the villa in via Bernini, but the carabinieri had requested permission to keep the villa under surveillance, to see who came to call. It seemed like an excellent idea – except that no agents were sent to watch the villa, and no search was ever made. By the time the prosecutor's office realized that the order had not been followed up, eighteen days had passed since Riina's arrest. When officers finally entered the villa, it was not only empty but had been remodelled: walls had been demolished and rebuilt, everything had been hoovered and repainted. It was no longer the same place where Riina and his family had lived. The hole where the safe had been was blocked up and plastered over. Caselli was incandescent and ordered an immediate inquiry. Two senior carabinieri were investigated for aiding and abetting the Mafia: both Sergio De Caprio (known as Capitano Ultimo) and Mario Mori had exemplary records of arresting mafiosi, and their failure to search the villa was baffling.

Their trial was a media sensation: the two men responsible for arresting Riina found themselves in the dock for protecting him. Capitano Ultimo, who had been a national hero when he stopped Riina at a traffic light in Palermo, now had to defend himself. Prosecutors claimed that there must be some mysterious explanation for this oversight, but in the end both officers were found not guilty of any intention to pervert the course of justice. They even received an apology from the court. Although the judge commented that not to search the fugitive's home was a professional misjudgement, it was found that no crime had been committed.

With the carabinieri exonerated, conspiracy theories focused on interference by the state. Years later, Giusy Vitale, sister of Riina's faithful killer dogs Leonardo and Vito, claimed that inside Riina's villa there had been 'documents that, if they'd been discovered, would have put a bomb under the state. If the police had got hold of them, it would have been a total disaster.'

The Caltanissetta judges who examined the events of this whole extraordinary period in their sentence for the via d'Amelio bomb noted Brusca's belief that 'Ciancimino was playing a double game. In fact, he helped investigators capture Riina, probably with Provenzano's consent. This way the state could be seen to make a strong response to the assassinations, while allowing part of Cosa Nostra – the part less compromised in the investigations – to survive.'

Although Provenzano initially supported the strategy of violence, he may have already begun to conceive his new strategy. And while Riina was threatening more terrible violence, Provenzano may have been talking a different language, to other ears, behind his back.

There were rumours among men of honour that Provenzano was talking to the authorities, possibly doing some kind of deal. Some were calling him *sbirro*, 'grass'. In a private moment Provenzano asked Giuffré whether he believed what people were saying. Giuffré, the inscrutable capo, assured the boss that no, he didn't believe it.

Brusca would not want to give Provenzano credit for such a bold move. But he had no doubt that Riina's arrest suited him. 'Provenzano wanted to take Riina's place.'

Was it possible that Provenzano would sell his troublesome friend when the going got tough? Riina, the peasant mafioso who took on the state, had finally been defeated – brought down by men on his own side, who could no longer go along with his violent strategy. Investigators set about recouping some of his ill-gotten fortune. Over the following months property and agricultural land worth £200 million were seized.

Not everyone gave credence to the rumour that Provenzano had 'sold' Riina, but it never quite went away. When Provenzano was arrested, his arrival at Terni prison was reportedly greeted by Riina's son shouting '*sbirro!*' Giovanni Riina apparently wanted to remind the inmates that the new prisoner had betrayed his father to the police.

It eventually emerged that the insult was an invention, a damaging rumour of the kind Provenzano himself specializes in. And, as damaging rumours often do, particularly in Cosa Nostra, the slur stuck. Some still believe the Boss of Bosses obtained his position by selling out his more powerful friends.

Riina's arrest, although it undoubtedly suited Provenzano, was by no means the end of his troubles. Aware that his former brother in arms had, if not caused his arrest, then failed to prevent it, Riina placed his military force in the hands of his brother-in-law Leoluca

Bagarella. A crude, hot-headed, violent man of inferior intelligence to Provenzano, Bagarella now wielded more power. And although he nominally occupied the top spot in Cosa Nostra, Provenzano was, for now, a general without an army. It would take all his dark arts of mediation and manipulation to prevent further disaster.

8

The regent

'EVERYTHING THAT Uncle Totò started, goes ahead; we're not stopping.'

Provenzano was addressing a meeting shortly after Riina's arrest in the early spring of 1993. He and several other capos were gathered in a warehouse in the Palermo suburb of Villabate. Provenzano's old friend Ciccio Pastoia owned a warehouse on an industrial estate, alongside workshops and small manufacturing plants. Amid the roar of engines and hammering Provenzano sat in a small office with his trusted allies Carlo Greco and Pietro Aglieri, a thoughtful, old-school mafioso, and with men still loyal to Riina – the attack dog Leoluca Bagarella and the portly Giovanni Brusca, perched uncomfortably on a desk.

Since Riina had invested Bagarella with his military force, Provenzano needed to find a way to work with him. He had to get Riina's loyal followers onside. What he lacked in firepower, he would have to make up by cunning, using all his dark arts of *tragedie*, play-acting and manipulation. He would start by reassuring the capos that there would be no U-turn. Who would suspect that he had guaranteed his own immunity in return for an end to Riina's bombing campaign?

In fact, everyone suspected that, and more. It was a tense period, a moment of fearful transition. The arrest of such a powerful, dictatorial leader left a vacuum. If Riina was feared, at least people knew what he wanted. Provenzano's line was not so clear-cut; he always prevaricated, weighing up the pros and cons, and those not in his inner circle did not know what to expect. Riina had controlled everything from the centre, and his men mistrusted Provenzano's more federal, *laissez-faire* approach. Brusca, without his godfather to protect him, felt fatherless.

He needed a strong leader. Provenzano was ill and very thin; his receding grey hair and glasses made him look frail.

Brusca was not the only one who felt bereft without their powerful leader. Giuffré recalls that Riina's arrest created considerable anxiety and restlessness; members wanted clear direction and needed to know who was giving the orders. While Provenzano's faction was held at bay by the Bagarella–Brusca camp, with a violent tendency matched by their superior firepower, Provenzano had to play it exceedingly carefully.

Cosa Nostra's senior capos split into factions, who would meet in secret, trying to figure out the others' next move. Giuffré had a meeting in Bagheria with Pietro Aglieri and Carlo Greco, who persuaded him to throw his support behind Provenzano. Giuffré, for all his diffident manner, had contacts in every part of the island, which was a great asset. 'Soon after that, we realized there was someone rowing against us . . . Bagarella was making moves to get control of the situation, with the help of Giovanni Brusca and other people close to them – and I'd have to say that to a certain extent, they succeeded.'

Giuffré got the impression that Provenzano was standing aside and letting Bagarella get on with it. This may have been partly due to his worsening prostrate trouble. It may have been a deliberate ploy to avoid being associated with this dark phase of Cosa Nostra's history, as he effectively removed himself from the front line. Indeed, the president of the anti-Mafia commission, Luciano Violante, announced, days after Riina's arrest: 'Provenzano is probably already dead or out of the game.'

'Whatever people say,' remembers Alfonso Sabella, who was part of the energetic new team of anti-Mafia prosecutors, 'when Caselli arrived in Palermo, Provenzano was not a big priority for us. Our priorities were Brusca, the Graviano brothers, Bagarella, any of the mass murderers who planted bombs . . . we had to stop the bombing.'

Bagarella was in some ways the natural heir to Riina: he shared his brother-in-law's single-minded enthusiasm for violence. Their family ties gave Riina access to information on the outside: he could send messages to Bagarella via his wife, Ninetta, who was close to her brother (she had pleaded for leniency on her brother's behalf in the past, when he had made mistakes in anger). There was also a close tie between Bagarella and Riina's son Giovanni, who worshipped his uncle. Bagarella had tutored the boy before his initiation to Cosa Nostra and taught him how to kill a man with his bare hands – he even took him to commit his first murder and was proud of how the boy got fired up. Since Giovanni was still allowed to visit his father in prison, Riina had another line of communication to Bagarella.

But Provenzano was still officially head of the commission and could not be swept aside. Brusca came to see him with a message from Bagarella, asking for a sit-down – to take the heat out of the situation, he said, and clarify a few things. But Provenzano knew Bagarella of old: they had grown up together in Corleone; Bernardo and Leoluca's brother had been best friends. He knew that Bagarella, unpredictable at the best of times, was dangerously out of control, and he would have to gain his respect. 'And if Bagarella doesn't agree with Cosa Nostra,' he sneered, 'what should I do? I'll be the teacher and give him a beating.'

His message was clear: I am Cosa Nostra. If Bagarella thought he had the measure of Uncle Binnu, he was wrong. Provenzano announced that he would be appointing a new boss of the Palermo area.

'I said I thought . . . I thought perhaps . . . he should discuss it with his *paesano*', stammered Brusca.

The two capos had a meeting to straighten out their position. The remaining Corleonesi from the original gang of four faced each other across a table, politely gauging each others' strengths while Brusca listened. Bagarella raised the subject of Riina's alleged discussions with the authorities, and his list of demands. He wanted to know what stage the negotiations were at.

'Provenzano claimed never to have heard anything about any list of demands.' As usual, Brusca commented bitterly, he feigned total ignorance. He, of course, revealed nothing about his own negotiations.

'I mentioned that there was no need to appoint a new capo for Palermo. But Provenzano didn't agree, and from that moment he became cold with us and closed, very closed. He shut us out.'

Tensions were mounting within the highest echelons of Cosa Nostra. As mafiosi behind bars continued to reveal its secrets, the organization needed a response. On 1 April 1993, two and a half months after Riina's arrest, a meeting of high-level capos was held to discuss strategy. Neither Provenzano (who seldom attended commission meetings) nor Brusca (who had fallen out with Bagarella) was present.

Since Riina's demands – overturning of the maxi-trial sentences and softening of the anti-Mafia laws – had not been accepted by the state, Bagarella insisted that Cosa Nostra continue with the strategy of violence. There were some chilling suggestions: they would leave syringes containing blood infected with HIV strewn on Sicilian beaches. They would poison children's breakfast brioches. Bagarella relished the idea of attacking people enjoying innocent pleasures. His suggestion was to blow up one of Sicily's most treasured tourist attractions, a heritage site of inestimable value: the Greek temple at Selinunte. The authors of the next phase in the war on the state would be Riina's men and leaders of the pro-violence faction: Bagarella, the young Matteo Messina Denaro and the capomafia of Brancaccio, Filippo Graviano.

When the upshot of this meeting was reported back to Provenzano, he was appalled. And though he was in no position to give Bagarella orders, he tried to limit the fall-out of the campaign by insisting, most politely, that any more bombings would have to take place outside Sicily. Cosa Nostra had been in the limelight too long; another spate of killings would further damage its interests and expose its members. Besides, Provenzano didn't really believe Bagarella would take on a bombing campaign on the mainland. In this, he was very much mistaken.

Bagarella's faction had a sense of omnipotence, a sense that, after the devastating results of the bombs that killed Falcone and Borsellino, Cosa Nostra could force the authorities to accede to their demands: 'We believed we could not lose.'

On 27 May 1993 a bomb exploded in the heart of Florence, killing five and wounding forty residents. The Uffizi Gallery was badly damaged; doors were ripped off their hinges, statues hurled to the ground. The nation was shocked: people dreaded a return to the nightmare of the terrorist attacks of the 1970s.

Provenzano sent for Brusca to demand an explanation. The fat, bearded killer shuffled in and answered in his halting, nasal voice the boss's furious questions. What did his *paesano* think he was doing? Did he want to ruin everything? How much pressure could Cosa Nostra be expected to take? When he was finally dismissed, Brusca reported back to Bagarella that Provenzano was furious.

Bagarella's response was defiant, revealing the depths of his scorn for the old man. 'Tell Provenzano he should walk the streets with a sign around his neck, saying, "The bombs have got nothing to do with me".'[20]

The killings continued relentlessly. In July another bomb went off in central Milan, killing five. And in Rome, in late July, the church itself received a warning: two bombs exploded below the walls of San Giovanni in Laterano, wounding three people and damaging the cathedral. In September Padre Puglisi, a tireless and courageous priest who had campaigned against the Mafia among the poor and disenfranchised, was shot dead at the door of his house in Brancaccio, a suburb of Palermo.

The bombings, striking at the heart of Italy's tourist centres, killing and maiming, quite deliberately, innocent members of the public, provoked outrage. The murder of a priest who did extraordinary work with boys in a blighted suburban area caused revulsion – even within Cosa Nostra. For many insiders this was not what the organization was about: by attacking the people, and the Church, they were striking at the Mafia's historic support system. Many of Riina's former followers were men who loved flash cars and ostentatious violence, and had little in the way of Mafia culture and tradition to fall back on in prison. The number of men of honour who 'repented' and gave information to the police continued to rise. With the harsher prison terms, by the mid-1990s more than 400 had 'repented' and agreed to talk.

Riina was not afraid of much, but he had a mortal fear and loathing of *pentiti*. He once declared: 'We've got to kill them and their relatives to the twentieth remove, starting with children of six years and over.'[21] One collaborator was dealt particularly savage punishment. In the autumn of 1993 a young boy, Giuseppe Di Matteo, was kidnapped on the orders of Leoluca Bagarella while grooming his horse at a riding stable in Villabate. His father, Santino, a former man of honour from Altofonte, a Mafia fortress in the mountains outside Palermo, had become a collaborator just a few months earlier and had revealed for the first time who had sat with him on the hillside above Capaci and activated the remote-control device that killed judge Falcone. After the child was snatched, his grandfather received a series of threatening notes, saying that if he wanted to spare the boy, Santino would have to recant.

The months went by, and Di Matteo showed no signs of retracting his evidence. He knew how these things went. In a heart-breaking appeal the boy's grandfather offered his own life in exchange for the child. Giovanni Brusca and his brother Enzo were keeping the boy, but Brusca never showed his face because the boy knew him: he had spent months in hiding at his father's house in Altofonte. Brusca had even given the boy a horse in gratitude for his family's hospitality; now he had him chained to a radiator in a darkened basement. Nino Giuffré and others, sensing the public horror at the kidnapping, or perhaps thinking of their own sons, felt that no good would come of this and sent a formal request to Provenzano to make Brusca release the child.

Brusca refused. Bagarella was insisting that the treacherous Santino be forced to give way. After two years chained up, Giuseppe, once a wiry outdoor type who loved his riding, was reduced to a frightened, flabby, whining creature. In early 1996 Brusca learned that he had been given a life sentence for the murder of the millionaire industrialist and mafioso Ignazio Salvo. Enraged at yet another strike against him, he gave orders for the boy to be executed. While one man held him down, another strangled him with a length of rope, and they dissolved his body in acid. It was as shocking and depraved a crime as had ever been committed in the name of Cosa Nostra and forced many within the organization to question their allegiance. The killing of a defenceless child threw Cosa Nostra into a new dark age. Few even tried to defend it.

In Bagarella's private life the kidnapping had a terrible effect: his wife, Vincenzina, who was desperate to have a child and had suffered the latest in a series of miscarriages, killed herself. According to one of Bagarella's closest associates, she felt that her inability to conceive was divine retribution for her husband's crime against a child.[22]

Provenzano had been keeping a low profile, staying away from big meetings, avoiding confrontation with Bagarella. To his satisfaction, his death had been reliably reported on several occasions. But he decided the time had come to take the reins of the organization. He must stop this destructive faction before they were all ruined. First he would let the Mafia capos know his intent.

On an April morning in 1994 Provenzano's 'postman' Simone Castello left his home in Bagheria and gunned his BMW along the motorway. He headed for Messina and took the ferry across to Reggio Calabria, on the mainland. There he stopped long enough to post a letter and knock back an espresso, looking out over the water towards Etna's dark slopes.

The letter arrived on the prosecutor's desk in Palermo two days later. It was from the fugitive Bernardo Provenzano, who had been on the run so long and so rarely sighted that he was assumed dead. The letter, signed in his painstakingly neat hand, merely announced Provenzano's appointment of his legal representatives. But in the massive publicity that inevitably followed, the real message reached its target. To the membership of Cosa Nostra, Provenzano's letter was proof that, contrary to rumour, he was not dead. Only a few people had seen him, but the Phantom, as he was called, was very much alive.

Provenzano's authority was accruing. People were increasingly turning to him for recommendations and guarantees. Men who had suffered years of imprisonment as a direct result of Riina's savage policies naturally gravitated to him on their release. In their eyes accusations that he had allowed or enabled Riina's arrest were no obstacle. Rightly or wrongly, Provenzano was not so strongly associated with the bombings, and he began to attract a more moderate faction – Giuffré, Aglieri, Raffaele Ganci. Benedetto Spera, capo of the strategic rural outpost Belmonte Mezzagno, an old-school mafioso, was beginning to prove a useful ally.

Aglieri had turned to Provenzano after a particularly bruising episode in the late 1980s: he had been sent to kill one of the surviving relatives of Salvatore Contorno, the supergrass who had done Cosa Nostra so much damage in the maxi-trial. Aglieri went armed with a gun to the intended victim's place of work, a greengrocer's. When he got there, the man was holding a little child, a four-year-old girl, in his arms. Aglieri, a man of strong religious convictions, walked away without firing a shot. When he told Riina what had happened, the boss screamed at him: 'Do you know what that little girl's surname is? Contorno!' Hearing this, Aglieri realized it was time he got some new friends.

Aglieri and Provenzano were natural allies; they shared traditional values and religious leanings, and after Provenzano sent his family away, they spent Christmases together. Aglieri's piety was a matter of deep conviction: he had always been a devout child and had attended a seminary (religion runs deep in his family: after his arrest, his sister joined a closed religious order). Aglieri is, in the words of his lawyer, 'orthodox': a man of honour. Provenzano learned from him how religion can lend a man an appearance of wisdom, enhance his image of peace and mediation – which became an essential part of Provenzano's make-up.

Provenzano had an extremely difficult job to do: he was sitting on a volcano that threatened to erupt at any time. It would require all his skill to outmanoeuvre Bagarella and keep a lid on the discontents and ambitions boiling up within the organization.

Although on the surface they managed to appear perfectly cordial, as was only proper in front of the other capos, a stand-off was developing between Provenzano and Bagarella.

One of the key strategic areas for Cosa Nostra at that time was Villabate, where the Mafia's infiltration of local government and industry meant a turnover of millions. The two dominant families at that time were in competition for their share of the profits, and the rivalry between them, bitterly fought inside the local council, was beginning to flare up into violence. The Di Peri clan was loyal to Provenzano. The Montaltos were on Totò Riina's side: the father of the family had betrayed his own boss to Riina and become known as *cane fedele*, 'Faithful Dog'.

On a November night in 1994 a man was frogmarched into a historic uninhabited villa in Palermo, one of the crumbling palazzi left to drift into ruin. The Mafia had turned this one into a fortress, with bars across windows and doors blocked up. Armed guards stood by the only entrance. In an internal room of the villa the man was murdered. He was Francesco Montalto, Faithful Dog's son.

It was not a move that could go unpunished, and Bagarella decided to go after the suspected killers. He sent a message, via Brusca, his own faithful dog, to Provenzano, saying, 'I'm going to make a move in Villabate. Is there anyone you want me to spare?'

Provenzano spied a trap. If he had given Bagarella any names of his people in Villabate, they would be the first to fall victim of the vendetta. He sent back a typically measured response: 'Everyone and no one.'

So Bagarella started to wreak his terrible revenge, executing anyone he believed to be loyal to Provenzano.

Investigators were alerted to a series of gruesome murders in Villabate, but for a while they were at a loss to understand the cause of the bloody feud, or who had ordered it. The explanation came from an unexpected source. Carabinieri investigating Salvatore Barbagallo, an accountant and rising star of the Villabate mob, had planted a bug in his mistress's bedroom. Like other men of honour, when Barbagallo was in bed with his mistress, he got carried away: forgetting the rules of Cosa Nostra, he told her all his most thrilling criminal secrets.

When the murders in Villabate began to pile up, assistant prosecutor Alfonso Sabella hauled in Barbagallo and let him read the transcripts of his pillow talk. 'I gave him fifteen minutes to decide whether to collaborate', Sabella recalls. 'I said, you can call your lawyer, whatever you like, but when this comes out in the papers tomorrow, as it inevitably will, the rest of Cosa Nostra will know that while you were screwing your girlfriend, you were spilling the organization's secrets. The choice is yours. A quarter of an hour later, he started talking. He told us all about the vendetta in Villabate, and who was behind it.'

A few days later Sabella issued arrest warrants for the key figures in the Villabate feud. The day after the police blitz, his driver Tony Calvaruso recalls, Bagarella was reading a copy of the newspaper with pictures of the wanted and arrested members of the Di Peri clan. He handed the paper to Calvaruso with an order for one of his capos: '*Ammazzali tutti*. Kill them all.'

Bagarella's reputation for violence preceded him. Two brothers from Villabate, recently released from prison on a technicality, knowing they were on his hit list, turned themselves in at the prison gate, begging to be readmitted.

Bagarella was finally arrested on 24 June 1995, near his apartment in the centre of Palermo – just across the piazza from a senior magistrate. The apartment looked scarcely lived in: elaborate Art Nouveau tables and chairs in pink, green and gold were decorated with glass vases and ornaments in the same style. A cabinet held their wedding china: a never used set of gold-rimmed dishes, delicate teacups and crystal. It was not exactly how one imagined the home of a man who wanted to blow up the ancient Greek temple at Selinunte. Carabinieri found a bunch of flowers in front of his wife's portrait on the mantelpiece.

Now Bagarella was behind bars, Provenzano's hands were untied. Almost immediately, and aided unintentionally by the authorities, who were arresting scores of men loyal to Bagarella, Provenzano moved to take over Palermo. The last of Riina's bully boys was Pieruccio Lo Bianco, capo of Misilmeri, who had been engaged in a long battle with Benedetto Spera for control of an area of strategic interest to Provenzano. Lo Bianco disappeared.

Giovanni Brusca was now dangerously isolated, his sense of alienation and mistrust intensified with the death of his friend and ally Lo Bianco. When Brusca protested, Provenzano claimed he had told Spera not to harm Lo Bianco, but 'he just wouldn't listen'. It was typical of Provenzano, fumed Brusca, that he would feign powerlessness at a moment like this.

'Pieruccio was a good guy, who followed the rules and killed a lot of our enemies for us', Brusca protested. 'Couldn't Provenzano have said a word on his behalf?' He believed the murder had been orchestrated to cut the ground from under his feet. He was afraid. Provenzano showed no gratitude, no bond of debt, towards a man who had done Cosa Nostra's dirty work for years – a lot like Brusca, *il boia* ('the Executioner').

'Like my father always said, Provenzano has a lot of sides to him – like a caciocavallo cheese', Brusca said. 'Several times I asked for an appointment to talk about Pieruccio Lo Bianco's case and to clear up the situation. At this point Provenzano sends me messages that he can't see anyone – and then I hear that he's been having meetings with Matteo Messina Denaro. When I met up with Matteo, we agreed to keep a close eye on Provenzano, and see what he was up to.'

By this stage relations between Provenzano's faction and those loyal to Riina had soured to the point of combustion. Brusca was so paranoid that Provenzano would have him killed that he was afraid to go to a meeting with the boss. Instead, he invited Provenzano to a meeting on his territory – planning to end the boss's career then and there. Two or three meetings were discussed, and a date arranged, but Provenzano always cancelled.

When Brusca received a summons to a meeting with the boss, he agreed, with some trepidation, to go. Knowing that an invitation to a friendly sit-down was one of Cosa Nostra's favoured set-ups for murder, he went armed. The meeting was in a village near Corleone, in an abandoned house on the site of a concrete plant – so there wouldn't have been any difficulty disposing of a body.

'I did have my suspicions. On Matteo Messina Denaro's advice . . . he and others told me I should be extremely careful. I didn't want . . . I just wanted to have this meeting without having to worry about . . . so I got my driver to take me over there, and we arranged that if anything happened I would throw my mobile phone out of the window and that would be the signal: they would come in shooting, and do whatever they could . . . I was armed, and so were they. But as it turned out there was no need, I could see there was no danger, so I came out again straight away and told him, "It's OK, you can go, it's fine".'

Thereafter Brusca, though often troublesome, was on Provenzano's side. Matteo Messina Denaro, a volatile capo whose obsession with childish things set him apart from the older bosses, was persuaded to make a deal and give up his opposition. Once he decided where his future lay, Messina Denaro became fiercely loyal to the Boss.

Provenzano's way was clear: anyone who stood between him and the leadership of Cosa Nostra had been eliminated, imprisoned or won over. But the organization was in chaos: the authorities were continuing to make arrests right across the Mafia's territory, and the mafiosi in prison were angry. It would take every bit of Provenzano's skill and experience to turn it around.

9

A new strategy

'I TOLD HIM, listen Binnu, we've only been doing this for two years . . . we don't have to agree with everything that's been done. Because good things have been done, but we have to admit, mistakes have been made. We've got to be patient. A lot of bad things have been done.'

Pino Lipari, Provenzano's consigliere, was describing a meeting of his inner circle. Relaxing with a friend at his villa in the holiday resort he owned in San Vito Lo Capo, on the north-west tip of Sicily, he was eager to show off how well he knew the boss, and how well he advised him. In his smug display of loyalty he unwittingly gave away a good deal of information to the police, who were listening to his every word.

'There are people who are feeling pretty let down . . . that's the truth! In fact, we're reorganizing ourselves a bit better, so we can say, "Now signori, let's not look at the mistakes of the past in isolation . . ." We need to say, yes, OK, mistakes were made . . . but the important thing is to keep moving forward . . . and we're working on it, but we need time.'

During the autumn and winter of 1995–6 the authorities were inflicting significant damage on Cosa Nostra. At one stage Alfonso Sabella's office was issuing twenty warrants every fortnight. 'We were cutting a swathe through Cosa Nostra like a hot knife through butter', he recalls.

Against a background of disarray and defections action was needed. Lipari was wrong: there was no time to lose. By waging war against the state, Cosa Nostra had destroyed its own defences, made new enemies and seriously damaged its business prospects. Provenzano, finally in sole command, began to formulate a new strategy. A period of calm was essential, in which the organization could be restored to strength, rebuild its people's shattered morale and (most important) start doing business.

'The moment Provenzano saw that Riina's strategy did not give the results he wanted,' Giuffré recalled, 'he took a step back and insisted that it was a mistake, and that we would have to pursue a different line . . . from this moment on he changed his position and pursued a new policy, not with bombs but with a strategy that would make Cosa Nostra invisible.'

The first step would be to limit the damage already done: he would impose a cease-fire. 'Provenzano's new strategy, which we called "submersion", had a clearly defined tactical approach', said assistant prosecutor Nino Di Matteo. 'Do not commit murder, particularly political assassinations; take steps to avoid going to war with the opposing wing of Cosa Nostra, and particular measures to avoid bloodshed within the organization.'

It was a long-term plan, which would require great faith from the men of Cosa Nostra. But Provenzano was determined that making great changes was the only way the organization would survive and regain its former strength.

'All the guys involved in implementing the changes called him *tabula rasa*, "clean slate",' said the *pentito* Salvatore Barbagallo (whose indiscretions in the arms of his mistress had caused so much trouble). Barbagallo added reverentially that he never heard Provenzano called anything so informal as 'Uncle Binnu'.

Investigators first learned of the new strategy through a police informer, Gino Ilardo. On his early release from prison on grounds of ill health in 1994, Ilardo had agreed to be an informant for Michele Riccio, a maverick colonel in the organized crime section of the carabinieri, known as the ROS (Ragruppamento Operativo Speciale). Ilardo, aged forty-three, from Catania, was a pedigree mafioso: his cousins the Madonia family were one of the strongest Mafia dynasties; Piddu Madonia, until his recent arrest, had been regent of Caltanissetta. Ilardo would not consider joining the witness protection programme – he was afraid his wife and children would never accept his defection. He could not face a scene like those terrible wailing women who disowned and denounced their husbands for treachery – he would wait until his wife was onside. But Ilardo was profoundly disillusioned with Cosa Nostra, as he said in a statement:

> I decided to collaborate formally with Justice after realizing what I have lost over these years apart from my family and my children, in the hope that my example will be of some help to young boys who feel that nothing can equal the honour of joining an organization such as this, just as I did . . . I hope that my collaboration will bear witness to how hollow and false it is, how the only reality is the wickedness that a depraved minority perpetrates, destroying everything that was good about this organization. Cosa Nostra has become an instrument of death, of lies and machinations. The evil deeds of the few at the head of the organization cast their guilt and shame over all the other members, for sadly, Cosa Nostra now consists of nothing but murderers and criminals . . . I decided to collaborate willingly with the Law, because I want to make a break with my past and hope to spend what remains of my life in peace, with my children.

This idyllic image of a family life beyond the reach of Cosa Nostra's fearsome revenge was the last thing that a Mafia informer could reasonably expect, and Ilardo was no exception. But as long as he remained beyond suspicion, as second-in-command of the Caltanissetta Mafia, he was an extremely well-placed informer. Diligent, pushy and proactive, he would ring his handler constantly from pay-phones or secure lines and meet him in bars, in waiting-rooms, in busy streets, to report the latest development, plot or rumour. Over the months he would try to draw Provenzano out of hiding to attend a sit-down, where the carabinieri could grab him. Riccio, whose high-risk strategies had occasionally won him rewards, could not put Ilardo on an official footing but allowed him to risk his life to bring about the result they both desired.

Ilardo revealed for the first time Provenzano's chief means of communication. The boss never used mobile phones, which he believed were too easily intercepted and could lead the police straight to him. He certainly did not like computers, and never used e-mail. He had perfected a secure means of communication: short letters closely typed on exercise book paper, folded as small as they would go, and sealed with Sellotape. The addressee would be marked as a number or a letter, and the *pizzino*, not much bigger than a cigarette butt, would be passed via a handshake along a sequence of trusted 'postmen' until it reached its destination. Ilardo gave Provenzano's postman, Simone Castello, his messages folded but not sealed, to make them easier to destroy (rip up, flush down the lavatory or swallow) if he'd been caught. Once Castello had safely met up with the next link in the chain, he sealed the letter with tape.

When the security forces were particularly active, the postmen would have to lie low, and a letter could take days to reach its destination, but because Provenzano had a close circle of trusted handlers it was still the most secure means of communication he could devise. (The recipients were always supposed to burn the letters when they had read and absorbed the contents, but some kept them safe. Giuffré stored a couple of dozen in a box in the farmhouse he called his 'office'. He claimed he needed to keep a record of agreed payments; in case of an eventual dispute, the parties could review the 'contract'. The letters were also an investment for the future: they might come in useful for blackmail, or revenge.)

Provenzano had left school at just seven years old, barely literate, but with his manual typewriter he could slowly bash out these closely typed letters, full of schoolboy errors, which his correspondents politely repeated. If anyone sent a scribbled note, he begged them to get hold of a typewriter, as he struggled to read handwriting. He showed great attention to detail, answering correspondents punctiliously, point by point.

The letters demonstrate how Provenzano brought about a change in leadership style. The following extract from a letter to Ilardo shows his emphasis on patience, negotiation and forbearance. A problem had arisen with an industrial plant in Catania: the manager was asking the Mafia for protection (from criminal damage and trade unionists), claiming he had already paid out. Various Catania mafiosi were accusing each other of appropriating the plant's money, and Ilardo was trying to sort out the mess. Provenzano writes:

Mio carissimo G. I received your letter with great joy, I am so pleased to hear you are in Good Health. I can assure you the same of myself. I know you were supposed to meet with MM [code for Mimmo Vaccaro, acting boss of Caltanissetta] and now I need you to confirm that you have indeed seen him, to sort out your situation. I hope you have an honest and straight collaboration. Even if we have a great deal against us, inside as well as outside ourselves, do try to salvage what you can from the present situation.

I hear what you say about someone trying to portray you in a bad light, telling lies about you, but I know nothing about this. I can't give you an exact response. I will try to help you in any way I can.

You ask me about the other question: the Riesani appropriating large sums, without asking permission. But listen these are things you must sort out between you, you know all about it and it's your business, besides I know nothing at all . . .

For the rest, it looks to me as though you're doing the right thing, just keep an eye on the situation.

The tone of the letter shows what a profound cultural change Provenzano was demanding. In contrast to his hectoring, dictatorial predecessor, he comes across as avuncular, pious, forbearing. He requires his men to resolve disputes and refuses to get drawn into their conflicts, but demands that parties sit down in a civilized manner to resolve their differences and find a peaceful solution.

He wrote to Ilardo, who had refused to attend a 'sit-down' with a Catania capo in the well-founded belief that he would be in danger:

Listen I have been informed about the appointment, and that you don't want to go. I can see your point, but since my aim is to restore peace wherever I can, and clear up any problems so we can continue to respect each other, this conflict is an absolute disaster.

Go and meet him, take 15 million with you and establish whether you have any genuine points of difference. Sort out the conflict between you, make peace with each other, and drink on it – but do it now. Send me your confirmation that this has been done, because they're expecting an answer from me.

I would love to see you before Christmas but I don't know how you're fixed, if we can, we'll see each other, if not, we should definitely be in touch, but in case you don't hear from me, Happy Christmas to everyone.

Provenzano used his fugitive status to great advantage: the letters carried his authority, and it was difficult to dispute his rulings by post. He could also claim (as in the Catania situation) to know nothing, when in fact he knew the whole story and was secretly working on behalf of one of the complainants. He finally confesses to Ilardo: 'It's true, I do know all about it, but I wasn't behind it, I kept him [the Catania mafioso in dispute with Ilardo] informed the whole way through. The fact is, that when I sent him my final solution, he didn't read it. His brother sent it back to me unopened, and you can check that with him.'

The art of *tragedie* could be most effectively practised in writing. For reasons of security Provenzano didn't hold big meetings and banquets, and was only ever seen in person by a few of his closest advisers. His elusiveness added to his reputation among mafiosi, who received his carefully worded instructions but never saw the Phantom.

Ilardo thought he could entrap the old man, but there were mysteries surrounding Provenzano that Ilardo could not have dreamed of. When Provenzano summoned him to a meeting, in the autumn of 1995, to expound his new directive, the carabinieri had an extraordinary opportunity to arrest one of Italy's most wanted criminals. A series of failures meant that the Boss of Bosses would remain beyond the grasp of the law for another decade.

Ilardo received his instructions from Provenzano's messenger, Catania mafioso and eye doctor Salvatore Ferro, to meet at the Mezzojuso junction in the early morning of 31 October. He called his handler, Colonel Riccio, telling him to come and meet him straight away, as this could potentially be a meeting with Provenzano himself.

Riccio took a plane from Rome and arrived in Catania the following evening. When they met, Ilardo was agitated by the magnitude of what he was about to do: to bring a company of carabinieri to the door of a meeting with the Boss of Bosses. He was risking his own life if the raid went wrong and his cover was blown. They agreed that Riccio's men would observe the other men of honour arriving at the junction and follow them to the meeting, but they would hold back if there was any sense that they knew they were being watched.

The following morning, early, Ilardo drove along the Palermo–Agrigento road, to the Mezzojuso turn-off. He pulled off the main road into the broad junction where two country roads joined the main drag, and parked behind another car. An old farm building loomed above the road, its windows dark. There were already two other cars in the lay-by, and two figures sitting in one of them to keep warm. The mountains lowered on either side, the shadows shortening as the sun climbed. Far away a village perched on its rocky slope, guardian of the valley. In the deep countryside there was no sound but the wind in the grass, and the occasional roar of a farm truck.

One of the men came over and introduced himself, and signalled to Ilardo to get in his car. Ilardo shuffled in behind Lorenzo Vaccaro, brother of the Mimmo in the letter and one of Provenzano's most assiduous attendants. The two men shook hands wordlessly. They drove towards Agrigento in silence for a few miles, then turned off a sharp right-hand bend onto a dirt road. A flock of sheep was grazing near by, their bells making the familiar tinkling sound as they trotted along, as much part of the ancient landscape as the stones themselves. The car bumped over a winding farm track, which dipped downwards before climbing towards the mountains. The driver pulled up outside a farmhouse that stood on the crest of a hill, with a sweeping view of the countryside all around: across the fields down to the main road, and over the rocky outcrops to the village above. No one could come anywhere near this place without being spotted. Ilardo wondered, would Riccio's men make it on foot?

Ilardo was shown into the farm building. In an upstairs office, sparsely furnished with a table and plastic chairs, an elderly man was waiting for them, dressed in simple country clothes: a polo shirt and V-neck sweater, working trousers and a heavy jacket. Ilardo realized with a shock that it was Uncle Binnu. He hadn't seen him face to face for years; he had grown old and thin, with sunken eyes and temples. His light brown hair was going grey and receding. The men joked about his excellent farmer's disguise, and the Boss agreed that he

made such a convincing peasant that he could go pretty much anywhere without being spotted. In fact, he boasted, just a couple of days
earlier, getting treatment for his prostate, he had had his catheter
removed, and had driven 25 km for an important meeting without
getting stopped. He did not say where he was living, but other shreds
of information convinced Ilardo he was staying in Bagheria, his long-
time centre of operations.

Salvatore Ferro, who had originally contacted Ilardo to make the
arrangements, arrived at 10 a.m., apologizing for his lateness, having
stashed his Mercedes in a barn down the road and picked up an old
banger to make the last part of the journey. All morning the four men
shut themselves in that small office and discussed some urgent issues;
the principal of these was the apparently unstoppable ambition of
Giovanni Brusca. The stocky scion of the San Giuseppe Iato clan was
throwing his weight around. Since Bagarella was arrested, he had lost
his brother in arms, his battering ram, who intimidated everyone into
submission – but he was not going to be left out in the cold. Brusca
was making moves to take over Agrigento, a strategically vital Mafia
stronghold. While they talked, Ilardo tried not to look at the door.

Provenzano was calling for the restoration of relations with Bagarella's
contacts in business, as a matter of urgency. Since Bagarella's arrest a
lucrative source of income had been lost, and it was vital to get these
onstream.

During the morning shepherds and farmworkers turned up from
time to time, some of them on foot, bringing food and drink. They
were all involved in organizing Provenzano's summit, and by lunchtime
there were three or four of them in the next room preparing pasta,
lightly cooked greens and cheese. Provenzano always relied on shepherds, a tight-knit community closed to the outside world, for support.
They were completely trustworthy and held it as part of their tradition
to help a Mafia boss in need. The shepherds were Provenzano's hidden
army.

Whenever someone new arrived, the host locked the office door.
A local farmer with white curly hair arrived at about eleven in a Fiat
Panda with the meat and proceeded to cook it, just how Provenzano
liked it: very rare, without salt. He was Cola La Barbera, who owned

the farm on the other side of the Palermo–Agrigento road. La Barbera was Provenzano's personal chef, providing for his particular needs and tastes.

They ate lunch sitting at the table, waited on by the shepherds, who brought dishes of fresh ricotta, pecorino and strong local bread, steamed vegetables and a vast platter of grilled steaks. There was local red wine, but Binnu drank only water.

After lunch Provenzano held one-to-one meetings to discuss his strategy for the organization, while the others waited discreetly in another room. Alone with Ilardo, he told him that whatever his grievances, and however much Brusca's behaviour warranted it, he must make every attempt to avoid going to war: the delicate political situation demanded stability for now. Ilardo was disillusioned to find his old friend less proactive than before, pressing for peace and preferring to wait for the other side to slip up instead of going on the attack. He said they had to wait for the political situation to improve. If necessary, Provenzano claimed, it would take between five and seven years for the organization to recover sufficiently to be able to do business again and overcome the current precarious economic situation.

On a more personal note, Provenzano asked Ilardo if he had ever heard anyone refer to him as *il ragioniere*, 'the Accountant'. His own accountant had started calling him that, and he had found it particularly irritating. Never, said Ilardo, politely. Provenzano, he knew, had been called 'the Accountant' for years.

At the end of the day, as it was getting dark, the driver came in and announced that now the men knew this place, when it came to the next meeting, they would be able to find it themselves. Ilardo nodded. He had taken in every detail of the place. But where was Riccio?

Riccio's men, it turned out, had spent the morning photographing the cars parked at the rendezvous, watched them out of sight and then gone back to base. When Ilardo got home at about ten that evening and phoned angrily demanding an explanation, Riccio explained he had been waiting for the order from Rome but claimed that he had been instructed not to move in. A week later, after dark, Riccio's men drove back along the Palermo–Agrigento road and tried to find the dirt track but, after driving up and down the road three times, were unable to find the turning.

A further breakdown in communications meant that investigators in Palermo were not to learn of these events for an entire year. As a result, the meeting place in Mezzojuso, although known to the carabinieri, was used repeatedly by Provenzano, with no surveillance in place. It was to be another year before the authorities received a request to put a bug in the chef La Barbera's car.

When it emerged that the carabinieri had had the opportunity to arrest the Boss of Bosses, the failure became a massive scandal. Riccio maintained he had orders from Rome not to raid the farmhouse.

'Ilardo was to meet Provenzano in the Mezzojuso area. I communicated this information to the ROS, proposing to carry out surveillance myself and conduct the whole operation [to arrest Provenzano]. But my boss had a different view and told me it was not my job. The day of the appointment at the Mezzojuso junction I was there but the means at my disposal (men and vehicles) were insufficient, and the only thing we could do was take a few photos.'

The response from Rome was swift. Riccio's superior officer, General Mario Mori, sued him for slander, saying there had never been any question of making arrests: 'Riccio told us specifically that if they'd raided the farmhouse, he had no way of protecting the source.'

The complaints and counter-suits have since been shelved, but the controversy still churns on. 'They didn't want to get Provenzano', Riccio, now white-haired, insists. 'It may have been incompetence, or they may have had another reason. Perhaps Provenzano had some task to perform.'[23]

Meanwhile, Ilardo's cover was still intact, and he continued to report to Riccio, providing a detailed picture of the daily administrative concerns of the organization and the changes being implemented as a result of Provenzano's directive.

The Boss's priority, in all correspondence, was to get problems sorted out quickly and peacefully, in order to let everyone get on with the real business at hand: making money. In one letter to Ilardo he wrote: 'You must do this quickly, so we don't lose the business . . . I beg you, don't make me look like an idiot, I am trying, with the will of God, to sort out everything I can, for you, for everyone.'

No problem was too small: 'Thank you for sorting out that firm I spoke to you about, but unfortunately, while I was looking into it, they had a jackhammer stolen, and two soldering irons, which you need to track down, and get them back. Once you've done that, let me know, everything should go through me.'

Provenzano was concerned that the firms they were squeezing for protection money should not feel aggrieved. Ilardo reported that one firm had refused to pay what he felt was a reasonable sum, £20,000. The Boss replied: 'We must be sure to ask the right amount, otherwise we get into a situation where we're putting ourselves in the wrong, pursuing them for an exaggerated figure, so ask for the right amount and we'll make sure they pay.'

While trying to impress on his cousin in prison that he was to be trusted to take over Caltanissetta, Ilardo fanned the flames of conflict with Brusca and the Agrigento clan, at considerable risk to himself, to try to force Provenzano to call another meeting and bring his collaboration to a speedy conclusion.

While Ilardo was still scheming how to force Provenzano out of hiding, word began to slip out that he was working for the police. At first it was just a rumour, odd snatches of hearsay, but in Cosa Nostra gossip can be lethal. Ilardo, now a marked man, blindly pursued his plan.

Brusca wrote to Provenzano saying he had had a request from the Catania clan to get rid of Ilardo, but he wanted the Boss's permission. Provenzano's response was typically measured: 'We must be extremely careful to avoid any unfortunate occurrence.'

Brusca's irritation turned to slow-burning anger. 'I wrote to Bernardo Provenzano for guidance, to see if he could shed some light on why the request had come from Catania, and not from him. I took a pen and paper and I wrote to Bernardo Provenzano that there was this problem we needed to resolve. His response to my question, was that he didn't understand what was going on. He said: "Let's see about this, as soon as we can." So he played for time.'

But Provenzano did not always prevaricate for the sake of it. While Brusca fumed, he was arranging for Ilardo to be swiftly dispatched.

Such profound treachery was deeply wounding, and damaging for the organization. He had revealed his plan to Gino Ilardo. The authorities would have his letters, would know more about him than they ever had in thirty years. He instructed Giuffré to find a secure, remote location. Giuffré, suspecting the purpose, found the perfect spot, out of sight of prying eyes, and told Provenzano it was ready.

In early May, Ilardo decided to put his collaboration on a formal footing. He asked to meet magistrates from Palermo and Caltanissetta to talk about his situation, and spent some hours with them at the ROS barracks in Rome, going over the details of his conviction, his protection and the information he could offer. He left that afternoon, with an agreement to reconvene in ten days' time, to finalize the arrangements for his, and his family's, protection. He took a plane straight back to Catania, hoping to get home before his absence had been noted. But the news was already out. The next day two gunmen accosted him outside his house in Catania and shot him several times from close range before making their escape.

Word of Ilardo's death spread rapidly through Mafia circles. Police recorded a conversation picked up by a bug in a mafioso's car:

'I saw Lucio yesterday evening . . . and he said to me: have you heard the latest about Gino? No, I haven't, I said. . . He said it seems he was an informer.'

'Who? Gino?'

'Apparently he was in direct contact with someone from the police. Looks like he was the one who got Mimì arrested . . . and Aiello . . . If they hadn't killed him he'd have let them have me, you and all our sons to the seventh generation . . . We don't know what they know. I feel like a complete idiot – my whole world's collapsed.'

Piddu Madonia was going wild with rage in his prison cell, betrayed by his own cousin, in whom he had placed his trust. The man described as the 'worm within our midst' had caused untold damage.

While Provenzano was digesting this disaster, Brusca, having made a show of pledging his loyalty, seemed to be acting on his own again. He refused to accept that he could not get any business in Bagheria – although he had never, by his own admission, been a part of that family, and he knew it was a closed shop.

The only way to prevent Brusca causing further damage, Giuffré concluded in his coldly calculating manner, would be to get rid of him. Obviously murdering Riina's godson was likely to be an unpopular proposition, and Riina, though in prison, must still be respected. But Giuffré remembered something Riina had said that made him think he might not stand in his way. Brusca had been demanding the right to collect extortion money on another mafioso's territory. Giuffré and Riina were discussing the protection rackets at a meeting in Palermo when Riina made a sardonic remark. 'The colt is beginning to paw the ground.'

Giuffré took this as explicit permission to get rid of the 'colt', adding that Riina never did like to show favouritism (on the contrary, he had never shown any compunction about killing friends and allies). But Provenzano did not buy Giuffré's rationalization and would not give permission for Brusca's murder, however much he would have liked to. He had other ideas for revenge.

'I wouldn't wish to cause trouble,' Giuffré said years later in his gravelly drawl, 'but if I was determined to think the worst of some people, I would say Provenzano was convinced that, as soon as Brusca was arrested, he would collaborate, and his thinking was, Brusca knows next to nothing about me.'

Brusca was in love with the power, the sudden wealth and the football star lifestyle that Cosa Nostra could offer. A gruff, greedy individual, he had a surprising weakness for comfort and expensive clothes. Provenzano figured that, as soon as the prison door clanged behind him, he would be a prime candidate for collaboration.

Brusca as an informer on the opposition: the prospect made him worth more to Provenzano alive than dead. It was, as Giuffré describes it, a case of particularly sharp far-sightedness. Brusca was duly arrested in May 1996 while watching a TV film about the assassination of Giovanni Falcone. And within a few months he did indeed collaborate.

There was a kind of morbid fascination, a compulsive repulsion, about the fat, bearded monster who had killed judge Falcone. In the early days of his collaboration Brusca told untruths and half-truths, and demonstrated a high-minded amorality. He said he was disgusted with the organization; no one followed the rules any more. 'I felt betrayed as a mafioso. Not guilty for what I had done.'

Magistrates who questioned him in the early weeks found an understandable reticence on some particularly hot topics, and anything concerning his father, but in general his memory of events was clear and well ordered. They also revealed that the man known as 'the Pig' scoffed biscuits between sessions.

Brusca's motive for betraying Cosa Nostra, his godfather and his own father, was his betrayal at Riina's hand. Brusca had read, in the confessions of another mafioso, that Riina had been angry with him for going behind his back on a drug deal, and had threatened to kill him.

Riina had known him since he was a child; his father had taken in Riina's whole family in times of trouble. 'This revelation made me so angry and upset, he might as well have killed me. I had lived in the cult of Riina, but from one day to the next he turned to dust before my eyes.'

Brusca, like so many others, would get his revenge. But in the meantime Provenzano faced another challenge. Vito Vitale, a young blood from Partinico, considered himself the natural successor of Riina and had no time for the old-style capos. He and his brother used to make a mockery of Provenzano's pious phraseology. He was a violent, hot-tempered man nearly thirty years Provenzano's junior, whose murderous talent was attracting a group of like-minded youths. He did not wait for permission to kill. He shot Nené Geraci, the patriarch of Partinico, whose position he had already usurped, on Riina's orders. He also got hold of a rocket launcher with which he intended to blow up the prosecutor Alfonso Sabella.

Provenzano heard rumours that Vitale was planning to take over the Mafia fiefdom of San Giuseppe Iato by executing any men loyal to Brusca and Balduccio Di Maggio. He wrote to a local mafioso in his steeliest tone: 'They tell me a certain Vitale from Partinico has been hanging around town. What is Vitale doing in San Giuseppe Iato?'

Provenzano also happened to know that Di Maggio had returned in secret to his home town and assembled a small and heavily armed force to settle some old scores. Provenzano, assuming that the *pentito* might also settle a new score, didn't try to stop him.

But before any of his enemies could get to him, Vitale was arrested. Provenzano, without using a gun, had seen off his last challenger. His circle of trusted allies was getting smaller, but they were men who understood what he was trying to do, who would work with him to accomplish his mission.

'After the arrest of Vito Vitale,' said Giuffré, 'Provenzano, Benedetto Spera and I had the field to ourselves. Provenzano set out to get Cosa Nostra under his control and make up for lost time.'

10

A management handbook for the aspiring Mafia boss

A FTER TOTÒ RIINA'S arrest Bernardo Provenzano was the unify-ing force that brought Cosa Nostra back from the brink of disaster. His followers within the organization bewailed the mistakes of the recent past, the policy of violence which had caused so much damage. 'Our toy is broken!' wailed Pino Lipari, Provenzano's long-term friend and business strategist.

The 'toy' had to be fixed. After taking over sole leadership Provenzano made his mission statement: 'We must do business'.[24] Anything that threatened the profit-making activities of Cosa Nostra had to be avoided. Provenzano set about halting arrests, restoring links in politics and business and reviving a culture of Cosa Nostra which had been lost.

His is an extraordinary achievement, based on his personal charisma and tactical skill, from which business leaders worldwide could learn much. The fact that he wrote his reforms by letter, means that we have what amounts to a manual of how to run a criminal organization, a steadily accumulating constitution.

Submersion

'Whatever the provocation, in the light of the current political situation we can't risk any armed conflict, we have to let it go. And if you hold your fire, in five, or maybe seven years' time the benefits will be felt by all our friends, we'll be able to do business again and overcome our present economic difficulties.'

In the mid-1990s Provenzano held a meeting at which he told his capos that if they followed his directives, their profits would eventually be restored. It could take years, he told them – no small matter for an organization accustomed to easy money. Provenzano gave his orders – *non fare scruscio*: 'make no noise'.

He took the organization below the radar of public security, ordering his men to avoid any kind of publicity, which meant no acts of violence. The policy of blowing up representatives of the state had caused so much collateral damage that Provenzano had to make urgent repairs. He wrote to Ilardo: 'We have many enemies who assail us, from outside and from within, but we must try to recover what we can.'

'We instigated a period of submersion, whose aim was to make Cosa Nostra invisible, giving us time to regroup', his lieutenant Nino Giuffré recalls.

From now on, before any act of violence could be carried out, there had to be a thorough appraisal of its usefulness. 'As far as Provenzano was concerned,' Giuffré said, 'it was essential to weigh up whether a person could do more damage dead or alive.' A magistrate investigating Cosa Nostra might do more harm as an 'excellent cadaver' than if he were allowed to do his job.

Cosa Nostra has historically used long periods of 'submersion' to secure its interests and stop a run of arrests. Unless Provenzano brought about radical change, there would not be a politician or businessman left who would be prepared to risk working with them. But his ambitions exceeded the Mafia's previous dealings with industry.

'The philosophy of submersion had the very clear aim of helping the organization cross over into running businesses', said assistant prosecutor Nino Di Matteo. 'The lines between Cosa Nostra's profit-making activities and legitimate business had to be blurred, or erased. It would no longer be forcing businesses to pay kickbacks; it would be running those businesses itself.'

In politics, the Mafia must not be seen to support candidates openly, or they risked ruining their chances. They were to approach apparently clean politicians and manipulate them from behind the scenes.

'Provenzano said that if a politician was seen to be supported by men of honour of a certain rank,' Giuffré explained, 'within twenty-four hours he'd be destroyed. That politician, our experience had taught us, would immediately be attacked by the opposition.'

Discipline was needed among the capos, who had been used to solving problems by sending in the boys to damage building sites and greenhouses if anyone refused to pay. Giuffré was responsible for putting the new policy into practice: 'We might have a problem with one of the businesses: even then we were absolutely forbidden to cause trouble. If one firm was a bit stubborn, and didn't want to pay, we had to find a solution without causing a row, without setting fires or smashing the place up.'

'This policy of submersion was particularly dangerous for us,' said Pietro Grasso, formerly Palermo's chief prosecutor, 'because it's more difficult to grasp what Cosa Nostra is doing if there is no violent crime. There was a danger that Cosa Nostra would drop out of our sights.'

Mediation

'I beg you to be calm, true and correct, correct and consistent, know how to turn any negative experiences to account, don't dismiss everything people tell you or believe everything you're told, always try to discover the truth before you speak, and remember that it's never enough to have just one source of information to make your judgement. To be certain, you need three sources to confirm it; you need to be fair, honest, and consistent.'

This letter was sent to Gino Ilardo, capo of Caltanissetta, who was seeking advice on how to resolve the problem of a large sum of money going missing, amid a storm of rumours and disinformation. Assistant prosecutor Michele Prestipino describes it as 'a manifesto of Cosa Nostra under Bernardo Provenzano, for whom mediation was the rule (although violence and terrorism were not ruled out if they became necessary)'.

'This letter gives us a snapshot of Provenzano the Mafia boss, at the height of his power', says Nino Di Matteo. 'What strikes me about this letter is his careful approach to directing the organization: he never takes a major step unless he is absolutely certain that it needs to be taken.'

Provenzano will go down in history as the 'guarantor of the pax mafioso'. He stopped the Mafia's war on the state and insisted on peaceful methods, instructing his men in the art of negotiation and the importance of dialogue.

Provenzano's lengthy and often difficult negotiations with Riina taught him a great deal about the essential skills of mediation: policy had to be thrashed out at the table, not at the end of a gun.

Provenzano was decisive and on occasions demanded swift and direct answers to his questions, but when it served him, he could come across as a ditherer. He was circumspect, added to which, the system of *pizzini* meant that he could choose whether and when to reply, sometimes remaining guarded even with his closest allies.

He wrote to Giuffré: 'You ask if I've got some advice to give you about this matter. I'm going to ask you the same thing, if you can advise me.'

On occasion he heard both sides of an argument, delayed matters by asking for more information and then gave each side contradictory instructions. He wrote to Giuffré: 'We must be patient, and hear the other side of the story, after which we'll see what we have to do.'

In a series of letters to Ilardo, who was trying to solve the disappearance of 500 million lire of protection money paid by a Catania industrial plant, Provenzano keeps the issue at bay, feigning ignorance of the issues. 'I'm not absolutely sure I know what you're referring to here', he writes. 'You want to clarify the matter, but what's to clarify? As I explained, I know nothing about this.'

Provenzano insisted that nothing was to be gained by falling out with each other. 'My wish is to make peace wherever possible, and keep everything clear between us, so as to maintain respect for each other.'

Differences had to be resolved, but because the organization was under intense scrutiny, top-level summits were out of the question. Provenzano urged his members to sort out their problems and revealed a steely impatience if there was any delay.

'You want me to give you instructions, or advice, but what can I tell you when there are two versions of the facts which contradict each other? You are the ones who can say, which is the correct version, not me.

'You must find a way to understand each other's point of view.'

Giuffré, watchful for signs of treachery, wrote to Provenzano expressing concern that his own trusted postmen had allowed more than one letter to get wet and become illegible *en route* to its destination. Scrupulously, he brought it to the Boss's attention, and was reassured by the reply: 'With his usual wisdom and diplomacy, Provenzano said: "Before we say anything, let's try and ascertain the facts, shall we? These things can happen, when they go through so many hands." '

All the time he was counselling moderation and straight dealing between warring factions, Provenzano was careful to keep himself out of the frame. It was one of his principles to stay out of relationships between families. 'It's between you. See if you can find a way to get everyone in agreement, all pulling in the same direction.'

Consensus

'The estate owner wants to give the administrator's job to one of our people. She can't get on with the current incumbent and wants him out of there', Provenzano wrote to Ilardo. 'We need to sort out a replacement. Let me know when you are able to give me a reply for this lady. Do forgive me for bothering you with these recommendations, but as you know, my aim is to serve.'

'We don't know whether the lady was making the request, or whether the Mafia got involved of its own initiative', observes Di Matteo. 'But it is extraordinary that today, on a big estate, they turn to Provenzano to let them know whom they can hire as a manager.'

Provenzano's letter makes clear, in his self-effacing way, that any requests for help, advice or recommendations from ordinary people must be treated as a priority.

One key step in the organization's recovery was recapturing the popular consensus, after Riina's bombing strategy alienated the population at large. The Mafia has always relied on the silent consent of the community, as an essential part of its social control. His ability to survive on the run depended on the full support of the communities in which he lived.

Provenzano was clear: the Mafia must appear a positive element of life, a mutual benefit for all. The Boss had to appear as a beneficent figure, an uncle whose advice and consent were sought on all matters – business and personal. Cosa Nostra has always portrayed itself as holder of the moral standard. Uncle Binnu accepted requests for assistance or advice from every level of society. Managers, landowners, employers, knew they could get a reliable recommendation from the Boss. Fathers whose daughters were getting married could discover if the young man in question had honourable intentions.

'Bernardo Provenzano, in these *pizzini*, replies to requests for help, advice and decisions', explains Prestipino: 'who gets permission to marry his girlfriend, who gets let off military service . . . he has a close and dynamic relationship with the community. He oversees everything, controls everything – his influence on people's private lives is pervasive. It's important for them to have his judgement on who marries whom, who they vote for, what to think, what to do. It's the basis of social control, and far more effective than military oppression.'

Investigators couldn't find Provenzano, but people who needed a favour knew how to get their request to him. Those who wanted to, knew his local representatives and turned to them with their requests for recommendations.

Parents of students appealed to the Godfather to make sure they passed their exams. This was a good deal more effective than dedicating an *ex voto* to Santa Maria: if the commission was accepted, a mafioso would speak to the professor and persuade him to give the boy a good grade.

'I'm sending you a copy of the response from your godson, and the Professor. So I'm pleased to say that the Prof did his duty and the boy did well in his exams . . .'

The aim is to penetrate social and economic relationships to such an extent that if a person wishes to exercise their rights, they can do so only through the Mafia. Cosa Nostra replaced the state, not battling against it but taking over from the inside.

Answering people's requests for help or advice brings them into a structure that they then implicitly support; this is the power of

Provenzano's system, the method by which the Mafia historically exerted social control. If you know about people's emotional lives, you have a hold on them. And if you help a businessman with connections, or recommendations, you have his complicity in the system. That ordinary people were once again turning to the Boss for help and favours in their daily lives was a sign that Provenzano's policies were succeeding.

The need for popular consensus also required a tactical change in the manner of extorting protection money. Instead of demanding ever-increasing slices of the profits until they drove companies out of business, Provenzano's watchword was 'everybody pays less, but everybody pays'. By demanding a figure businesses could afford, he restored the sense that it was on the whole much less trouble for companies to pay up quietly, month after month. His pragmatic approach made it advantageous for companies to deal with the Mafia.

In a letter to one of the Palermo capos Provenzano explains that paying protection is not an imposition but an opportunity: 'Let me know whatever they need, they must expect nothing but good from us.'

'Provenzano's skill was to keep everyone happy,' says Pietro Grasso, 'he managed to resolve everyone's problems.'

Keep God on your side

'May the lord bless you and keep you . . . know that where I can be of use to you, with the will of God, I am completely at your disposal . . .'

Provenzano's letters, each one signed off in the same way, read like the parish priest's homily. He would send tracts copied from the Bible to his followers. His show of religious fervour was an important part of the process of rehabilitating Cosa Nostra after the devastation of Riina's regime.

The Mafia has always laid claim to the religious high ground. 'The mafioso has God behind him', writes the editor of the Catholic magazine *Segno*. 'His life is at one with the will and the law of God, in relation to which his role is as a kind of official priest and representative.'

The Church has traditionally been reticent about the Mafia: one priest regularly heard the confessions of Pietro Aglieri; another performed the marriage ceremony between the fugitive Totò Riina and Ninetta Bagarella. But Riina's war against the state finally stirred the Vatican out of its torpor, provoking a surprisingly strong attack from the Pope. In May 1993 John Paul II visited Sicily and made an emotional speech, waving a defiant fist and decrying the Mafia's inhumanity, its culture of death. 'Mafiosi, you must convert!' he cried out.

Re-establishing an ideology rooted in Catholic principles appeared to be an important part of Provenzano's strategy, and he adopted a pastoral role that would appeal to many of his men: 'With the will of God I would be a servant. Command me and, if possible, with calm and caution let's see if we can make progress and work together.'

His pastoral role clearly had the desired effect on some of his followers. His loyal friend Lipari wrote to him: 'You are altruistic, wise, you take life as it comes, like a gift from God. Your faith is strong and sustains you. God has enlightened you . . .'

In his letters Provenzano invokes the Lord's good offices in matters of security: 'It would give me great pleasure to see you in person, but at the moment this isn't possible, but we will meet, if God wills it, and soon.' He also invoked God in matters of violence, when necessary. When Provenzano's aggressive war against the violent splinter groups in Gela was brought to an end, at a cost of 300 mostly young lives, he praised God: 'I thank you from my heart, if this is true as you say, but for now no compliments, let us pray to our Heavenly Father, who guides us to do Good Works.'

In one of the letters discussing a murder plot, Provenzano writes: 'I've got nothing to say except let the will of God be done.' With this, the Boss's implied consent, the man died.[25]

While Provenzano's use of pious language was an effective public relations exercise, adding authority and *gravitas* to his letters, it has been given a more sinister interpretation. The only thing Provenzano has requested in prison is a Bible – not just any Bible, but his own – the one he had underlined, annotated and scribbled on during his years of composing and decoding *pizzini*. Investigators were convinced that a man so intent on restoring the Mafia's good appearance would use a Bible to construct his secret code.

But it seems increasingly likely that Provenzano's Bible was, in fact, just a Bible. After making a thorough search of the volume, the Servizio Centrale Operativo (SCO), the police organized crime unit, reported that Provenzano seemed to have combed the Bible for texts to sustain a Mafia boss in his endeavours, and give him strength. 'In general, one observes a certain attention to rules, to punishments, guilt, and vengeance, as though he were searching the book for some inspiration and authority to support him in his responsibilities and the decisions which were a necessary part of being the head of an organization.'

Reinvention

'I beg your forgiveness for the errors in my writing . . .'

Every letter from the boss ends with the same sign-off: a saintly and affectionate benediction and an apology for grammatical errors. The bad spelling and schoolboy mistakes detracted nothing from the authority of its writer. For a man who moved easily in the worlds of business and politics it was apparently part of an elaborate disguise.

One clue comes to us from a recorded conversation between Provenzano's long-time associate Pino Lipari and his son, in which Lipari instructs his son to make deliberate grammatical mistakes when writing to Provenzano, as he himself does.

'It's all spelt badly, the grammar's all wrong . . . I put the bad grammar in . . . it's done on purpose, do you see? Get some verbs wrong, the odd word . . . do you see what I mean, Arturo?'

This could mean that Lipari has understood by osmosis the political advantage of imitating your superiors, but it could be so that the police would think they were looking for an illiterate clod.

One of the major reasons Bernardo Provenzano managed to live undetected for so long was that people still thought of him as a brainless killer, thanks to Luciano Liggio's deathless phrase: 'He shoots like a god, shame he has the brains of a chicken.' Investigators spent decades trying to locate a dumb bully boy. When police wires picked up mafiosi talking about *u ragioniere*, 'the Accountant', whose advice and adjudication was sought on matters of business and finance, it never occurred to them it could be the same person. According to super-grass Tommaso Buscetta, if you asked most mafiosi they wouldn't be able to say whether Binnu was an idiot or a genius.

The man known as 'the Tractor' disappeared before his twenty-fifth birthday, when he was running a political campaign for Luciano Liggio's favoured candidate. During his career in Cosa Nostra he transformed himself from a hired killer setting fire to hayricks and stealing cattle into a business investor, political mastermind and, ulti-mately, strategist and leader.

When he was arrested, his expensive clothes and toiletries revealed he was used to a comfortable existence in the salons of Palermo, wearing silk and cashmere, and Armani aftershave. As the most pow-erful Mafia boss of the last generation, and the longest-surviving fugi-tive from the law, he was also a hardened survivor, living in a freezing mountain shepherd's hut stinking of cheese, eating maggoty greens.

'When I got out of prison in 1993,' Giuffré recalled, 'I found a changed Provenzano from the warrior he was; now he was showing signs of saintliness. After the bombings, he was urgently looking for a remedy. He became a different person, above all in the way he expressed himself.'

'We have an image of him bashing a man's brains out with the heel of a gun', says police chief Giuseppe Gualtieri. 'Now he's become a political strategist.'

With Provenzano's new directives, not only did the headline-grabbing violence cease, but Provenzano managed to dissociate himself from the violence that had gone before. Among all the col-laborators who were giving their version of events to investigators, there was not one who could recall a meeting at which Provenzano gave an explicit order to kill.

The new boss had an acute sense of public relations and the impor-tance of creating an image. Giuffré was impressed: 'Lipari and Cannella [Provenzano's strategists] helped him get his virginity back; like everyone else, he had emerged from the bombings with his reputation in tatters. They had to restore his image. So this little group was identified as having been against the bombings – which was not true at all; Provenzano, in matters of politics, and therefore of political assassinations, had always been number one.'

Provenzano's transformative genius enabled him to live for forty-three years as a fugitive from justice. He became known as The Phantom of Corleone, since many believed that he had never strayed far from his home town, and yet no one could find him.

'It's not that he changed, he just understood what was required at the time, and responded to that', wrote the Mafia expert, sociologist and anti-Mafia campaigner Umberto Santino. 'He's been a man for all seasons: killer for Luciano Liggio in his youth, bomber with Riina in the '80s and early '90s; when Cosa Nostra was beaten and had to put a brave face on defeat, he became a moderator . . . he showed yet again how the Mafia can keep transforming itself and stay the same.'

Modesty

'They want me to tell them what to do, but who am I to tell them how to behave?' Provenzano wrote to Giuffré.

Many of the letters have the solemn and affectionate tone of a father writing to his children. Provenzano never wanted to be a tyrant; he wanted to be a 'kindly dictator'. In deliberately avoiding the hectoring tones of Riina, Provenzano adopts an earnest modesty.

'I can tell you what I tell you, that is, in your position I would do this, not that you must do it . . . I can't give orders to anyone, indeed I look for someone who can give orders to me.'

This manner sets a tone of modesty and forbearance that is a tremendous asset in tackling disputes. 'With the will of God I want to be a servant', he writes to Ilardo 'command me, and if possible, with calm and reserve we will make progress. My typewriter stops here, but my heart carries on.'

'The greatest quality in a Mafia leader is to know how to co-ordinate the activities of different groups, without imposing his will', says Professor Lupo.

'He was the uncontested boss of Cosa Nostra,' says Prestipino, 'but he wanted to give the impression that his decisions were reached after long consultation. He had learned how to be the antithesis of Riina. His ostentatious modesty becomes part of his character in his personal relationships. Others, like Riina and Brusca, have an obsession with being great, looking powerful. He deliberately comes across as being down at heel.'

Living simply, in a humble rustic setting, could be seen as a deliberate choice, setting an example of true leadership, particularly in a Christian context – surrounded by weeping Madonnas and Jesus pictures. It sent a message both to mafiosi enduring hard times in gaol and to those who loved to live extravagantly, quaffing champagne at casinos.

Provenzano's letters speak of a humility apparently incompatible with a boss of his status, but make him sound all the greater for that: 'I ask nothing, I was born to serve.'

One young mafioso turned *pentito*, Salvatore Barbagallo, attested to the Boss's reputation for fairness and conciliation: 'I've got to say that within Cosa Nostra I always heard good things about Provenzano; people said he used the expression "Eat and let others eat"' which underlined his willingness to share the money he made from crime.'

Provenzano's simple lifestyle gave the signal that he was frugal and hardy; people who came into contact with him were impressed by his toughness. As his last hideout testified, his power was to be measured out not in fancy possessions but in the loyalty he commanded.

Don't let political beliefs get in your way

'We didn't create Forza Italia', Nino Giuffré told the court in one of his first appearances. 'We merely put our resources behind the party most likely to succeed.'

Provenzano never held a strong preference for one political party. His predecessors had tended to favour the Christian Democrats, the party of tradition, with a strong Catholic heritage, but he had no such party loyalties. He looked for the individual politicians who would best serve the Mafia's interests.

Cosa Nostra's way of doing business required politicians of the right disposition to smooth the way. Giuffré was the principal exponent and apostle of Provenzano's thought, and of finding trustworthy people to pursue it. 'It's important to have the right political experience,' said Giuffré, 'to know how to get things done behind the scenes, to steer particular debates that might have an impact on public works, health, agriculture and everything that we have an interest in. There has to be a certain aptitude on both sides.'

During the years when some within the Christian Democrats were doing Cosa Nostra's bidding, and the reforming Communists were considered a threat to the Mafia's stranglehold on industry, Provenzano had his moles in the Communist ranks. In Bagheria and Villabate Communist-controlled councils were infiltrated by Cosa Nostra's friends and business partners.

Siino recalled of Provenzano: 'A sophisticated mind like that of Signor Provenzano decided to cover his back by bringing in the Communist co-operatives, while Riina, the clod, had thrown them out.'

Provenzano had learned early in his career to change parties when it suited him: Liggio had decided to support a Liberal candidate against the Christian Democrats in the 1958 elections because he was promoting a potentially lucrative construction project. From this episode Provenzano learned a lesson in politics that he would never forget: that the only ideology is Cosa Nostra's, and that any political belief is as good as the next, as long as it makes money.

When Riina decided to back the Socialist Party in 1987, Provenzano was against it because most of the Mafia's powerful contacts were still Christian Democrats, and he could not see any benefit in dropping them.

When he took over the organization, the prison population was deeply unhappy with the way they had been neglected. The only way Provenzano was going to be able to appease mafiosi serving long sentences was to bring about some changes in the harsh anti-Mafia laws.

He needed new political contacts, who would be open to negotiating. For a short time he toyed with the idea of joining forces with a growing far-right separatist movement.

But when Forza Italia was founded in 1993, Provenzano saw a new political party on the landscape and recognized that a number of its local politicians were willing to do business. 'From then on', recalls Giuffré, 'our people had to forget about their old friends in the Christian Democrats – it was all Forza Italia.'

Security

'Tell the others they mustn't talk inside their cars or anywhere near them, and at home they must be careful as well, they mustn't talk loudly near any houses, construction sites or abandoned buildings.'

This letter from Provenzano to one of his managers followed a tip-off that police had bugged their meeting place – a farm office out in the country.

Provenzano was obsessive about security. Wherever he went, he carried a little backpack, a sleeping bag and a wand for detecting bugging devices, and he was constantly on the look-out for new and more secure meeting places.

Giuffré described a meeting with Provenzano and Pino Lipari in which the main topics were security issues. As Giuffré recalls, he reminded them repeatedly 'to be careful never to talk about certain things, to try and find some protection against being bugged, for example with one of those instruments that locates bugs, and at the same time to try and find new people, with no record, who could move freely without being spotted by the forces of law and order, to protect both fugitives and people who shouldn't be seen in contact with them'.

With so many penitent mafiosi revealing the organization's darkest secrets, Provenzano had to find a secure means of communication, to stay ahead of police investigators.

'New technology is a minefield for anyone with security worries', points out General Angiolo Pellegrini, who was tracking Provenzano in the early 1980s. 'Mobile phones can be pinpointed, landlines are no longer secure; we put bugs in their cars, and we can follow them with GPS, e-mails can be intercepted, computers can be taken apart. Anything they do we can intercept. By the time it's legal to plant listening devices in houses, well, at this point, the less we talk, the better. So I write a note on a piece of paper, and I send it to you.'

Provenzano's simple method of communication, no more sophisticated than the one used by schoolchildren in class before mobile phones, revolutionized the running of Cosa Nostra.

Provenzano kept the *pizzini* circulating, come what may – as symbols of his authority and reminders of his continual presence – advising, answering, cajoling and, occasionally, making demands. He used code numbers and initials to conceal the identity of the addressees. 'Zio' ('Uncle') signed on and off in similar, generic vein, avoiding any personal detail that could have identified the recipient.

He advocated extreme caution in business dealings, as an essential part of his no-risk, no-noise policy. He wrote to Brusca, who had invited him to join a drug deal: 'This is the second time you've invited me to invest in this deal with you, and I thank you for it, but if you would listen to my advice, at this moment in time, if we can't hand-pick the people we are doing business with, we should do nothing. The people who you are in contact with are fine, I know who they are. But what about the people they are in contact with? We don't know them, so I don't want any part in this.'

Brusca recalled this rebuttal years later: 'He insisted that before we made any kind of investment, he wanted to know who we were doing business with, where we were going, what it was all about . . . he wanted to know the whole story from A to Z.'

If any of his men proposed to make political contacts without the necessary caution, they could expect the same grilling. Provenzano sent his man in San Giuseppe Iato, Salvatore Genovese, a chilling rebuke.

'You tell me you have a high-level political contact who would put you in a position to manage major projects, and before going ahead you ask me what I think. But without knowing this person, what do you want me to tell you?

'I would need to know their name, and who their contacts are. These days we can't trust anyone. They could be a trickster, a cop, an infiltrator. They could be wasting our time or plotting our downfall. More than that, I can't honestly say.'

Provenzano had been highly disciplined and autonomous, even in earlier days on the run. Brusca remembers: 'I would say that man is prudence personified. We would go out and about, taking the usual precautions, usually in the early morning, but he was capable of going to ground for months at a time. He walled himself in. When we saw him again, his skin was as white as paper.'

Provenzano never let even those closest to him know where he was staying. He was good at letting the people think that he was staying in the place where they met. His driver would be from that village, and his associates would naturally assume he was staying there. That was what he wanted them to think.

Although they were close associates, there was a deep-seated, quite mutual, sense of caution. 'If he had ever needed somewhere to stay as a matter of urgency,' said Giuffré, 'I of course told him he could stay with me. But he didn't know where I lived because I didn't tell anyone that . . . not even Provenzano. He did ask me once but I didn't tell him, because he didn't need to know. There are some things you don't ask.'

Taking the best of old and new

'How can you ask for a discount, when our people are inside? You are like a rock in the middle of the sea, with the wind battering against you from all sides. Please, stop getting in the way of what I'm trying to do and sort this out for me.'

Provenzano had set up a fund for imprisoned members of Cosa Nostra, paid for from the profits of racketeering. When Palermo capo Nino Rotolo asked permission to give one of the businesses in his territory a discount, Provenzano chided him for neglecting his brothers in prison.

The new boss had no military power, and a diminishing number of capos. He had to deal with a decimated, demoralized, even traumatized, army, and his first priority was to stop any more mafiosi turning state's evidence. By giving prisoners their due, Provenzano showed he was prepared to pay attention to the old way of doing things. It was important to reinstate the old rules and the old way of managing Cosa Nostra – such as the mutual fund for all the families in Palermo.

Provenzano proved a master at combining old and new: modern business methods with old-fashioned typewritten notes; new business strategies with old-fashioned patronage. In the process of rebuilding an army, he combined the knowledge of the old guard with the energy of the new.

'The apparent equilibrium within Cosa Nostra rests entirely on the recognition of Bernardo Provenzano's authority', a secret service report notes. 'He continues to be the connecting link between the traditional Mafia and the more aggressive factions.'

After Bagarella's arrest Provenzano called a summit. Present were senior men of honour Provenzano knew he could rely on. 'All the men on this new-style cupola were so old,' wrote the examining magistrates in their report, 'it should have been called a Senate.'

Provenzano restored a sense of hierarchy. He recruited the old guard who had been out of the country, or out of favour, for a decade, and who were appalled by the turn Cosa Nostra had taken under Riina.

'Provenzano's strength', explains Nino Di Matteo, 'has been his ability to surround himself with apparently respectable people perfectly capable of interacting with the institutions of power, to discover what he needed to know.' Di Matteo observes that Provenzano rebuilt the commission on new guidelines, avoiding old clan enmities and feuds: 'Provenzano gathered together a close group of men, often not even formally affiliated with Cosa Nostra, a group that comprised members of several families, across different *mandamenti*.'

In so doing, he revived a culture of working together for a common aim. It was not always easy to do. In Palermo there were some, such as Rotolo, who found it impossible to forget the past and unite. 'We must do it for everyone's good', Provenzano wrote to him.

Political and business contacts appreciated the change of regime and understood that these were people they could do business with, without jeopardizing their careers.

The magistrates investigating Provenzano's supporters described his successful process of recovery and rehabilitation: 'A Cosa Nostra, directed by Provenzano, fully operational, run on a hierarchical model, whose ruling group, once they have processed the fall-out from the "mistakes made" in the recent past, acknowledge the need to stitch up old wounds, in order to mend their "broken toy" and get on with achieving their goals: wealth and Mafia power.'

Politics for Pragmatists

Cosa nostra's desertion of its traditional political allies the Christian Democrats did not assist the Mafia cause. New anti-Mafia laws passed by Giulio Andreotti made life very uncomfortable for the prisoners and their families, who were now separated by Perspex screens on their monthly visits and body-searched on their way in and out. The authorities seized their businesses and – more painful still for those, like Riina, of peasant stock – their land.

'What do they think, that the prime minister's forgotten they voted for the Socialists? They were a thorn in his side, and he's got rid of them', Salvo Lima scoffed to Angelo Siino.

Riina had put too much pressure on his political contacts, who had ultimately snapped. 'He had pulled the rope too tight,' said Giuffré, 'particularly in connection with control of public works contracts. The politicians got irritated; they felt bullied and threatened.'

Although Provenzano had never set much store by any of the parties, he needed a new political alliance to consolidate his position and realize the next phase of his plan. While he consulted his contacts in search of new political partners, in early 1990 Leoluca Bagarella, always inclined towards the dramatic, started taking an interest in the idea of a coup d'état. He asked Tullio Cannella, a contractor, to seek out any separatist tendencies and find out if they were serious. Cannella duly spent some months and a lot of money founding a new separatist party. He later confessed: 'I worked on the plan to build an independence movement that would hand Sicily over to Cosa Nostra.'

Among those he canvassed for selection was a prince who had expressed an interest in starting a Southern League. At supper with the prince, who liked to be addressed as Your Royal Highness, Cannella told him bluntly that if they were going to get him elected, they would have to do a deal with the Mafia bosses, to 'kiss some hands', as he put it, however disagreeable this might be. At this point His Highness paled and politely declined, and said, 'We never had this meeting.'

The attraction of a separatist movement was, to Provenzano, the ideal of controlling a political party from the inside. Cosa Nostra had a new ambition, 'in which men of honour would be able, directly or nearly, to make their voices heard and impose their will'. But such a movement could take years to get going, and the man at the helm of Cosa Nostra was in a hurry. Just when he was running out of money, Cannella was contacted by Bagarella, who said that they had a solution, more concrete and immediate than the project he'd been working on, and he should not waste any more time on it. 'Bagarella told me they were supporting a new party, Forza Italia. Apparently there were members of Cosa Nostra who had links to some of the candidates, who had made some kind of electoral pact, had undertaken a commitment, so they were going to vote for them.'

Provenzano's top priority was to get the anti-Mafia laws changed, to lessen the power of the *pentiti* and to soften the harsh conditions for mafiosi in prison. In January 1993 Provenzano summoned Giuffré and told him he had found a new political reference, one that within a decade would have made all the concessions they demanded. As the judges later put it: 'The new political line was good news for anyone who needed to move vast amounts of capital, and would raise the threshold of impunity.'

'The leaders of Cosa Nostra had made contact with a very senior figure in Berlusconi's entourage, someone beyond suspicion', the informer Gino Ilardo told his carabiniere handler, Maresciallo Riccio. 'In exchange for their support in the elections, I was told they had received certain guarantees.'

So, Riccio asked, who was Berlusconi's man at the meeting? Was it Marcello dell'Utri?

'Ah, Maresciallo, nothing gets past you!' Ilardo replied.

Dell'Utri had been a banker and was now director of Berlusconi's advertising agency, Publitalia. In a clever stroke for a football-mad nation he came up with the idea for a political party called Forza Italia! (Go Italy!). Prosecutors dated dell'Utri's links with the Mafia back to his days as a football coach in Palermo in the 1960s, and he had hired a man of honour, Vittorio Mangano, to work at Berlusconi's country estate in the '70s.

It was later claimed that dell'Utri hired Mangano in the 1970s not for his skill with animals (he could not even ride a horse, and as one mafioso put it, 'Cosa Nostra doesn't clean stables for anyone'[26]), but as a representative of Cosa Nostra, to protect Berlusconi and his family from kidnapping. Berlusconi has insisted that he had no idea about Mangano's links with Cosa Nostra and recalled that, as estate manager, he was exemplary.

For the rich, kidnapping was a real threat at that time: after the commission outlawed his favourite way of making money on Sicilian soil, Luciano Liggio had moved his operations to the north. 'First we threatened them, then we offered them a guarantee of safety; it worked every time', said collaborator Francesco Di Carlo, capo of Altofonte, who was later arrested in London for drug trafficking.

Di Carlo claimed sensationally that Berlusconi's fears about a member of his family being kidnapped led to an extraordinary meeting in 1974 between Berlusconi and the rather eccentric and self-important Palermo Mafia boss Stefano Bontate. The meeting, as described by Di Carlo, was held in a Milan office and convened by the Mafia capo Dr Gaetano Cinà, at dell'Utri's request. Di Carlo, a detached and amusing narrator whose account of events has been hotly contested by dell'Utri, said he was only invited along to make Bontate look good.

'I shook dell'Utri's hand, but I didn't kiss him . . . I've never really gone in for all that kissing. Besides he wasn't Cosa Nostra . . . if he had been, I suppose I'd have been obliged to kiss him.'

Bontate, who believed Berlusconi had a low view of southerners, was very conscious of his status. He expected to be addressed with the formal '*lei*' throughout the meeting, while he used the familiar '*tu*': 'Bontate had these affectations of grandeur', said Di Carlo.

According to Di Carlo's account, which reads like a film script, Berlusconi explained his concerns about kidnapping, and they discussed protection measures. In a relaxed moment at this improbable-sounding gathering Bontate and Berlusconi sparred.

'Why don't you come down and build an industrial plant in Sicily?' asked the Palermo boss.

'What do I need to come down there for? I've got enough trouble with Sicilians already', answered the industrialist with a wry smile.

'Ah, but if you came to Sicily, you'd be the boss!' protested Bontate mildly. 'We'd be at your disposal . . .'

'In the end, Berlusconi said he too was at our disposal for anything: we just had to let Marcello know what we needed. And I don't know whether the Milanesi mean something different by "at our disposal" than Sicilians do, because for us, when someone says they are at our disposal, in Cosa Nostra that means for anything and everything.'

Dell'Utri's lawyers, who are appealing against his conviction for Mafia association at the time of going to print, claim to have documentary evidence showing that Bontate could not have been in Milan for this meeting since he was under special surveillance in Palermo and attending a Mafia trial. Whether or not the fabled meeting of Titans took place, Mangano was hired as estate manager at Arcore, where his duties included driving his boss's daughter to school every day. After dinner, every bit the faithful retainer in immaculate tweeds, Mangano would set off round the gardens accompanied by his Neapolitan mastiffs. But soon enough there was trouble.

On a December night in 1974 Berlusconi gave a grand dinner at Arcore, which Mangano attended. Late at night, as he was leaving, one of the guests was kidnapped. Outside the gates his car was blocked in by two others, he was forced into another car and driven off. But snow was thick on the ground, and the driver lost control, slid off the road and crashed into a bank. The kidnappers made off on foot, and the victim, shocked and a little battered, was rescued. In the ensuing police operation it was discovered that Mangano had a criminal record, and shortly afterwards he left.

Mangano kept in touch with his old friend dell'Utri, however, and in the summer of 1993 the connection probably saved his life. Mangano had just finished an eleven-year sentence for drug trafficking and had returned to Palermo. His ambition was on fire after being out of the game for so long, and he had become very close to the boss of Porta Nuova, Salvatore Cancemi. But Cancemi had aroused the wrath of Leoluca Bagarella – not a difficult thing to do at the best of times – and he was invited to a meeting to clear up a misunderstanding. Cancemi, remembering the Corleonese family's peculiarly violent methods of clearing up misunderstandings, knew he was unlikely to survive the meeting and turned himself in to the carabinieri. (His subsequent collaboration would give the authorities their first concrete evidence that Provenzano was not only alive but actually running the organization.)

At this point it would have been Mangano's turn to die – except that now Bernardo Provenzano had a political project, and Mangano's powerful contact was needed.

According to a note on a telephone pad produced by the prosecution, Mangano and dell'Utri met twice in 1993. One collaborator claimed these meetings were to discuss a political contract, under which dell'Utri promised legislative change, including 'softening of the law on confiscation of assets; and release of all those convicted of Mafia association . . . At the same time, dell'Utri told Mangano that it would be good if everyone could stay calm, that is, avoid any acts of violence, which would not contribute to the success of political projects favourable to the Mafia organization.'[27]

Dell'Utri said later that he and Mangano may have met a couple of times during the period, but only to discuss Mangano's personal problems. Dell'Utri's legal team now say that the telephone notes are totally unreliable as evidence of meetings.

Provenzano's choice of Forza Italia was a decisive moment in his leadership. He could at last separate himself definitively from Riina's politics; he also believed he had found a solution to the organization's immediate crisis: a high-ranking official in a political party who was willing to support changes to the law in their favour.

'At last Provenzano announced we were in good hands,' Giuffré recalled, 'and we could trust them. For the first time, Provenzano committed himself, assuming personal responsibility for the guarantees he had received. And from that moment, we're on the move, promoting the Forza Italia line within Cosa Nostra, in order to take it to the rest of Sicily.'

The organization got behind Provenzano's decision. Even Bagarella agreed to support the new party, providing they kept their promises – on pain of death. Provenzano's pursuit of a non-violent strategy had a political sponsor. The bombers had lost.

'Provenzano called a halt to the Mafia's strategy of attacking the institutions of state', says assistant prosecutor Nino Di Matteo. 'This paved the way for him to reach an agreement with political representatives. Under the terms of the deal the Mafia had to disappear from the public arena and must support Forza Italia in the '94 elections. In exchange, according to our information, within a decade Cosa Nostra would receive certain benefits.'

Although dell'Utri's links with Cosa Nostra have been proven (he was sentenced to nine years in 2005 but is appealing), there is no evidence that Berlusconi ever courted the Mafia's support for Forza Italia. Giuffré described Cosa Nostra's relationship with Forza Italia as a case of jumping on the bandwagon: 'We have always been smart enough to be on the winner's side, that's how clever we are. When we went with the Socialists, you could see it wouldn't work. It's not that we control Sicilian politics, but when we back the winners, we're in. We didn't create Forza Italia's success. People were fed up with the Christian Democrats, people were sick of politicians – *unni putieva cchiù*, they couldn't take any more. So they saw in Forza Italia an anchor to grab hold of, and everyone was talking about it, and it was all new, a new hope. And we, smart as we are, caught the ball on the rebound.'

It has been suggested that with his inflammatory claims about Berlusconi sitting round a table with men of honour, Giuffré was merely making trouble for Cosa Nostra's political friends, who had failed to deliver any benefits for the organization. Contrary to guarantees Provenzano had allegedly received, there was no let-up in the most draconian anti-Mafia laws. Provenzano had committed early on to improving conditions for prisoners, but when Falcone's law on maximum security terms for convicted mafiosi was upheld at review, the captive members of Cosa Nostra began to feel sorely neglected.

Although the law did not change fast enough to placate the prison population, Provenzano had more success in other areas. 'At last the conditions were right to press ahead in Provenzano's specialist sector, that is, contracts', Di Matteo explains. 'Once he'd got the right people in place, he could subvert this system of power that allowed him to be the master.'

To exploit their links with the ruling party, Cosa Nostra needed people who knew how to operate in the political environment. One of these was the eminent doctor and mafioso, the boss of Brancaccio, Giuseppe Guttadauro. In spite of his homely looks – he was short and rotund, with a double chin – his pedigree was excellent: his brother-in-law was Trapani boss Matteo Messina Denaro.

Giuffré recalls: 'Provenzano's policy was to reverse Riina's strategy of violence, and he found in Dr Guttadauro a perfect pupil, who would pursue his pacifist politics in the best possible way. To initiate the process of remodelling the image of Cosa Nostra, Guttadauro made contacts in business and started a debate on how best to apply peacefully the process of silent reconstruction of Cosa Nostra.'

Guttadauro had plans for a huge development in Brancaccio: a shopping centre and multiplex cinema. He planned to sell developers his own land, and then become the guarantor for protection of the site, while making sure that a significant number of Mafia people were employed. It was the perfect business plan for Provenzano's philosophy.

Provenzano's political ties enabled him to push through the next phase of his revolution. The election in 1994 was won by Forza Italia with a narrow margin. After that, Cosa Nostra's strategists started thinking about how to cut out the middleman. One magistrate said, 'the Mafia has decided it no longer needed intermediaries between itself and the political world. Mafiosi are now being elected directly to political office.'[28]

While state subsidies and European funding were pouring into Sicily, the Mafia began to dispense with the system of supporting politicians and began to field them from its own ranks. Local councils in Mafia strongholds such as Bagheria and Villabate were infiltrated by mafiosi: Provenzano's men were green-lighting devel-

opments, awarding contracts, channelling agricultural and development funding towards Cosa Nostra.

The first Forza Italia association was founded in Villabate by Nino
Mandalà, the local Mafia boss. Known as 'the Lawyer', Mandalà was
respected and feared: he had a violent temper and a vindictive mind.
If there was any hold-up in the council for one of the Mafia-backed
projects, he would scream abuse at the councillors. He once threatened to punch a councillor, and boasted that he had made a Forza
Italia senator cry.

Giuffré claims that councils such as Bagheria became fortresses,
closed shops operated from within the local administration. Anyone
who lacked the right connections had no hope of getting a contract.
'I challenge you', Giuffré said under cross-examination, 'to find a
single company working on a public contract during the mid-'90s
that had no links with the Bagheria family.'

But while Provenzano's people did good business, investigators
were tapping their phones, recording their conversations and reading
their bank statements. By November 1998 Ilardo and Brusca's detailed
accounts of the principal players in Provenzano's court finally came to
fruition. Early one chilly autumn morning, police raided forty-seven
addresses across Bagheria and Villabate, kicking in doors and hauling
out mafiosi in handcuffs.

Simone Castello, Provenzano's postman and factotum, whose
links in politics and international business had served his master
so well, was led away. He would have to endure the nauseating
experience of reading hours of conversations that police had
recorded in his car.

Enzo Giammanco, head of the council's technical office, which had
rubber-stamped so many building contracts on behalf of Cosa Nostra,
was another one rudely awakened. Just a few months earlier, the feisty
Nino Mandalà had been picked up in Villabate. Provenzano's political network, and his logistical support, had been savaged. Bagheria,
for years his impregnable territory, was no longer safe. From now on
he would have to look for logistical support where he could get it.
The men at his disposal would not necessarily be the ones he would
choose.

Nino's son Nicola Mandalà had followed his father's footsteps into a career in organized crime and, once the old man was arrested, stepped into his shoes. Nicola was a keen gambler and big spender; he would take last-minute planes to watch important football games on the mainland and visit casinos. Weary agents conducting surveillance never knew where he'd be going or, once he'd started partying, whether he'd keep going all night.

Mandalà was another one who couldn't help telling his mistress everything. While they snorted cocaine, he recounted the story of his initiation: 'You prick your finger, the blood comes out and you hold the picture of a saint . . . Then you set fire to the picture, and pass it from one hand to the other, repeating three times, "if I should betray Cosa Nostra, my flesh will burn like this." '

Mandalà confided to his girlfriend that he was the *de facto* boss of Villabate, with control over the administration: 'They do whatever I tell them, see?'

'He was like the prince of the *1001 Nights*: hotels and women and cocaine and champagne.' Mandalà's friend Francesco Campanella shared his passion for gambling and occasionally flew with his flash friend to the casino in Val d'Aosta, but he was was shocked by Mandalà's extravagant lifestyle. He berated his friend for the brazen way he flouted Cosa Nostra's security rules, ran up massive credit card bills and cashed enormous cheques. Not to mention that he had a child with his mistress.

Mandalà had an excellent contact in Campanella, whose meteoric political career in the Christian Democrats had taken him to the top of Villabate council. He was a good friend and former hustings partner of the ex-regional president, Salvatore Cuffaro, who had been a witness at his wedding.

One of Campanella's great coups, pre-empting a move to disband the council for Mafia infiltration, was to launch a cultural anti-Mafia initiative. It was exactly the sort of PR gambit that met with Provenzano's approval. In a cynical move the council invited a top actor to receive an anti-Mafia award for his portrayal of Capitano Ultimo in a film. The actor had no idea he was being exploited in this way, but the sham was exposed, and the council was disbanded shortly afterwards.

Campanella subsequently confessed that Cosa Nostra's policy of submersion 'was intended principally to pave the way for the organization's direct running of business'. Nino Di Matteo recalls: 'The aim was to blur the line between legimitate income and income from business that was apparently legal. The Mafia need no longer limit itself to traditional activities like extorting protection money from businesses, but should be part of those businesses themselves.'

Ambitions in Villabate were running high, and Provenzano was eager to move on from its recent ugly past. In a conversation intercepted by investigators Mandalà passed the Boss's message on to Campanella: 'The old man says, we must run businesses, we must infiltrate every important commercial enterprise. Our priority is to do business.'

The projected shopping centre in Villabate is emblematic of how the system worked. The massive development, worth £200 million, with a multiplex cinema, shopping centre, offices, businesses, car parks and so on, was proposed in the mid-1990s by a company based in Rome, Asset Development, and welcomed by the council.

It was a complicated project, involving the acquisition of a large number of properties – a matter almost impossible for an outside firm to sort out but simple enough for the local Mafia, who quickly dispensed with any objections on the ground. Under Campanella's direction a legal contract was signed (amazing though it may seem) between the developer and Mario Cusimano, representing the Villabate Mafia.

'We found the evidence on a computer used by one of the intermediaries', recalls Di Matteo. 'There was actually a written deal: "You, the northern developer, will make this investment; we, the Mafia, guarantee to make all the arrangements for your acquisition of this plot of land. Then if there is any problem with the bureaucracy in the council administration, I will sort it out, because I know which strings to pull. I will permit you to do business, but you must employ my people, and buy cement where I tell you . . ."

'The Mafia infiltrates the business and exploits it from the inside. The private contractors had to do what Signor Mandalà told them to do: they had to employ at least 20 per cent of workers named by the Mafia. They had to rent out 30 per cent of the office space to firms chosen by the Mafia. The Mafia was taking control of a major development from the inside. Such an operation could only be possible with political contacts.'

The commercial development was a monster, in a small suburban residential area, and would cause pollution, not to mention traffic chaos, and starve out any small businesses in the immediate area. But planning permission would not be a problem: for a consideration of £150,000 the Mafia's contacts in the planning department would take care of the application. The kickback had to be paid via untraceable companies, which received an invoice for an initial €25,000 for telecommunications consultancy from a fruit and vegetable merchant.

One major sticking point was transport: the centre would need a number of access roads linking to the motorway, which had been ruled technically impossible. And yet, using the letterhead of ANAS, the national road construction company, Campanella granted all the necessary permissions.

The shopping centre's inexorable progress was halted by the dissolution of the Villabate council and the arrest of Francesco Campanella and Mario Cusimano, both representing the Mafia's interests in the deal. Pierfrancesco Marussig, a director of Asset, was also accused of corruption but denies the charges. After ten years being forced past every legal challenge, the development was finally stopped.

Provenzano had been alerted to the fact that Guttadauro was planning a development on a similar scale in Brancaccio, and that these two massive projects could potentially be in competition. The Boss ruled that they should both go ahead, in case one failed to get the green light. Guttadauro's arrest put paid to his hopes of the greatest employment opportunity seen in years.

One of the men accused of enabling Provenzano to make major investments was Michele Aiello, known as 'the Engineer', a resident of Bagheria who had begun his career building single-lane country roads. In the early 1990s he made a massive investment in a private health clinic – a payment investigators considered far too great to have been made from laying asphalt on sheep tracks.

He subsequently built a state-of-the-art radiography centre, with equipment the public hospitals couldn't afford in their wildest dreams. They sent their patients to him, and he fixed the prices for the state repayments. Aiello's contacts on the Bagheria council would accept the overblown figures without a murmur. He also allegedly recommended that his clinics bought their equipment from Provenzano's favourite nephew, Carmelo Gariffo.

Provenzano wanted his own 'minister of health', a representative on local authorities who would appoint hospital directors and medical fund managers. It did not take long to find one.

The Ospedale Civico in Palermo is a sorry place. People sit for hours in the dirty corridors in plastic chairs, waiting for tests or treatment. Waiting lists for operations are hundreds of names long, and new requests are greeted with grim resignation. Equipment is out of date, in need of repair. It is desperately in need of investment.

To deal with the shortcomings in staffing, beds and equipment in public hospitals, the regional government pays for patients to receive private treatment. The Mafia's investment in state-subsidized private clinics and diagnostic laboratories has forced up prices and immobilized waiting lists, draining the lifeblood from the public health service.

After a number of deaths apparently caused by lack of resources, the head of the anti-Mafia commission denounced the Mafia's control of private health schemes. 'Sicily has about 1,800 private health centres, compared with 150 in the rich northern region of Lombardy. Instead of reducing the workload for public hospitals, they have diverted funds away from those hospitals, which are falling into a state of disrepair', he said. 'Sicily is the first region in Italy for the financing of private health centres and the first for patient deaths.'

As far as Giuffré is concerned, if anyone embodies the Mafia's new way of operating from within the institutions, it is Dr Mercadante, fifty-nine, director of the Ospedale Civico, radiologist and Forza Italia politician elected to the Palermo council in 1997. Long suspected of involvement with the Mafia, Mercadante became head of the anti-corruption commission set up to ensure transparency and financial propriety in the administration. His name appeared in a letter to Bernardo Provenzano from his son Angelo – the first confirmation of the doctor's rumoured links with Cosa Nostra.

His uncle was Tommaso Cannella, Mafia boss of Prizzi and Provenzano's strategist. Mercadante would brush off questions about his criminal connections with the old adage 'You can't choose your relations'. But his relations were pleased to have him, and his potential value to Cosa Nostra increased exponentially when he was elected to the regional parliament for Forza Italia in 2001.

When police bugs planted in the secret meeting place of Palermo boss Nino Rotolo picked up numerous references to the 'doctor's orders', investigators believed they had enough solid evidence against Mercadante to arrest him for Mafia association. While awaiting trial, Mercadante has resigned from his position as regional deputy. In a statement he said that he wanted to focus his energies on clearing his name.

Giuffré reported that Provenzano constantly complained about the new raft of politicians. 'A subject he brought up time and again was that certain politicians couldn't be trusted, and he complained particularly about their inexperience.

'It's important,' said Giuffré, 'to know how to get things done behind the scenes, to steer particular debates that might have an impact on public works, health, agriculture and everything that we have an interest in. There has to be a certain ability on both sides, a *savoir-faire*. And I have to say that frequently, in the case of some politicians, Provenzano was pretty unimpressed.'

The disbanded Christian Democrats reformed under the banners of several centre-right parties. Giuffré described how, in the run-up to the elections for president of the region in 2001, Cosa Nostra made the decision to vote for Salvatore Cuffaro.

'There was an agreement within Cosa Nostra to support the election of *l'onorevole* Cuffaro – as usual, from behind the scenes. As far as Provenzano was concerned, it was the right decision, and he told us that, wherever we could press Cuffaro's advantage, we should do so. We were to do whatever we could to ensure that the candidate opposing Cuffaro – Leoluca Orlando, if I remember rightly – would lose.'

Cuffaro has always denied any knowledge of whether the Mafia supported his candidacy or not. When he was asked whether Cuffaro was aware of Cosa Nostra's support, Giuffré replied: 'I don't know if he was aware of it, but every politician knows that if you take a position of power at that level, you have to have Cosa Nostra's protection, otherwise you upset the balance.'

For the next few years the balance would go very much in Cosa Nostra's favour.

12

Treacherous friends

SHELTERING A FUGITIVE is not an easy job. Angelo Tolentino and Nino Episcopo, joint bosses of Ciminna, managed the seventy-year-old capo Benedetto Spera's life in hiding for seven years. Although they initially enjoyed the status this role conferred on them, their charge was excessively demanding, and the life of service began to get them down. They were on call day and night, organizing his meetings and bringing supplies.

Ciminna is a remote mountain town across the valley from Mezzojuso, reached by small, winding roads through the sheep pastures. Tolentino and Episcopo were required to drive Spera to meetings, speeding along the treacherous and often unpaved country roads in the darkness before dawn, with the added anxiety of avoiding detection on the roads. Every time they saw an electrician working on the telegraph poles, they were afraid it might be a police detective installing a camera. If the weather was bad, the potholed tracks became impassable, and they'd be pushing the car out of the mud while the boss sat furiously inside.

When they got to the meeting place, they'd have to wait an entire day outside in the car or in a nearby farmhouse or livestock pen, as it might be, for hours on end. There was fresh food to be bought and prepared, and every other kind of special need – batteries, typewriter ribbons, toothpaste. If Spera wanted to see his wife, they had to arrange everything, fetch her and deliver her to one of the farmhouses before first light.

The carabinieri had planted listening devices in Tolentino's home in Ciminna and in a farm building they used for meetings, and were monitoring their every conversation. They heard a lot of complaints about the men's troublesome charge.

'We've looked after him for five and a half years', Tolentino moaned. 'And as you know, five and a half years, day and night, I've barely been home. He gets me out at one or two in the morning. I'm always with him. I'm the real fugitive here!'

'All these years we've been his slaves', Episcopo agreed.

The two men had no choice in the matter: Spera was the *capo mandamento*. 'Like it or not,' recalled Giuffré, 'Tolentino and Episcopo had to obey him – and Spera could be despotic.'

Spera had been lodging with Episcopo's family, running the women ragged with his incessant demands. The strain was taking its toll on Episcopo's health, and his long mountain drives became more infrequent.

The Belmonte capo had secured a string of lucrative contracts across the Palermo hinterland, and his base, a small mountain town, boasted an unusually large number of millionaire businessmen. While he was enjoying the hospitality of the Ciminna capos, Spera demanded a kick-back from public contracts issued to firms on their territory. It was a presumption that outraged his hosts. 'It's the nastiest thing he could have done', lamented Tolentino. 'While we looked after him in our homes, he mugged us.'

Not only did Spera claim money from his hosts, but he then found another mafioso from the same area to arrange his meetings and employed him as his driver. The jealousies and rivalry this created in Ciminna were a dangerous distraction. The two men talked about the difference between Spera and their other boss, the old man Bernardo Provenzano, who had also passed through their care. 'How could he have anything in common with that animal? Binnu is much more affectionate in his letters.'

'No comparison', the men agreed. To Uncle Binnu they were loyal servants. Agents listened in as they slowly and deliberately dictated their letters to the boss or whooped with excitement as they sorted through his post and found *pizzini* addressed to them.

Provenzano always took particular care to treat his hosts with respect: because he was forced to move house so frequently, he needed people who would be prepared to support him, turn over their houses to him, bring him food and deliver his letters, at considerable risk to themselves.

'My brother's been a fugitive for many years', his brother Simone told a reporter. 'The man had to eat. If he was as bad as people say he is, who would have taken the trouble to bring him food?'

Giuffré related that after the regular meetings between himself, Provenzano and Spera, the Boss of Bosses would give orders: 'You wash, I'll dry, you sweep.' Three of the most powerful criminals in Sicily would roll up their sleeves and set the cottage to rights, polishing the last glass and sweeping under the table. Provenzano always wanted to make sure he'd be invited back. His needs were not excessive, even when he was in poor health; he lived like a monk, showing his people by example that power was not about exhibition.

The Ciminna bosses were not the only ones to be enraged by Spera's lack of respect. Spera had been embroiled in a long-drawn-out campaign against the Lo Bianco family, his rivals for control of the Misilmeri district. In 1995 Provenzano had allowed Spera to get rid of his long-time rival Pieruccio Lo Bianco because Lo Bianco was one of Riina's old guard, close to Giovanni Brusca. Provenzano needed to send a message to Brusca that his – Riina's – faction was finished, and Spera was a willing accomplice.

But the disappearance of Lo Bianco was not the end of it. After Provenzano's peace directive had gone out, forbidding any kind of violent action likely to attract attention, Spera pursued his bid for control of the area. There were deaths on both sides. 'Benedetto had gone over the top with his military offensive,' said Giuffré, 'and the way he went striding all over everything in hobnail boots was causing trouble. I could tell the effect it was having on Provenzano when he said in a meeting, "Benedetto, please remember, I rule with my head."'

Those mild-sounding words betrayed a darker intent. This was a direct warning, Giuffré explained, not to let personal ambition get in the way of progress. 'The situation in Belmonte Mezzagno had become – dare I say it – untenable within the context of Cosa Nostra, because it was in direct conflict with the politics of submersion, of making no noise, not attracting attention from magistrates and law enforcement. That is, to create a calm environment, with the express purpose of getting to work quietly behind the scenes. Riina had crowned Spera *capo mandamento*. But Provenzano, if he wanted, could depose him.

'At one meeting we talked about contracts, and we also talked about the situation in Belmonte Mezzagno, which had become a bit – a bit! – extremely complicated, because it had begun to create problems outside. Problems in the sense that it was attracting attention from law enforcement – particularly after they started killing businessmen. Then the situation got really heavy.'

Someone was slowly picking off wealthy businessmen who had close ties to Spera. It was not a massacre – the deaths were spread out over many months – but it was enough to do him serious economic damage. And he was convinced he knew who was behind it.

The man emerging as Spera's main rival as boss of Belmonte Mezzagno was Ciccio Pastoia, Provenzano's former driver and a man very much in his mould. They were of the same generation and understood each other instinctively; he has been called Provenzano's 'alter ego'. 'Provenzano trusted Pastoia blindly', Giuffré said, implying that his faith was perhaps misplaced. (Events would prove him right.) Pastoia arranged Provenzano's meetings, which were held in his office in Palermo. Capos could make an appointment, through Pastoia, to see the boss or they could leave their letters with him. No one got to Provenzano except through Pastoia. He stayed in the background, never throwing his weight around, but the low-profile, dependable Ciccio became the reference point for contracts and protection payments across the whole *mandamento*.

Spera and Pastoia's rivalry became intense. Meetings between Provenzano, Giuffré, Spera and Pastoia's representative got extremely heated. Spera couldn't abide Pastoia's man, and there was a lot of shouting and arguing as Provenzano tried to bring the two sides to an agreement while surreptitiously finding a way to put his own man in power. Police discovered a massive arsenal in the countryside near Misilmeri: buried inside a greenhouse, they found shotguns, sub-machine guns, ammunition, rocket launchers and bazookas. Investigators believed it was Spera's arsenal.

The peace plan did not go well. Spera confided to Giuffré that he intended to murder Pastoia without telling Provenzano (Giuffré, who valued Spera's trust, decided not to bother the Boss with this detail). Police agents monitoring the Belmonte clan heard the two rivals swear vengeance.

'I'll kill him, that bastard', Pastoia confided to his son as they drove through heavy traffic.

'The old fool, he's going to disappear', Spera told Giuffré as they talked in a remote shepherd's cottage.

The boss demanded a sit-down to prevent any further escalation of the war, but Spera refused. Provenzano wrote to Giuffré: 'What can I do about Ciccio? They want to know from me how to resolve this issue. But who am I to tell them what to do? I have already told BN [Benedetto] how he should behave, and as you are my witness, he has not listened to me. I hoped he would understand and follow my direction, but sadly this has not happened. He wants me to meet Ciccio alone, which I will not do. I told him, "If you are present I will meet him, but if you're not there I will not meet him, and my word on that is final."'

Pastoia, recently released from prison, was under special surveillance, so his movements were restricted. Spera and Provenzano, both fugitives, continued to meet in conditions of heightened security. Their drivers would drop them off before dawn at one of the shepherds' cottages in the middle of the countryside and leave them to discuss business and politics during the hours of daylight. Spera's plot to kill Pastoia was coming together: he had the gunman and the place. As the situation became increasingly volatile, there was an added complication. Spera, who had been on the run for seven years, needed medical attention.

Investigators had been led by the supergrass Giovanni Brusca to the area around Mezzojuso; Brusca had revealed that the farm buildings dotted across the mountainous countryside provided discreet meeting places for the boss. It was ideal terrain: the main Palermo–Agrigento road ran through it, if they needed to get away fast; isolated farm houses high on the slopes commanded a good view of anyone approaching. It was at the turn-off to Mezzojuso that the carabinieri had watched the mafiosi gathering for a meeting with the boss in October 1995. It was here that the informer Ilardo had sat through eight hours of meetings with the boss, poker-faced, waiting for the carabinieri to burst through the door.

Provenzano's cook, the sheep farmer Cola La Barbera, used to host meetings in a remote farm building in the area, believing it was safe from investigators' bugs as there was no electricity. However, the crack troops selected from the Palermo flying squad and dedicated to catching fugitives, known as the Catturandi, successfully planted a bug inside the building and on a December morning recorded a meeting between La Barbera and an unknown doctor. Shortly afterwards the two were joined by another man. The agents heard references to prostate trouble, for which the doctor gave him various prescriptions. Could it be Provenzano?

The Catturandi had been watching a doctor, Vincenzo Di Noto, who seemed to have some interesting patients and was suspected of diagnosing mafiosi with conditions that meant they could serve their prison sentences under house arrest.

One of the Catturandi's most experienced agents, code-named Bloodhound, recalls: 'We knew that Provenzano had already had an operation on his prostate, and we had information that this particular doctor was treating an old man with prostate problems. We intercepted a conversation in which they made an appointment with Dr Di Noto, for a particular day in January, at a farm cottage belonging to Nicola La Barbera, near Mezzojuso.'

La Barbera (known as 'Cola Truppicuni', after his family nickname 'the Bunglers') had been under surveillance since the mid-1990s, when Gino Ilardo told the carabinieri about his support role. They knew from Ilardo's revelations that La Barbera was Provenzano's meat man, responsible for providing, and often cooking, his steaks, just as the boss's delicate health required it: bloody, no salt, no fat.

'On the morning of 30 January', Bloodhound recalls, 'we followed him to the meeting place, and let him go in.'

The Catturandi, dressed in black, wearing balaclavas, crept up the hillside and surrounded the little farm building. When they heard voices inside, they burst in through the windows and the door, shouting: 'Freeze! Police!'

They found three men and pinned them to the walls, hands behind their backs. To the Catturandi's disappointment the old man with his trousers down wasn't Provenzano. The one they led away in handcuffs was another on their most wanted list, Benedetto Spera, the notorious boss of Belmonte Mezzagno. His host, Cola La Barbera, was in the next room. When agents searched La Barbera, they found his pockets and unlikely corners of his clothes were stuffed with *pizzini*, sealed tightly with Sellotape.

If the Catturandi were disappointed by their catch, there was further mortification to come. A few days after his arrest, Spera was visited by family members in prison. The table where they sat was equipped with a hidden microphone, which picked up their conversation. At one point Spera lowered his voice, and said: 'And to think, he was just 200 metres away.'

'He' could only mean Provenzano. The Boss had been hiding just a few hundred yards away in another anonymous, dilapidated farmhouse, waiting in the dark for the doctor to finish with Spera before he joined them for a meeting. When he saw the police arrive, he stayed where he was, and hours later was rescued by his driver when the last police car had disappeared slowly down the farm track.

In the aftermath of Spera's arrest a major row erupted between police and carabinieri, with the Catturandi squad criticized for doing their own thing and jeopardizing other investigations. Half of the flying squad had not even been informed about what the other half were doing. And as it turned out, the carabinieri were working on their own line of investigation, conducting close surveillance on La Barbera. The Catturandi were accused of destroying years of detective work and bungling an operation that would have ended in the capture of the Boss of Bosses.

In the midst of this storm investigators opened the *pizzini* confiscated from La Barbera and found positive confirmation that Bernardo Provenzano was alive, if not quite well, and living in the area. One indicated that he had recently met up with his son Angelo. There were several letters from Angelo and his younger brother, and from his wife, all expressing concern about his health and discussing everyday family matters. The discovery of these *pizzini* re-ignited the row between law enforcement groups: La Barbera was one of Provenzano's 'postmen' – if the Catturandi had not been so impetuous, he might have led them to the Boss.

Provenzano must be in the area. But in this rural part of the island, intelligence was hard to come by. The hillsides were scattered with hundreds of shepherds' cottages, huts and sheep sheds in varying states of repair: some were in use, others were little more than crumbling shells. Any of them could have provided shelter for clandestine meetings. With no inside information there was no way to search them all. The Catturandi and the carabinieri were doing their utmost, planting listening devices like seeds across the landscape, but there had to be another way.

The man who had tracked Provenzano's infiltration of the health sector in 1983 was invited back. Angiolo Pellegrini returned to Palermo in 2000, to search out property secretly owned by Provenzano. He set about tracing the ownership of plots of land between Mezzojuso and Corleone.

'He has lived much of the time in the remote countryside,' said Pellegrini, 'in those rural areas, where he has an endless number of villas, houses and cottages at his disposal, on land he owned through intermediaries. There's a strip of land that goes from San Giuseppe Iato to Caltanissetta, and I did a check on all the land ownership there. I was convinced that he was just moving on his own property. He definitely had support. And since he didn't have great needs . . .

'From what my sources have told me, he was capable of staying indoors, with the windows shut, surviving on whatever he had to eat, with the radio on . . . he always listened to the radio. He was capable of living alone for long periods, in the dark.'

Somewhere out in the rugged landscape Provenzano was living with the radio on and the lights turned off. But where? Even if he wanted to tell, Cola La Barbera, his faithful retainer and cook, did not know. He had only ever seen him at prearranged meeting places during the day.

After the arrest of Spera and La Barbera there was a period of hush as replacement postmen and suppliers were urgently sought and Provenzano's men laid low to avoid police activity in the area. In

Belmonte Mezzagno, which had already seen dangerous conflict, there was a scrummage for power. To avoid further bloodshed and settle the leadership contest for this strategic district the boss had work to do. In his remote lodging out in the hills his typewriter click-clacked into the small hours.

Provenzano's long-term plan was to install his old friend and 'alter ego', Ciccio Pastoia, as head of Belmonte Mezzagno. But Giuffré had other ideas. He favoured another man, who, although not a man of honour, was *au fait* with Spera's business dealings and had the partic-ular virtue of being almost unknown to the authorities. In the weeks that followed, both men tried to promote their own candidates – without letting on. It became another game of *tragedie* and bluff. Provenzano, while sticking to his plan with steely resolve, put on a show of humility. He wrote to Giuffré: 'They ask me how they should conduct themselves. But who am I to tell them what to do?' 'This', Giuffré comments, 'is the role Provenzano plays. He deliberately wants to take a back seat, in order to disguise his intention of taking the situation in hand.'

In the world of Cosa Nostra, particularly where several of the most senior members are in hiding, information is power. Between the Boss and his various *capi mandamenti* there was a constant manoeuvring to get information by any possible means. Provenzano wrote to Giuffré: 'Listen, I've received word from a friend who had made some recom-mendations to BN [Spera] and he wants me to take care of it but I don't know anything about it. Could you do me the courtesy, if you had some business with BN, to let me know what it was, and if pos-sible tell me the name of the firms and what agreements you've made? Let me know your response as soon as you can.'

Giuffré, re-reading the letter years later, laughed. There was no 'friend'. It was a fishing exercise, he recalled, a subtle trap to get Giuffré to tell him about Spera's business and pass the information on to him. In the end Giuffré was outmanoeuvred, and his candidate was, as he put it, 'cut off at the legs'.

Provenzano had rolled out a successful strategy for the organiza-tion, while Giuffré was busy setting up his own power base. He may not have been preparing a challenge; it may have been mere contingency planning, should anything (God forbid) happen to the Boss of Bosses. But the exchange of letters between Provenzano and Giuffré reveals just how much continual intricate plotting went on between the various factions, even within each group of supposed allies.

Uncle Binnu ruled with an open hand, giving as much leeway as he could and encouraging families to settle their own disputes where possible. He tried to make sure that profits were shared, that prisoners were taken care of. He cultivated the image of a strong but benevolent leader who inspired trust. So when he suspected treachery in his ranks, he was devastated.

When the key position of Cosa Nostra's regional representative in Agrigento became vacant, the scene was set for some frenzied plotting. Agrigento was one of the most important areas for Provenzano's faction to conquer. The Valley of the Temples, with its magnificent ancient Greek ruins bestriding the hills, has been in Mafia control for years. The evidence is plain to see: what should be a protected site has been built up, with sprawling developments crowding over the landscape.

Provenzano's candidate in Agrigento was Giuseppe Falsone. Giuffré, for his part, had been cultivating Maurizio DiGati, sending him information about Palermo companies doing business in Agrigento from which he could demand protection money. While Giuffré was quietly building up his man for the regional job, another Agrigento family, the Capizi, made a serious challenge for the leadership. At this point there were three different factions, all squaring up for the fight.

DiGati was determined to face down the challenge. He wrote to Giuffré threatening that, if the Capizi family did not back him, he would execute every last one of them. In the frantic negotiation that followed, capos from different areas tried to settle the matter in their candidate's favour and avoid another war, without involving Provenzano.

Two of Giuffré's allies from Palermo, who supported DiGati, came up with an audacious plot. They called a meeting with the Capizi family, claiming to be emissaries from Provenzano, and announced that the Boss had a message: he was supporting DiGati. Knowing that they would be going head to head with the Boss, the upstarts stepped down.

'When Provenzano found out,' said Giuffré, 'all hell broke loose.'

The next letter Giuffré received from the Boss was entirely unlike his usual cordial formality. He was furious:

'There is a topic I have to raise, which is painful and suspect, but I can't say I'm surprised.' He quoted an intermediary who gave him the whole sorry tale of the two Palermo capos passing themselves off as his ambassadors and concluded: 'There is much to reflect on and analyse here. But I pray to God to let me know how much more slander and lies these troublemakers want to spread about me.' Provenzano, as the king of *tragediatori*, was practised in the art of deception. Finding his own techniques used against him was devastating.

Giuffré was unrepentant. 'The Agrigento question was settled, because there were three or four of us who decided what was going to happen in Agrigento, and that was the end of the matter. There was nothing Provenzano could do about it. He had to fall in step with us, and everything had to go through me.'

Eventually, and inevitably, Provenzano discovered the extent of the betrayal: that his own right-hand man had been among those plotting against his candidate. Years later the two men confronted each other (via video conference) in court. While Giuffré was talking, Provenzano seemed to be having trouble following the notes in front of him. His lawyer, seeing he was in difficulty, phoned him from the courtroom.

'I can't hear very well. They seem to have missed a bit', he said.

'Is there something specific?' she asked. 'You've got all the papers there.'

'I think you're missing one of the papers, one that was taken from my house', said her client.

After the call the lawyer figured out what Provenzano was referring to. On a newspaper article found in his hideout he had written a single word over Giuffré's picture: 'Traitor'. It was a message he wanted to relay to his former friend. When the court reconvened, she asked Giuffré how he would describe his conduct.

'I'd call it betrayal', she announced. Provenzano's message was delivered. It had the desired effect on Giuffré.

'He was supposed to stay in Corleone, *e basta*', he replied curtly.

The Agrigento episode showed up some deep cracks within the new, peaceful and prosperous Cosa Nostra and demonstrated how, skilled moderator though he was, and mild-mannered though he seemed, Provenzano was not prepared to see his orders counter-manded.

'I don't want to be the axe man *at the moment,*' he had written, as his frustration over the Agrigento situation mounted, 'but we'll see how it goes.'

Giuffré knew the Boss's true colours, and he wasn't fooled: 'It's all there, in those three little words. He didn't want to be the axe man for now. He didn't want to go after these people for the time being, he would wait until the time was right.'

13

Letters home

LETTERS FROM PROVENZANO'S family members, confiscated by the police, revealed a disjointed family life in which his wife and sons maintained the premiss that he was the head of their family and continued to make decisions that mattered. And yet the reality was that ordinary life had to go on, and he was not there to oversee it. The older son, Angelo, was under a lot of pressure and clearly struggling to find his place in the world. Meanwhile Saveria sent letters full of touchingly domestic detail, as though their life were quite normal:

'My life, the holidays are past and I received a short visit on new year's day everything's fine here, work is going ahead, Paolo is starting his studies, I will go to Catania on Friday with Angelo, and we'll see if they can do anything my Love you know five hundred is here, we went to visit, she's done up her house it's lovely she invited us for a meal but we had to go to Tina's and so we couldn't go this time now angelo's going to go because my brother wants to talk to him but we don't know when. My Life I will close with the Holy Blessing that the light of the Lord shine on you and assist you and may give us the strength we need and give us faith.'

Saveria's letters followed a rudimentary code ('five hundred' is presumably a relative or an associate) and express the same religious fervour as her husband's, invoking God's blessing in times of unjust persecution. They allowed a glimpse into the couple's domestic arrangements and the family's reduced circumstances. She wrote about the clothes she had found for him, particularly suitable for life on the run and for someone suffering from incontinence, whose clothes would need frequent washing. He was obviously troubled by the cold and was apparently living in Spartan conditions.

Saveria led a strange, isolated life, sustained by her love of Bernardo. Despite being forced to live apart, the couple still had a passionate relationship. Her letters to her husband began 'Carissimo amore mio' ('My dearest love') and ended with 'I love you always'.

'They have a very tender relationship', said police chief Giuseppe Gualtieri. 'We've got letters between husband and wife that we haven't made public, because they're too personal, and they reveal a great love, a great respect for each other.'

In a letter dated 15 January 2001 she wrote: 'My life, I have sent you socks and I wanted to send you another pair of those thick ones but I couldn't find any. You'll need to wash them by hand in warm water. I'm sending you 2 pairs of knee socks which are good to keep out the cold and you can wash them in cold water . . . you wanted a pair of trousers that you can wear in the snow, I found some with a bib so I got you those, there's a fleece as well if you want it. . . . My life I'll sign off with the Holy Blessing that the light of the Lord shine upon you and help you, and give us faith and strength to carry on. My life I send you a big hug and if I've forgotten anything, let me know.'

Angelo's difficulties were not only existential but also practical in nature: he wrote to his father complaining of money worries. 'You asked me about the launderette, papà, for the moment we're just about managing to cover our outgoings, but only just, and some months we have to balance the books using money out of our own pockets.'

Investigators who had long suspected that the launderette in Corleone was a front for a money-laundering operation tried to decipher any hidden code. But what these letters revealed was the strain under which Angelo, now twenty-six, was living. As the elder son of a Mafia boss, raised outside Cosa Nostra but denied the freedom to operate as a normal citizen, Angelo had been trying to sort out his prospects. It was proving difficult, as his father's advisers had warned, to get a business off the ground, and he was trying to circumvent the anti-Mafia laws. His close relationship to the Mafia boss, which would have guaranteed him success in any illegal venture, ruined his chances in the straight world.

And although his father was still around, he was not actually there, and Angelo needed to assert his identity as the man of the household. He wanted to invest in property and had found some land (albeit of poor quality) for sale. He and his father had evidently had a disagreement about this before, and Angelo, with some trepidation, had decided to go ahead. It was a rare moment of rebellion. As in other letters, Angelo uses a numerical code to conceal names.

'I've been a bit disobedient, just before Christmas I met the interested party 512151522 191212154 and we left it that after the holidays we would meet to talk it through. I don't want to have to justify myself, but if I don't start looking after our needs, you might as well stop me having access to our family funds. This is incredibly serious for me, I'm looking at my reflection and I'm worse off than when we last met and I can't bear it much longer so I'm asking you, if I can't manage this by myself I beg you at least to help me not to do any damage because maybe there's some truth in the proverb, you can't put a square peg in a round hole. That said, I would like your view on something I've done on my own initiative.

'You remember that bit of land I spoke to you about at Scorciavacche which you advised me against as you said the land was no good. Well I kept track of the deal and they've just let me know that the owner will sell all 38 hectares for 400ml. Of course I know I haven't got the money and that the land isn't particularly good, but I know there are people who have done deals over similar plots of land for more money, so I've asked around to find out how to go ahead, and I've been told I could do it if I had a political contact . . . also through Agenda 2000 [the European Union funding initative].

'This is where my doubts start, as I could go to the person I spoke to you about, since he has done this before and he could make it happen – that's one route. In the meantime, I've told uncle Paolo [Palazzolo] about it, and he's got a possible contact.

'I've never been able to do anything that was my own idea before now.'

This last, politely assertive but plaintive sentence gives an idea of how difficult Angelo's position is: he needs to assert his individuality, prove his worth to his father the Mafia boss, but without using the

Mafia's clout – in fact, handicapped by his infamous surname. The anti-Mafia law makes it difficult for him to obtain finance, and he can't put his name to the transaction.

The unfortunate Angelo's efforts to earn some respect in his father's eyes and get a business venture of his own off the ground were stymied once again when his tremulous letter to his father fell into police hands. There would be no chance of a deal after that.

His younger brother, Francesco Paolo, now aged eighteen, wrote to his father about how he had been contacted by a young woman who claimed that, in a dream, she had received a message for him from the Madonna. The whole family was in a ferment over this personal contact from the Virgin. Knowing Provenzano's tendency to use the same religious phrases in his letters, cryptologists searched for a hidden meaning. Angelo wrote soon afterwards, to report their disappointment that the young woman had not shown up to a meeting. The brothers' letters displayed varying degrees of curiosity and scepticism about this holy message. Eventually they suspected a set-up.

'I wanted to find out more about this business. I mean, is there anyone here in town who would hold a grudge against us?' asks Angelo, with startling ingenuousness. This episode shows how vulnerable the family was, hidden away from the world but exposed to anyone who wanted to exploit their weaknesses. Judging by Angelo's tone, his father's letters were full of reproach. He apologized for the slow delivery of his messages and for troubling his father with his investment worries.

Provenzano, preoccupied as ever with health matters, had to be updated about his wife's medical appointments. Angelo had gone with his mother to visit a doctor in Catania about her constant headaches: she was suffering from sinusitis, which was aggravating her painful condition. He asked permission to contact 1012234151512. 14819647415218. 'As for the other doctor I asked your permission to contact, I found him in the phone book, I'm glad to say he is still practising and I'll make an appointment as soon as I can.'

Saveria has had problems with her health: surgery to unblock her intestine went wrong, and she had to undergo a second operation, by the specialist Giuseppe Guttadauro, a close associate of her husband.

According to Nino Giuffré, the reparatory operation was so successful that the doctor won Provenzano's gratitude for life. When the
doctor's enemies (Giuffré included) were plotting to get rid of him,
the Boss ordered them not to touch him.

It seems strange that Angelo would need his father's permission to
see a particular doctor, but there is a studied reverence in the son's
tone. Was Provenzano excessively cautious and controlling, or was this
another hidden message? Investigators worked on the numerical code
and cracked it without too much trouble (A was 4, B was 5, C was 6
and so on). The doctor Angelo wanted permission to consult was
Giovanni Mercadante, a Forza Italia politician and nephew of the
senior Mafia strategist Tommaso Cannella. Investigators had been circling Mercadante for years, but this was the first time he had been
explicitly linked to Provenzano. The family letters began to look less
innocent and domestic.

Bernardo's sons were not the only ones struggling to negotiate with
the absent family member. All was not well between Binnu and his
brothers. A letter from Salvatore referred to an ongoing family feud
over an inheritance. This quarrel had been rumbling on for years, in
spite of Bernardo's talents as a mediator. Salvatore's querulous letter
did not stint on emotional blackmail:

'My brother, I don't want to quarrel with anyone, I am just hurt
that because of something said out of turn or misunderstood, there's
a great drama blowing up, because I really believe we both want the
same thing, or anyway to settle this issue between us, but we have a
different way of figuring out how to get there, with the result that we
can't understand each other; I am not saying this because I want to
quarrel with you, I repeat – I don't, it's just that when you try to
explain what you want, I don't understand what you're trying to say,
I'm referring in general to our correspondence, and I hate to talk like
this, but it's the truth and you might as well hear it.

'I will close wishing you the grace of God, may He watch over you
and protect you wherever you are, we send you our dear and
affectionate greetings and kisses with all best wishes for the new year,
may it bring you joy and peace, a brotherly hug from your affectionate
brother.'

Such avowals of fraternal love bely the irritable tone of the rest: Binnu's family was clearly under undue and unwelcome pressure, and – Saveria excepted – didn't mind him knowing their grievances. Saveria's letters are mild, fond and cheery, maintaining a housewifely tone that must have required heroic efforts to achieve.

The Provenzano family kept a low profile in Corleone. They wrote to the absent father and made arrangements for him where they could, trying to take care of his failing health and his security while avoiding the attentions of law enforcement. When they were forced to talk to the police, for a minor traffic violation or a parking offence, they were unfailingly polite and well mannered. They had very few people around them: their cousin Carmelo Gariffo was in and out of prison and offered little in the way of support. Saveria was almost never seen around town: Angelo would drive her to the shops, and she would stay in the car while he went inside. He drove her to Cinisi to visit relatives, but otherwise, like so many housewives in small towns in rural Sicily, she ventured out only very rarely. Most of the time she stayed indoors, preparing meals, polishing ornaments or writing letters.

Less than a year after Saveria and the boys took up residence in Corleone, the Riina family had come back to town. The two families could not have been more different.

After her husband's arrest, Ninetta Bagarella, deposed as first lady of Cosa Nostra, hurriedly left the villa in central Palermo the family had occupied for the last few years of their comfortable life as privileged fugitives. She and the four children, aged thirteen to nineteen, were collected by one of Riina's men, who packed them and everything they could carry into the back of his car and dropped them at the railway station. There they got a taxi home to Corleone – a winding little road over the mountains, a long, uncomfortable hour's journey crammed into a stranger's car. The taxi dropped them outside the family house in via Scorsone, a narrow street in the old part of town. After twenty-three years living as a fugitive, under an assumed name, Ninetta Bagarella was home.

Despite their shared history, Ninetta the schoolteacher and Saveria the seamstress did not meet for coffee and chats about the old days on the run. Ninetta engaged with the press, fought rhetorical battles with prosecutors and followed her husband's legal processes assiduously. Every court appearance he made, every time he angrily rejected accusations of involvement with Cosa Nostra or accused magistrates of communist activism, his wife was there in the public gallery – a formidable figure in sun-glasses. Saveria doesn't go to court, according to her lawyers, because she's just not interested in drama. She never speaks to reporters. Her husband is known as the Phantom of Corleone because, although his presence was suspected, he was never found; but she is the real phantom – a shadowy figure haunting the town, guarding her silence. The only recent photo of her has been the subject of a legal injunction.

According to insiders, the presence of the two women and their children in Corleone was proof that their husbands, once brothers in arms, were now enemies. According to supergrass Tommaso Buscetta, Provenzano had a deal with Riina, under which their family members would be protected on their home ground.

Saveria dresses simply, and never gets her hair done: she only visits the hairdressers on rare occasions, to have her greying curls cut short.

When Riina's men cleared out his villa in Palermo after the arrest, they found a whole room full of furs, and a safe containing jewellery. Ninetta may have started out as a schoolteacher, but she has evidently acquired a taste for the finer things in life. Saveria and Angelo had opened a launderette, The Splendor, on the outskirts of town, which barely covered its costs.

Giovanni and Salvo Riina opened a business selling agricultural equipment on the main road into town. In a place where Alfa-Romeos and tractors are parked side by side, it blended in perfectly. The company was also a cover for the Riina boys' movements: they had clients in Palermo, Trapani and all over the rest of the island, whom they had frequent reason to visit. It took a few years for the authorities to close the business on the grounds of extortion, money-laundering and Mafia association.

Maria Concetta Riina was elected class representative at Corleone High School, which caused a huge row. Were the children in Corleone's classrooms obeying the old Mafia hierarchy? One magistrate implored the children of mafiosi to renounce their fathers, to state on record that they rejected organized crime. Maria Concetta wrote an impassioned riposte, defending filial bonds and daughterly devotion. Angelo and Paolo Provenzano kept their heads down, studied hard and learned to loathe their father's world. Nobody ever voted them class rep.

When her son Giovanni was arrested in June 1996 for Mafia association and suspicion of murder, La Bagarella issued an emotional plea for his release. Her letter to the press was a beautifully calculated example of the Mafia's appropriation of religious language for public relations purposes, reasoning that whatever he had done, the boy was redeemed by his mother's love: 'I have decided to open my heart, the heart of a mother overflowing with grief at the arrest of my son . . . In the eyes of the world, my children were born guilty. We have brought up our children making enormous sacrifices, overcoming tremendous difficulties, giving them every possible love and support. We have raised them to respect the family and love their neighbour . . . The motto of the Riina household is "Respect everyone and everything".'[29]

The wife of the boss of San Giuseppe Iato, Bernardo Brusca, kept a low profile while her husband was boss of the local clan. But when her sons were arrested in 1996, she came out with a firebrand speech in their defence. Giovanni was Totò Riina's hit man, known as '*lo scannacristiani*', the strangler of Christians (i.e., men of honour). At the time of his arrest he had killed, by his own admission, more than 150 people but fewer than 200 – he couldn't remember an exact figure. As far as his mother was concerned, he was innocent, because she had brought him up in the Church. His arrest was an aberration, a matter of spiritual blindness. Signora Brusca told journalists: 'If the Holy Spirit will enlighten our minds, and the judges' minds, my sons will not be convicted.'

A mafioso's life of violence does not preclude religious faith. In fact, it is a central part of the culture of Cosa Nostra, although in a form most people would not recognize. The mafioso believes himself the executor of divine justice. If he kills, he is doing nothing less than God's will.

Ninetta Bagarella invoked the divine law in her plea for her son's freedom – the law that protects the family bonds above all else, including mere laws of state. All human beings are born free, she continued, life is a gift from God . . . in this vein she enters an unfathomable realm of denial.

She cited the commandments, the holy bond between parent and child, and a higher order of 'justice'. She accused the judges of visiting the sins of the father on the son. The attribution of the sins of the father is a vexed question. Hardline anti-Mafia campaigners demand that the children of mafiosi disown their fathers and disavow any links with Cosa Nostra.[30] Others maintain it would destroy the very fabric of society if children were set against their parents. The law remains on the side of the family: you cannot be prosecuted for aiding and abetting your father – and yet, as Angelo discovered to his cost, there are ways in which the sons' very DNA is contaminated by the father's crimes.

Angelo found that, as the son of the fugitive boss, his efforts to be law-abiding would never be enough. He would fail again and again to get a commercial licence since it was assumed that his father would use any family enterprise to launder money. In the past he had done exactly that, but Angelo felt the whole thing was massively unfair. Although Angelo's family connections have effectively ruined his life, he has no one but the family to protect him.

'I am against every form of violence', he protested in a rare interview. 'And on a personal level, my actions speak for themselves. I have had a moral education, and I believe I have always followed my principles. I have made my choice. But how am I supposed to defend myself against the accusation that my chromosomes are contaminated?

'I have no criminal convictions. Let me make my living honestly, that's all I ask.'

Riina's sons had no such compunction: they were involved in contract-fixing in Palermo, and eager to be initiated into Cosa Nostra. Giovanni was taken under the paternal wing of his uncle Leoluca Bagarella, a man of ill temper and unpredictable violence.

Saveria Palazzolo has never written to the papers, nor has she made use of the many requests for interviews she received over the months and years to defend her husband's name. She focused on keeping her sons out of the public eye as they tried to establish a normal life for themselves. Occasionally journalists would wander into the launderette, posing as customers with dirty clothes, and then, once they'd got the proprietor chatting, make a bid for an interview. Saveria would generally give them short shrift and shut the door firmly behind them.

Possibly the only journalist to engage Saveria Palazzolo in conversation, just before lunchtime closing at the launderette, was *La Repubblica*'s grand old man, Attilio Bolzoni. He portrays her as the stereotypical Mafia wife and martyr, campaigning against her husband's unjust persecution.

'My husband has been persecuted since he was a boy', ran the story, 'since 1963, when terrible things started happening here in Corleone and they put the blame on him. Since then, no one has left him in peace, no one has left me in peace, and above all, no one has left my sons in peace.

'Ask the old people here in town who know him, ask them what they think of my husband. I know what they'll say. They'll say Bernardo Provenzano is a man who has always worked for a living. He worked in the fields from dawn till nightfall.'

This interesting picture of bucolic innocence is not entirely accurate, considering that Provenzano, as a young man, sowed terror among the farmers for miles around, looting, stealing sheep, smashing wine barrels and setting fire to corn stacks. The Mafia wife in her media incarnation waxes eloquent with overblown piety, a high moral tone and intense focus on the family.

'This persecution isn't justice. I know only divine justice; I don't believe in what they call "justice" in this world. I answer only to God, and He alone will judge us.'

One of the main functions of Mafia women is to perform as the intermediaries between men of honour and the outside world, making statements and appeals on their behalf through the media. Lawyers for Saveria Palazzolo maintain this interview never took place but point out that its publication shows what a self-effacing person La Palazzolo is. 'Do you think anyone would have got away with writing that stuff about Ninetta Bagarella? They'd have been trussed up and strangled.'

'The role of Mafia women has always been as keepers of the culture, knowledge and values. It's women's job to pass on Mafia culture, above all in the education of their children', wrote magistrate Teresa

Principato. As the principal educators, mothers are also uniquely qualified to vouch for their sons.

In her letter to the papers Ninetta Bagarella portrayed her older son as a paragon of local youth, unjustly persecuted by the state: 'Justice demands that people should know that my son Giovanni is a normal, open, happy, easy-going boy. He works hard in the fields, and when he comes home he meets up with his friends.'

If you asked anyone other than his mother, since the moment he arrived in Corleone, Giovanni had sought to establish his credentials as the boss in waiting. He was taught to handle firearms and command respect. By the age of nineteen Giovanni had been initiated into Cosa Nostra, surrounded by mentors and friends of his father's and invited to formal feasts with other men of honour. He 'made his bones' two years after his father's arrest, under the guidance of his uncle Leoluca Bagarella, by strangling with his bare hands a man accused of talking to the police. Giovanni was overweight and unfit, and struggled to dispatch the victim. But when he had stopped the man's breath, he was, as Brusca later described him, 'excited as a child'.

He attended summits with senior Corleone bosses. He did wheelies on motor cycles in the main square. If the police stopped him for questioning or caution, he was insolent and sarcastic: 'Yes, sir, is there anything at all I can do for you today sir?' When the plaque in the centre of Corleone commemorating the sacrifice of judges Falcone and Borsellino was ripped up, Giovanni Riina was the prime suspect.

While the Riina boys roared around town on their motor bikes and picked fights in the bar, Provenzano's sons studied hard and kept themselves to themselves. Angelo Provenzano was raised to do things differently. When his car was stolen, he reported the theft to the police – an action that would have branded a mafioso as a *sbirro*, a spy.

At a club night held near Corleone a confrontation between the brothers highlighted their essential differences. Angelo wore his usual preppy uniform of polo shirt and jeans and chatted to friends about his passion – Milan football team; Paolo wore his jeans trendily low slung, with lashings of gel in his hair. They were standing near the bar when they were aware of a row going on at the door. The Riina brothers were refusing to pay the entrance fee, insisting that their status as the boss's sons be recognized. When Angelo heard what was going on, he picked his way through the throng and took Salvo aside. 'Don't be an arsehole. If you behave like this, it reflects really badly on all of us. We paid to get in, and you're paying.'

However much the Riina boys threw their weight around in town, they acknowleged the Provenzano boys' authority – rather than start a fight, they paid for their tickets.

Once Provenzano's law of 'submersion' had come into operation, the Riina boys' thuggish behaviour was no longer indulged. Word reached Provenzano that Giovanni and Salvo were destroying the carefully constructed *pax mafiosa* that had been maintained in Corleone for decades. He wrote to Brusca: 'I am dismayed by what you tell me about our dear friend's son, who seems to be behaving very badly, and from what you say, has been even worse lately. I need you to give him a message from me, ask them to stop causing problems. In the meantime, I need details: what have they done, exactly? How have they been making so much trouble? Make absolutely sure that what people are saying is true, but at the same time, tell the boys they've got to limit the damage they are causing. It's got to stop. That is my fervent prayer.'

By the age of thirty, Giovanni was serving a life sentence in a maximum-security prison, for murder. Totò Riina, so bitter about the old, privileged Palermo families, had transformed his dirt-poor peasant heritage in one generation into something terrible and self-destructive. Giovanni's younger brother Salvo seemed to see the world exactly as his father taught him, despising Mafia collaborators as *malantri e spiuni*, 'evil-doers and spies'. Police who planted a bug in his car heard him boast about the Corleonese clan's triumph in the bloodbath of the second Mafia war, as though it were a football match. 'Excuse me, in Sicily . . . In the whole of Italy, who have always been the winners? The Corleonesi!! So, who did you think was going to win?'

On one occasion Salvo and a friend, 'C', were driving along the A29 towards Palermo while agents strained to hear their conversation. As the two men drove past Capaci, Salvo noticed bunches of flowers placed at the site of the bomb blast that killed Falcone, his wife and his police escort. He had evidently been fighting off the growing belief within Cosa Nostra that the bombs had been a disastrous mistake.

> Riina: God . . . they're still leaving wreaths for this thing.
> C: What do you think about it? . . . Things have got worse since then, haven't they?
> R: It's not that they've got worse . . .
> C: Prison conditions, stuff . . .
> R: No, but prison conditions wouldn't have got worse if there hadn't been such a heavy reaction that made them back off . . . In May there was this bomb, in July there was the other one, then they arrested my father in January, understand? That was a blow . . . I don't know how it would have ended up, if we hadn't forced the state to back off.
> C: You're right.
> R: We had to tell them, 'we're in charge here'.
> C: So outsiders were saying, fuck, they got it wrong . . .
> R: Right! And it's not true, because we told them, 'We're in charge here, you might be in charge up north, but down here, we're in charge'.
> C: Yeah, 'cause the guy who took over didn't have . . .
> R: Didn't have the guts to carry on . . .
> C: So the state and everyone in it could say, 'Fuck, they got it wrong'.
> R: A colonel's got to make the decision and take responsibility. And the decision was: 'Shoot them!' And they shot them down!'

Salvo is clear that Provenzano, 'the guy that took over', let the organization down by failing to carry through the violent strategy started by his father. Totò Riina's children have shown how a family raised within Mafia culture behaves: they proclaim themselves unjustly persecuted and assert their own, separate, brand of justice. They are united against the world, and they are secure in their identity. Angelo and Paolo don't have that luxury. Provenzano's sons are unhappy, resentful and muddled about their place in the world.

Both Provenzano and Giuffré's sons struggled to lead legitimate lives with some semblance of normality. As the operation to catch their fathers intensified, they were constantly watched, and the strain sometimes showed in strange ways. One night a police surveillance unit watched Giuffré's son get into his car in Caccamo in the early hours of the morning. They followed him at high speed across the island, becoming ever more convinced that he would lead them to his father. When he arrived in Messina, four hours later, the young man walked into a bar and ordered a coffee, then turned and gave his pursuers a wave, before getting back in his car and driving all the way home.

Police surveillance was making Angelo and Saveria's lives extremely stressful. Bernardo's prostate trouble was getting worse, which was deeply worrying. They knew he paid attention to his symptoms and consulted his medical dictionary all the time. As the months went by, his health would become a matter of urgency, continually increasing his risk of exposure.

14

Spies and leaks

'I F YOU CAN get the others to do as you say . . . get them to see if, around the office, someone could have put a camera, or more than one, close up or a bit further away, get them to have a really good look . . . . Tell them what to do, and don't thank me, thank Our Lord Jesus Christ.'

Provenzano's letter to Carmelo Umina, owner of the office, was not a general warning but a very specific instruction. The rural farm office where Umina was to host a meeting of senior capos had been under surveillance for some time by the Raggruppamento Operativo Speciale (ROS), the anti-organized crime section of the carabinieri. One day, quite suddenly, the agents' screens went blank. Someone had searched the place and found micro-cameras hidden in the furniture. The tip-off had probably come to Provenzano from his sources inside the carabinieri, and he had passed it on. It was just one of several secret cameras and listening devices that Provenzano's men had discovered and immediately dismantled.

Someone was watching over the Boss. Provenzano's frequent religious invocations revealed a close connection to the Lord, who was very attentive to his needs: 'I don't need that house, Jesus Christ has found one for me', he wrote. Closer attention indicated that Jesus Christ was probably a code-name for one of Provenzano's informers, who often came to the rescue in moments of crisis.

Provenzano's preoccupation with security, already high, intensified after the discovery that law enforcement were planting bugs like wildflowers around his favourite meeting places. He lost no opportunity to remind his men not to lower their guard.

Provenzano didn't always meet his lieutenants in sheep sheds in the middle of the country: one of their favoured places was a driving school right in the centre of Palermo, between handbag shops and upmarket groceries in via Daita, behind the glorious Politeama theatre, with its prancing bronze horses. Around the corner was via Libertà, Palermo's most fashionable avenue, lined with plane trees and smart clothes stores, Max Mara and Tod's. The driving school was owned by Carmelo Amato, sixty-four, a quiet man who hung posters bearing spiritual slogans on his office walls. He was a man nostalgic for the old Mafia and bewildered by how difficult the world had become since the bombings, but he was happy enough to host meetings for the Boss.

On a given day Giuffré and the other capos would turn up and wait for their appointments, sitting on a sofa under the stairs. At various times Giuffré recalled seeing Provenzano's old friend and former driver Ciccio Pastoia and his consigliere Pino Lipari coming or going. Then he'd be called in for his private meeting with Uncle Binnu.

The carabinieri listening in on Provenzano's strategist Tommaso Cannella's phone heard him say he was going to 'Amato's, to see about Binnu'. Agents followed him and kept the place under surveillance for weeks. Through their micro-cameras they watched mafiosi coming and going but never caught a glimpse of Provenzano. Then suddenly the visits stopped. One afternoon Amato's son-in-law walked over to the television and turned it around. Agents held their breath as he inspected the back and eventually found the bug. In the surveillance room the screen went blank.

'I got a call to let me know that the meeting place had been discovered by the police', Giuffré later recalled. 'After that we found a new place to go. No one went there again.'

Fast as the carabinieri implanted listening devices and cameras, the Mafia seemed to find them, but still Provenzano was afraid his capos weren't taking the matter seriously enough. Security had become something of an obsession, and Giuffré began to find it slightly wearing.

'He had one of these devices . . . I actually gave him one of these things back in about '96 or '97, I gave him one of these instruments to search for bugs. It wasn't anything particularly sophisticated, a bit of plastic, let's say, nothing very . . . I remember it because it was a time when he was holding meetings in my area. He would bring this instrument, which was a little receiver, like a transistor radio, with an antenna . . . not really an antenna but a bit of red wire sticking out. And he'd always have it with him in his jacket pocket. As soon as he set foot indoors, he would go over the whole room, going "all right, all right, all right". . . and he'd do the same thing with all our cars. He was increasingly fearful, during this period, and would never get in a car without sweeping it for bugs with this machine. Honestly, his obsession with this thing was just crazy. And pointless, because even though he told the men hundreds of times, they just didn't take any notice and just carried on talking, and he'd end up shouting, "Would you just stop talking!" '

Provenzano and the investigators who sought him constantly tried to outsmart each other. The long-term fugitive thought and planned long and hard about how to protect himself and avoid detection while keeping the flow of essential correspondence going. The judges wrote: 'Over the months and years he recruited different people, ever careful continually to bring in new "filters" between himself and people assigned the dangerous task of collecting and delivering the correspondence.'

Meetings between Provenzano and his closest aides always revolved around the same problems of security and restricted contact, as Giuffré recalls: 'We were told to be careful about broaching these subjects, not to talk, to try to find a defence against mobile phones that could be used to locate us, and to try to find new manpower, men with no record who could move around without being under the glare of the investigators, so as to protect those in hiding.'

Provenzano told his men that good days for meetings were hunting days in the forests around Palermo, since people got used to seeing strange fellows in tweed jackets wandering about the woods. But then he received a tip-off that not only mafiosi but also the police were taking advantage of the hunting days to wander about in the woods, disguised in green hunting jackets and hats, shotguns and game bags slung about their shoulders. Instead of game, they were hunting fugitives. A new directive went out: no one was to move on hunting days.

In spite of the investigators' best efforts to keep pace, a number of near misses gave them an idea they were being handicapped. In September 2002 a patrol acting on a tip-off that Provenzano might be in the area spotted a jeep that was driving through the dark with no lights. As the patrol got closer, the jeep disappeared from sight and the mystified carabinieri couldn't figure out how it had vanished – until the following morning, when they returned in the light and found a farm track. It later emerged that Provenzano had indeed been travelling in the jeep, and his driver had been forced to make a quick turn-off. It was a close thing. In a letter to Giuffré, he thanked Our Lord Jesus Christ, who had helped him make his escape.

His driver, Angelo Tolentino, was deeply shaken by the experience. 'I thought we'd had it this time', he told a friend. 'I've never been so scared in my life. The Accountant was in that car.'

Tolentino and Episcopo used to use a farmhouse in the Ciminna countryside to go through Provenzano's mail and compose their replies. The carabinieri had their bugs in place and were listening to the men's idle chat, when suddenly they heard a shout: 'Fuck! These wires are connected!' Detectives heard a lot more swearing before the wire was cut.

Provenzano's men came up with ever more sophisticated ways of evading the authorities' attention. His faithful friend Pino Lipari was arrested at the end of 1998 and declared himself proud to serve yet another sentence on Uncle Binnu's account. Ever conscious of Uncle's security concerns, Lipari spent hours cutting up his letters to Provenzano and stitching them into the hem of his trousers, which would be picked up by his wife with the laundry. His son would piece together the scraps of the letter and rewrite it, as though from himself.

Lipari later came up with the brilliant idea of pretending to collaborate. His whole family had been arrested, and, although he expected no favours for himself, he was eager to secure their release. He had also understood the role of sabotage in Provenzano's new strategy: it was better to derail a police investigation than to put a bomb under the station. Unfortunately for him, the government spies had already planted their bugs under the table in the prison visiting room. 'I'm only telling them stuff done by dead men, trials that are over and done with, people who've already got life', Lipari confided to his wife and grown-up children. Thanks to the little listening device, Lipari's plans to fake a collaboration were exposed.

Provenzano's main weapon against being caught was not a dodgy electronic device running on batteries but, according to prosecutors, allegedly corrupt carabinieri and politicians who passed on key information about investigations into his whereabouts and activities, allowing him to stay one step ahead of the police. The magistrates' case in this regard has been revealed in the course of a long trial brought against the alleged Mafia associates.

At the centre of a flurry of leaks and counter-intelligence was Michele Aiello, the private health entrepreneur recently convicted of being Provenzano's key business contact. The prosecution claimed that Aiello sought out an old connection, Maresciallo Borzacchelli, a senior investigator of corruption in public administration and a centre-right member of the Sicilian regional assembly (or, as he was described by one magistrate, 'another of those bastards who took the piss out of us'). Borzacchelli had known Aiello for over ten years, and prosecutors claim that during this time he gave the developer the benefits of his excellent contacts, as well as information on investigations into his activities, in return for money, use of a villa and other perks.

It was Borzacchelli, according to prosecutors, who introduced Aiello to another maresciallo of the carabinieri, Giorgio Riolo. Riolo would prove an invaluable asset, being one of the carabinieri's foremost experts on installing bugs and secret cameras.

They were an ill-matched couple: Aiello tall and thin, scratchy and irritable, with thinning hair and glasses; Riolo short and round-faced, with curly hair and dark, beady eyes. He confessed he was flattered by Aiello's attention, and the power information conferred on him. In exchange for details on investigations into Cosa Nostra's activities, Riolo was given money, a car, an entrée into a different world.

Aiello, who investigators revealed had been working as the legitimate face of the Bagheria Mafia for over a decade, was anxious to avoid risks and greatly appreciated his friends' advice. He was careful to pass the information along to Provenzano's men. But Provenzano's security arrangements were suddenly, devastatingly, breached when, in April 2002, the carabinieri arrested his right-hand man, the capomafia of Caccamo, Nino Giuffré.

The carabinieri at Termini Imerese had received a mysterious phone call informing them that they would find Giuffré, a fugitive for eight years, on a nearby sheep farm. One report later said that the anonymous caller had tried to make a deal: he claimed that if they did not touch, or read, any of the letters in Giuffré's possession, the caller would reveal the whereabouts of another fugitive, currently hiding out in the same area.

Giuffré had been living for over a year in a villa in Vicari, a sprawling village of houses and farm buildings by the river San Leonardo. His guardians were the local capomafia, Salvatore Umina, and his nephew Carmelo, a headstrong young man who drove a roaring off-road police jeep (much disapproved of by his uncle) or galloped around the valleys on horseback. Giuffré had taken a shine to him and employed him as his driver and his postman; he even gave Carmelo his sawn-off shotgun to look after (this favouritism, he admitted, caused jealousy among his entourage). Drivers had to be intimately familiar with the terrain: their charges moved only at night-time, without headlights. Easter had come and gone with the usual festive greetings exchanged by letter and a cake sent by the mafioso, who had finally agreed a price for the contract to build a new waste disposal site. Giuffré had let the delivery man keep the cake. There were few enough perks you could give the people you depended on in this situation – even an Easter cake counted for something.

On the morning of 16 April Carmelo had collected him before dawn as usual and driven him across country to the converted barn he used as his office. He had appointments lined up for most of the day starting at 6.30, with one empty slot: Domenico Virga had written to cancel, for the second time running.

As soon as he had got himself organized, with his list of appointments, and Carmelo had roared off, the carabinieri crashed in. He remembered the apocalyptic moment: 'Complete earthquake, blackout. I couldn't understand what was going on, the carabinieri turned up, and goodnight . . .'

The carabinieri searched him and found, in the pouch he wore round his waist, a gun and a few newspaper clippings. In his pockets were eight *pizzini*. All bar one of the letters were from Provenzano; one carried the previous day's date. The two men had met and spent a whole day in private discussion just over a week earlier, close to where Giuffré was staying.

Giuffré thought about who might have phoned the carabinieri to give him away. Then he remembered: one of his deputies had changed his appointment and then failed to show up – Virga. Giuffré had recently taken him and his brother to task for behaving like cowboys – demanding protection money from companies that had already come to an arrangement with the local Mafia or others that didn't fall within their jurisdiction – and causing no end of trouble. Giuffré had to make a calculation about how best to come out of this situation. If he had been set up, he might as well gain some advantage, since he evidently had enemies within the system. No one knew more about Bernardo Provenzano's regime than he did. There was another urgent consideration: if he collaborated, his sons would be barred from Cosa Nostra, and this might be the best thing he could do for them.

'He was worried his sons might become part of Cosa Nostra', said chief anti-Mafia prosecutor Pietro Grasso. 'He wanted to stop this happening before it was too late.'

In a statement Giuffré said: 'I have decided to collaborate for various motives. Finding myself completely alone, and quiet, perhaps for the first time in my life, I found the time to dig deep within myself, a thing I've probably never had time to do before. I thought long and hard about what I have done in my life. From these thoughts, and this painful search within myself, I understood that a lot of things I have done have been wrong, and so, without asking for any reward, either in terms of my release or money, I began my collaboration.'

Magistrates kept Giuffré's collaboration secret as long as they could, to protect his family. If they could get to August, his wife and sons could leave Caccamo to go away on holiday as usual and then disappear. It would certainly be better than a dawn raid, with all the publicity that would entail. His wife still lived in the centre of Caccamo, on the top floors of a large house overlooking the main square. A flight of broad cobbled steps swept right past her door, where the name Giuffré was still marked on Dymo tape beside the bell.

'I spent the worst summer of my life', recalls Grasso, 'travelling up to the prison in Novara every weekend, in the heat, covered in mosquitoes . . . we went at the weekends so no one would know. The only people in the prison who knew were the governor and the director.'

Another reason for the intense secrecy was that Grasso was hoping Giuffré could lead them to Provenzano. His men followed Giuffré's description of their last meeting places and staked out the area. But after Giuffré's arrest Provenzano did not go back. By mid-September the news was out. Word spread among mafiosi that Giuffré's wife and sons were no longer in Caccamo.

If Provenzano was fearful of listening devices, he was far more afraid of collaborators. He had made great efforts to re-establish a positive culture within Cosa Nostra, to revive loyalty to the organization and prevent any more mafiosi turning state's evidence. Now Giuffré, who had seemed to be old-school, who apparently lived and breathed the values of the honoured society, who had been so ambitious as a young man that he had married into the powerful Stanfa family who ran Philadelphia, had joined the ranks of the traitors. Provenzano had hours to sit in the dark, alone, and contemplate Giuffré's betrayal. He would say he was doing it for his sons, but he had always encouraged one of his boys to follow his footsteps. Thinking about it, he had his finger in pies all over the place, a contact in every major town. Perhaps he had been thinking of trying to destroy Binnu, even before his arrest.

There was a copy of a newspaper special, *Antimafia 2000*, on Provenzano's desk, with a photo of Giuffré on the cover. His eyes looked staight to camera, cold, expressionless.

'Traitor', Provenzano scrawled across his face.

The man with the crippled hand had been an integral part of Provenzano's machine: there was not much he did not know. As Giuffré himself put it: 'He is the director, and I'm the one who puts his politics into practice.'

The treacherous Gino Ilardo reportedly told his carabiniere handler: 'In Sicily the capimafia either kill each other or they sell each other out.'

Giuffré had avoided death and had opted for betrayal. Once he had decided to talk, there was nothing he would not say.

One of the first names Giuffré mentioned in his long, detailed statements (with lengthy digressions and occasional rhetorical flourishes) was Michele Aiello, the former road builder, now a private health magnate. He confirmed Aiello's status as a front for the Mafia boss: 'Aiello is the flower in Bernardo Provenzano's buttonhole.' Aiello denied he was ever working for the Mafia, but the judges did not agree. He has been sentenced to fourteen years.

Health was a matter very close to Provenzano's heart. He laundered money through the health system, but more importantly, after he had started experiencing problems with his prostate, he needed access to private healthcare in a discreet and safe environment. His postmen also used hospital lifts to exchange letters. Two apparent strangers were observed getting into the lift together on different occasions. When detectives put a camera inside, they witnessed these two strangers, as soon as the lift doors closed, embracing and kissing each other on both cheeks, then passing one of Provenzano's *pizzini* from hand to hand. When the lift doors opened, they emerged poker-faced and went their separate ways.

Following Giuffré's revelations, agents started intercepting calls to Aiello's home and to his office. When the ROS decided to pursue their investigation further, it was Riolo they approached to plant bugs in the clinic. Towards the end of 2002 Maresciallo Borzacchelli allegedly broke the news to Aiello that, as a result of Giuffré's evidence, he was under investigation.

Aiello had another mole inside the judiciary. Giuseppe Ciuro worked for the revenue and had been seconded to the anti-Mafia section, the Direzione Investigativa Antimafia (DIA). He had been working for Borsellino's former pupil the assistant prosecutor Antonino Ingroia, who had always believed him to be a person of utter integrity. Such faith made Ciuro exceedingly well placed to leak highly sensitive information.

Right: The aftermath of the shoot-out in viale Lazio, Palermo, on 10 December 1969. Provenzano led a group of gunmen disguised as policemen. When his gun jammed, he pistol-whipped Mafia capo Michele Cavataio (pictured) to death.

Below: National hero General Alberto Dalla Chiesa and his young wife, Emanuela Setti Carraro, were ambushed by mafiosi with machine guns in September 1982.

Leoluca Bagarella, Totò Riina's brother-in-law from Corleone, who took over the clan's military leadership after Riina's arrest in 1993. He pursued a reckless strategy of violence, jeering at Provenzano's peaceful approach.

The aftermath of the bomb at Capaci, near Palermo, that killed anti-Mafia judge Giovanni Falcone and his wife, Francesca Morvillo, on 23 May 1992. Riina and Provenzano were both convicted of ordering the killing, which resulted in a massive crackdown on the mafia.

Giovanni Brusca, boss of San Giuseppe Iato and one of the Corleonesi's main allies, after his arrest in June 1996. He pressed the detonator that set off the Capaci bomb. Behind him is a photograph of Giovanni Falcone with Paolo Borsellino.

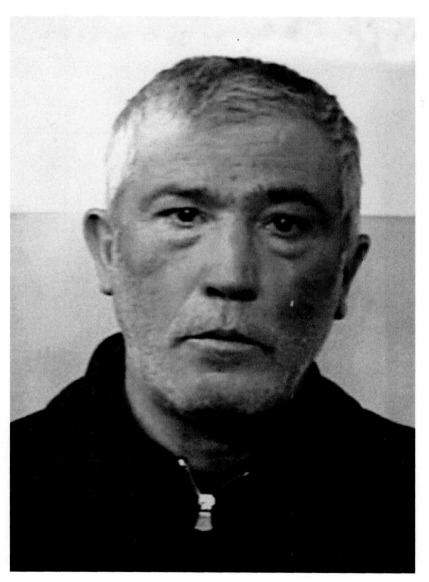

Nino Giuffré, boss of Caccamo and Provenzano's right-hand man, on his arrest in April 2002. He later became one of the most important mafia collaborators, revealing much about Provenzano's personality, his obsession with security, his ill health and his fears for his sons.

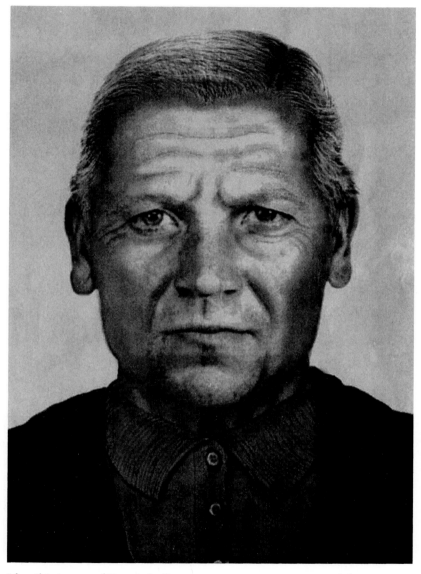

Identikit image of Bernardo Provenzano, computer-generated from descriptions by collaborators in 2002. Police intercepted mafiosi discussing the likeness: 'He's got more hair... his neck's too thin.'

Giovanni, the eldest son of Totò Riina, riding his motor bike around the Corleone cemetery on the day of Luciano Liggio's funeral, 1994. He was eager to take his father's place, and when he committed his first murder was said to be as 'excited as a child'.

Provenzano's sons, Angelo and Francesco Paolo, giving their first-ever interview, to the BBC. Having been kept out of the Mafia, they are struggling to find their way in the straight world.

07-01-2002.

Carissimo, con l'augurio, che la presente, vi rrovi
a tutti in ottima salute. Come grazie a Dio, al
momento posso dire di me.
Senti, non rigordo se già, te ne avessi parlato,e
pregato. Mà a scanzo d'equivoci, ti prego, senti
che io rigordi? non mi rigordo, Matt. mi dici che
C'è L'imp. Sabo di Favara che ha finito da poco
un lavoro a Partanna di TP. Si Tratta di Capannoni,
l'importo' era un miliardo e seicento milioni. Sono
andati via e non hanno dato niente. Se per favore
può vedere se si possono recuperare queste cose.
Ripeto, che io non rigordo, se io ti avessi pregato di mettere questa Impresa apposto? mà ora ti

Above: One of the hundreds of letters written by Provenzano, with instructions for his capos. It is full of his characteristic errors and mis-spellings. They were written on his manual typewriter, folded up small and sealed with tape.

A5 - B4 - C3 - D2 - E1
6F - 7G - 8H - 9I -
10L - 15M - 14N - 13O
12P - 11Q - 16R - 17S
18T - 19U - 20V
21Z

Right: The code Provenzano used in his letters to disguise the names of people mentioned. When anyone close to him was arrested, he would change the code in case they revealed his secrets.

From their espionage activities Ciuro and Riolo received various benefits: jobs for family members in Aiello's company; cars, jewellery and introductions to politicians, in particular to the president of the region, Aiello's old friend Salvatore Cuffaro. Ciuro was so grateful that he declared lifelong fealty to Aiello ('my life is in your hands', he wrote). Aiello for his part claimed that he was an innocent victim of blackmail.

A few weeks after Giuffré began his collaboration, he directed carabinieri to a glass jar stashed under a pile of terracotta tiles in his former hiding place. On a night raid police found the jar containing sixty-eight *pizzini*, mostly from Provenzano. Like other senior members of Provenzano's entourage, Giuffré kept his letters. Now he handed the whole lot over to investigators, to be pored over, analysed and taken down in evidence. The contents were entered on the carabinieri computer system, many of them still classified as part of ongoing investigations. Riolo copied the files and sent them to Aiello.

Ciuro was the one with best access to information: he discovered that Giuffré was saying Aiello had paid out large sums of money to the Bagheria Mafia.

Aiello maintained he was a target for extortion, but prosecutors claimed the payments were part of a multi-million-pound healthcare scam. Realizing the operation was in danger of being uncovered, according to the prosecution, Aiello's gang held a crisis meeting at which each was assigned a different task: Ciuro would look for information, using other people's passwords, on the prosecutors' system; Riolo would be an informal propagandist, softening attitudes in the justice department towards Aiello's crimes. He had, in fact, thoroughly confused his roles: 'I kept Aiello up to date with the investigation as if he was one of us, really.'

In the middle of June, Ciuro was intercepted calling Aiello at the clinic, saying he was going to Rome with Dr Ingroia to interview a collaborator who had 'bad things' to say about him, and he would let him know what they were. Ciuro's colleagues began a secret investigation into his espionage activity. The operation was conducted under conditions of utter secrecy, since he was bound to find anything written or logged against him in the system, but if they denied him access to all material, he would be alerted that they knew what he was up to.

At the DIA the discovery of a traitor in their midst was disappointing, but no surprise. 'We had always known that part of Cosa Nostra's remit is constantly to find ways to infiltrate the judicial system,' says Grasso, 'so it wasn't a surprise. We knew it was happening; the hard thing was to find out who, and where.'

They also discovered that, ironically, much of the time Ciuro was bluffing, inventing meetings and conversations to report to Aiello, to calm his mounting anxiety about the investigations in the hope of bigger rewards.

Since the group knew all their telephone calls were intercepted, Ciuro had the bright idea that they set up a restricted circle of mobile phones, registered to blameless individuals, on which they would only call the other three mobiles. If no one called one of the intercepted landlines from these phones, in theory, the restricted network would be impenetrable.

The plan worked splendidly for two months, until Ciuro's wife, tidying up, found his mobile phone on his bedside table and used it to call him at his office. He was furious, since he'd already given her strict instructions never to use that phone. Agents listening to their conversation on the office line wondered why he should be so concerned about her using this particular mobile. They checked the number and found the phone was registered to one of his employees. Once they had that mobile under surveillance, they were able to intercept the other 'restricted' phones.

For two weeks detectives listened to the gang of four talking openly, several times a day, discussing the progress of their efforts to access information on the investigations. They talked about the health scam and about the fugitive Trapani boss Matteo Messina Denaro. His fiancée, Maria Mesi, had already been arrested once for aiding and abetting. Her sister Paola was Aiello's secretary. Cameras were even trained on Paola Mesi's house in Bagheria by investigators hoping the Trapani boss, Messina Denaro, might pay an unsolicited visit. Borzacchelli allegedly, drove by with a scanner to check if the cameras were on.

While detectives were uncovering private health fraud, another investigation was under way, into the Mafia's infiltration of politics.

Giuseppe Guttadauro had only recently been released from prison, and yet, in the run-up to the elections in 2001, his grand Palermo villa had been the meeting place for mafiosi, politicians and opinion formers, who would drop by to discuss the latest developments on the campaign. One of the candidates standing for the regional elections was the leader of the newly formed centre-right party the UDC, the big, blustering political heavyweight Salvatore Cuffaro. He and the stick-thin millionaire Michele Aiello were old friends, and Aiello was financing the party, which had swept up the remnants of the old Christian Democrats.

Investigators instructed the carabinieri to place a number of bugs in Guttadauro's elegant sitting-room. Guttadauro had acquired some of Provenzano's attention to security: he had bought an electronic wand for detecting bugs. He had not yet learned how to use it, but as it turned out, he did not need to. The officer chosen to the install the bugs was Giorgio Riolo, the expert technician with a weakness for publicizing his work.

One of Guttadauro's most frequent visitors was Mimmo Miceli, an ambitious young Palermo councillor who had good links with Cuffaro and was hoping to get a seat on the regional parliament. The two men discussed issues of burning importance to Cosa Nostra: candidates for regional elections and hospital directorships, development plans for new shopping centres. The most pressing issue for Guttadauro was to improve prison conditions for convicted mafiosi. He needed to find a political contact who would start the ball rolling on changing the anti-Mafia laws. He confided to Miceli: 'I need to create a relationship with Cuffaro, via you . . . if he responds, and offers us some guarantees, it won't go any further.'

Miceli promised to pass the message on to Cuffaro, but word never came back. (Cuffaro was recently cleared of accusations that he had done any favours for the Mafia.)

Just days before the election the agent on duty suddenly heard shouting, as a row broke out at the Guttadauro house. The bugs had been discovered.

On the evening of 24 June, Cuffaro hosted a dinner at the Richard III restaurant on the hillside above Monreale in anticipation of the party's victory. The guests ate swordfish carpaccio and fresh tuna, beef steaks and slabs of fresh tomatoes in the warm summer air, drinking golden Sicilian wine, looking down over Palermo's Golden Basin. But not everyone was having a good time. After the meal Miceli motioned one of his associates to step outside with him for a moment and broke the news that Guttadauro's place had been bugged.

Agents back at the ROS were wondering how they had found out. At the DIA Ciuro continued his undercover work. He discovered that one investigation was looking into the connection between Aiello and Cuffaro. By the end of the year Guttadauro was back in prison, charged with Mafia association. Miceli was arrested the following summer. At the same time, a formal investigation was launched into Cuffaro's role in the leaks of information.

Riolo kept busy playing hide-and-seek, planting bugs in cars and houses, and informing the owners that they should take a look around. He learned about a bug in an Opel belonging to one of Provenzano's top managers in Bagheria and let Aiello know it was there. The bugs, which had been recording highly incriminating conversations, were located and quickly removed.

By the summer of 2003 Riolo was suffering from acute anxiety. He had so thoroughly abused his position of trust that it would be only a matter of time before he was found out. He was in such a state of fear that Borzacchelli allegedly put out feelers to see if his friends could not give Riolo a cheque big enough to calm his nerves and make the risk worth his while.

When the region adjusted the tariffs that would fix the repayments for highly specialist radiotherapy treatment, Cuffaro and Aiello had long discussions about the tariff levels. Aiello's clinics stood to earn millions from the state health pay-outs, but they had other urgent matters to discuss. At the end of October they made an appointment at a clothes shop in Bagheria. Cuffaro dismissed his armed escort and let Aiello know that he was under no circumstances to tell anyone where he was going or whom he was meeting. During their thirty-minute tryst in the shop, as they examined jackets and felt the thickness of collars and cuffs, Cuffaro told Aiello he had heard Ciuro and Riolo were under investigation. He had got the news 'from Rome' – that is, from government contacts. (This was the version of events

Aiello gave magistrates under questioning. He later denied that they had talked about any investigations, saying his ill-health had muddled him.)

Cuffaro later denied revealing any news about the investigation, claiming they had met merely to discuss the private health tariffs – a significant matter for a politician responsible for a black hole in the region's health budget.

On the evening of 4 November, Ciuro was alarmed to see that an urgent meeting had been called between magistrates and the director of the police organized crime unit and rang a friend at the DIA to find out what it was about. His colleague (as directed) gave him a reassuring answer. 'OK then,' Ciuro replied, 'I can go and eat my dinner in peace, because they won't be arresting me this evening.'

His optimism was misplaced. Ciuro was arrested the following morning, along with Riolo and Aiello. Aiello was charged with being a front man for Bernardo Provenzano; Riolo and the others with aiding and abetting a fugitive. Three months later Deputy Borzacchelli was also arrested. The trial of the mafia's 'moles' was a massive operation, which resulted in convictions for Aiello (14 years for mafia association) and Riolo (7 years). Cuffaro was convicted of revealing official secrets, however the judge ruled that his actions benefited individual mafiosi, not the organization. After a fast-track trial Ciuro was convicted of aiding and abetting; at the time of writing Borzacchelli is awaiting the judges' verdict.

'I'm so ashamed of my disgraceful conduct', Riolo confessed in court. 'I feel utterly contemptible. I let myself be drawn into a world of power games, money and crime which has nothing to do with me. I stupidly believed I could do my job and still be able to use my contacts to build myself up and curry favour with important people.'

He claimed that he had done it all for *protagonismo*, to make himself the centre of attention – but the car, and the money, spoke for themselves.

'The trial of the spies in the institutions gave us an insight into how deep and pervasive Cosa Nostra's contacts were, throughout the system', the prosecutors wrote. 'Unusually we have seen evidence of relationships between a defendant accused of Mafia association (Michele Aiello) and one convicted of the same crime (Giuseppe

Guttadauro) with politicians of the highest level, with businessmen, professionals and journalists, with employees and directors of public administration, with people who work in the prosecutor's office and with members at every level of seniority of the police force.'

In the judges' motivation for the sentence against the politician Mimmo Miceli, published in May 2007, they reiterated that Miceli, as Palermo's local minister for health, was the go-between for the mafioso Giuseppe Guttadauro and the president of the region, Salvatore Cuffaro. Cuffaro remains under a separate investigation for aiding and abetting the mafia.

After the round-up of Provenzano's informers, investigators discovered there were other shadowy officials in Cosa Nostra's pay, passing him news about plans for his capture, helping him keep one step ahead of arrest. While investigators were on high alert for leaks, at least one other attempt to arrest him would be scuppered by 'the good Lord Jesus Christ', the spy in the system.

15

Prostate trouble

PROVENZANO'S HEALTH PROBLEMS, which had been troubling him for some time, were becoming urgent. Ever attentive to his failing body, he needed to see a doctor with increasing regularity, and his letters were full of arrangements for clandestine medical appointments.

Visits to private clinics had to be arranged, analyses of bodily fluids had to be organized; at some stage he had an operation. In April 2001 his loyal friend Pino Lipari wrote, in one of the more unlikely descriptions of the Boss of Bosses, 'Our kitten has been unwell . . .'.

Lipari had everything prepared; an ambulance was ready. His wife was going to go along, pretending to be the sick man's companion. But there was a last-minute cancellation, as so often happened; the doctor couldn't make a consulting room safe for a high-level fugitive to visit without arousing suspicion, and Provenzano was back in his old refuge, managing his symptoms with diet and drugs.

After their galling near miss when they followed a doctor and arrested the 'wrong' patient, the police were taking no chances. They followed leads to urology departments all over Italy and further afield. An agent from the Catturandi went to London after receiving intelligence that one of Provenzano's relations was booked in for prostate treatment in a private London clinic. The Sicilian pensioner in his private room was extremely surprised to receive a visit from the police – but he was not the fugitive Boss.

Following the arrest of so many of Provenzano's closest associates, he was thrown back on his oldest allies. Ciccio Pastoia, an old-school mob boss who had moulded himself in Provenzano's image, had become capo of Belmonte Mezzagno after Spera's arrest, with Provenzano's support. Now he took on the Boss's day-to-day management. He got in touch with his godson Nicola Mandalà, the womanizing, coke-snorting, gambling king of Villabate. Two men more different in style one couldn't imagine, but Uncle Binnu needed them, and together they took on the difficult task of managing Provenzano's life in hiding.

As Provenzano's spokesman, Pastoia contacted capos all over western Sicily, organizing his postal system and letting his will be known. 'Pastoia became Provenzano's alter ego', says prosecutor Michele Prestipino. 'He was the closest in character to Provenzano. The others had delusions of grandeur, they were power-crazed. Provenzano, and Pastoia, to a degree, were the opposite: they had this ostentatious modesty. Pastoia was capable of great self-sacrifice; he could operate behind the scenes, let someone else be the boss, but he was by no means powerless.'

Pastoia waxed lyrical on his relationship with the Boss: 'We're the same, we are the same deep in our souls, he and I . . . for that reason whatever happens in life, nothing and no one can come between us . . . no one can put . . . they've tried . . . that bastard from my town even tried . . . but he couldn't do it . . . because he'll tell you, "I don't believe Ciccio would ever betray me . . . me or anyone else".'

Pastoia was now involved in trying to organize Provenzano's cure. Agents listened in as he and Mandalà discussed how to get him a doctor. They feared he would need further treatment, perhaps even surgery.

Mafiosi are particularly vulnerable to health problems, and not just because they're liable to get shot: life in the Mafia takes its toll both physically and mentally. In the USA many mafiosi have sought help for stress-related conditions, including diabetes and depression.

The supergrass Tommaso Buscetta has spoken about the punishing reality of life on the run: 'When you know they're after you, you can't sleep, you never have a moment's peace. Every night, before you go to bed, you think about what could happen to you during the night. I travelled all over the world as a fugitive for forty years, in a state of constant anxiety. Life on the run is very tough. You can do it for a month or two, no problem. But to keep it up for a lifetime is incredibly stressful. You get used to it – but basically you get used to the stress.'

In every letter Provenzano and his ageing supporters and friends inquired tenderly after each other's health before getting on to the question of murder. His helpers were sent off with shopping lists in search of medicines, syringes, pills and incontinence pads. The sickening Boss, living apart from his wife, was becoming increasingly dependent. He continually recruited new supporters and 'postmen' to deliver his letters along their complicated routes, creating a vast and complex structure whose main aim was his own protection.

By his late sixties he had become obsessive, full of anxieties, afraid that he would start forgetting things or leave out something important in one of his messages. As his fear of forgetting became a fixation, his letters set out the points by number. Of course, being Provenzano, it was probably an act, to create a fictional image of a bumbling old man to get maximum support and indulgence from his friends and lull his foes into a false sense of security.

'I hope I haven't forgotten anything, my memory does play tricks on me', he wrote. 'Please do make sure that anything I've forgotten, if you remember, remind me next time.'

By 2003 Provenzano was a sick man, in urgent need of medical intervention. There were logistical problems: he had been a fugitive for forty years, leaving no official record of his existence anywhere. How does a man get medical help if he has no records?

Nicola Mandalà, who loved to party and flash money around, was one of Provenzano's key protectors and managers. One morning in June 2003 Mandalà called on his good friend Francesco Campanella, former leader of the local council, in his office at Credito Siciliano's modern, orange-clad concrete block in Villabate. The two men were in business together, running an operation that included concessions on phone shops, bingo halls and betting shops. But since Mandalà had come in on the business, he had taken out large sums for his and his entourage's expenses and massively expanded the gambling side of things, and it began to make a loss. To shore up the plummeting bottom line, Campanella went behind his bosses' backs to siphon off money from savings accounts deposited by legitimate clients. Campanella always intended to pay them back, but the company's finances went from bad to worse.

As Mandalà swung into Campanella's office, the bank clerk dreaded what was coming. Before he said a word, Mandalà threw his jacket over the CCTV camera that perched, beady-eyed, in the corner and shut the door.

He handed Campanella a document: it was an ID card belonging to an old man by the name of Gaspare Troia. 'I need you to fix this ID card, and I'll need a couple of mobile phones', said Mandalà, giving his friend a passport photo of a grey-haired pensioner. 'To be honest,' Campanella later confessed, 'I didn't know who it was in the photo.'

Mandalà spoke in a whisper in Campanella's ear: 'And watch it, because if you get caught with this photo you'll get thirty years.' Campanella understood this must be a high-level fugitive, and as he looked at the photo again, he realized it was the Boss himself.

Campanella had witnessed just how terrifying the Boss could be if you messed up. 'Mandalà had been to a top-level meeting,' he told magistrates, 'and I assumed it was with Provenzano. He met us for dinner at the Mata Hari restaurant in Bagheria, and he was holding a note, a *pizzino*, sealed. At dinner he talked about other stuff, he didn't mention Provenzano or anything about him. Then we drove back to Villabate, and we'd just got to the motorway when he realized he had lost the note. He frantically checked his pockets and searched behind the car seats, shouting: "I'm dead, he's going to kill me, this *pizzino* is incredibly important, if I don't find it, I swear he'll kill me." He started looking along the road, we went back the way we came, all the way back to the restaurant. At last he found it under the car mat.'

After Mandalà had unhooked his jacket from the surveillance camera and left, Campanella put the documents carefully in an inside pocket and hunted through his desk drawers for an official stamp. He did not have anything that would make the right impression. He knew the office where the registration stamps were kept, and what sort of stamp they used – but he had not been able to get access to them. The guy in charge of the official stamps at the bank was an old political adversary, so there was no way he could ask a favour.

He took an early lunch break and went across the road to his old office in the city council. Taking out the documents, he glued the new picture in place and rummaged around in boxes to find an official stamp. It was the wrong sort, but it said 'Comune di Villabate', so it would have to do. He needed another which would leave a raised impression. For that, he tried pressing down on the paper over a €2 coin. The result was a mess. It didn't look right at all. He went back into town, feeling extremely apprehensive, to meet Mandalà and apologize for the botched job. With Mandalà were his closest associates in the Villabate mafia, Mario Cusimano and Ezio Fontana, both of them on the Provenzano protection detail. Fontana was known as Provenzano's 'minister of post and telecommunications'.

'Look, I haven't got the proper stamps,' Campanella babbled, 'the official ones, I can't get hold of them, I'm not allowed to use them, there's no way I can do a good job on this.'

Mandalà took the ID card and gave it a cursory glance. 'Looks all right.'

Campanella, relieved, felt bold enough to ask who it was for, and Mandalà, without using the name, made it clear it was for the Boss. 'He's got to have an operation urgently, so we're taking him abroad.'

'How the hell are you going to get there?' Campanella imagined Italy's most notorious fugitive might have a problem leaving the country unnoticed.

'Same way as I've done for the past few years', replied Mandalà. 'I'll drive him in my car, easy. Don't worry about it.'

Mandalà's confidence was well placed. Over the years Provenzano had moved freely around Palermo in no apparent danger of being arrested. He had been stopped at road-blocks, treated in clinics, even gone to the cinema, and had never been recognized. He did have a mortal fear of having his picture taken, which is why this fake ID was such a dangerous document. He had managed to stay at liberty for over forty years because the only photo of him dated from the 1950s. Mandalà told Campanella that the ID card would do fine if they were stopped on the journey.

The Boss's deteriorating health was well known. Investigators were aware that he had problems with his kidneys and his prostate. They were also aware that he had contacts in the health sector.

The *pentito* Angelo Siino revealed that, approaching old age with failing health, Provenzano considered it a sensible idea to buy a private clinic. The suspicion was that by investing in Aiello's Santa Teresa clinic in Bagheria, that was more or less what he had done.

When Provenzano's need for surgery became a matter of urgency, he was convinced he would be at risk of discovery in Bagheria: by this time it was well known that the Palermo suburb was his base of operations. His aides located a private clinic in Marseille that, on presentation of a doctor's referral letter, did not require any other ID.

The man recruited to help Provenzano get to this discreet establishment on the French Riviera was Salvatore Troia, a wealthy associate of the Villabate Mafia and a resident of Marseille, where he and his wife owned a bar.

In July 2003 the Mafia boss, in constant pain, with aching legs and unable to sleep, set off for France in a convoy of two cars, with Mandalà, Fontana and his 'son' Salvatore Troia. For security reasons Saveria did not go with him. Provenzano, whose favourite reading was the Bible and who spent most of his time completely alone, sat, suffering, in the back, while Mandalà – the high rolling, fast-living, night-clubber – drove. There could not be two more different characters in the ranks of the organization, and here they were, shut in a car together for whole days: Provenzano, who liked to turn matters over in his head, in silence and solitude; Mandalà, who always wanted a mate to go to the casino with him, and a mistress, and a woman in his hotel room. It must have been a very quiet journey.

In Marseille the team hooked up with Troia's glamorous French wife, Madeleine Orlando, who was needed to interpret for the patient. Mme Orlando claims not to have known the true identity of the mysterious sick man, but must have been aware that the old fellow was not, as his ID card announced, Gaspare Troia, her father-in-law. Provenzano was examined at La Licorne clinic in a small town just outside Marseille, by doctors who, considering how serious his illness, were surprised at how strong his constitution was. They found problems with his arteries and diagnosed hepatitis B and C; he also suffered from rheumatic pain (exacerbated by living in basic accommodation in the mountains in winter). Doctors informed him that he urgently needed surgery to remove his prostate.

The patient insisted he could not be treated straight away; he had urgent business at home to attend to. The Boss instructed his helpers that he had to get back to Sicily immediately. He could not be away from Sicily for long: he was needed to oversee business, make decisions and give advice. Surgery would have to wait; Cosa Nostra could not.

In October he was back, again driving through Italy and along the coast of France, to another clinic, La Casamance, east of Marseille. There he spent nineteen days as a tourist, staying in a borrowed apartment in the centre of the city before undergoing surgery. When he came round after the first operation, to remove a lesion on his arm, he asked nurses to take the phone out of his room. He never used the phone for fear of being intercepted by the police. While he was recovering, Troia, Fontana and Mandalà spent their nights at the casino.

The Boss returned to Sicily in a much more comfortable state and spent some days convalescing at Mario Cusimano's villa outside Bagheria: an elegant place (in a style much imitated in the subsequent illegal building boom all around it) amid the lemon groves that slope down towards the sea at Ficarazzi, with a swimming-pool. Before the operation he had followed a strict diet of fish and steamed vegetables; afterwards he continued to eat healthily, even in difficult circumstances. In his rural hideouts there was usually fresh fruit and ricotta cheese available. In spring he sent a request to his temporary landlord to pick wild chicory and dry the seeds for him, so he could grow his own – he found it refreshing and had read that it has a cleansing effect on the urinary tract. 'Not the stuff you buy in plastic bags,' he wrote, 'but the plant in its natural state. I need the seeds.'

He sent out for a particular kind of honey with health-giving properties. One of his men managed to source forty-six jars of the precious stuff and had it taken to his hideout.

The middle-aged man who took Provenzano his meals was impressed by how tough he was. In a conversation recorded by police Stefano Lo Verso, forty-four, called the Boss 'Rambo' because of his strength under duress and his ability to survive the harshest living conditions. Unlike the younger, fast-living generation of capos, Provenzano did not need comfort, let alone luxury hotels and fancy restaurants. Lo Verso recounted an occasion when he was in one of Provenzano's hideouts, cleaning the larder, and the Boss told him off for throwing away the outer leaves of vegetables and greenery with bugs in it. 'Don't waste it, I've eaten worse', he said.

Provenzano's multi-million Euro deals did nothing to change his attitude to money: he always behaved as though he was earning no more than one of his faithful shepherds. On his return from his operation in Marseille, under the borrowed identity of Gaspare Troia, he applied for reimbursement under the regional health scheme. Given the way Cosa Nostra has stripped the public health system of funds, nothing could have been more natural.

Salvatore Troia, tanned and wealthy, was rewarded for helping Provenzano get to Marseille with membership of the Villabate Mafia. He returned to Sicily and invested some of his wealth in a gleaming ultra-modern bakery and French patisserie called La Baguette. On a prominent corner of the market square the bakery was brightly painted in orange and black, with a broad curved frontage.

By now the police were watching everything that went on in Villabate. Provenzano's postmen had led them to Pastoia, whom they knew as an old Mafia hand. The investigation was homing in on his contacts. There were bugs in their cars, bugs in their homes, on their phones. As they made every effort to avoid detection, the police became more and more ingenious. Pastoia used a ruined house out in the country for his meetings. The Catturandi put listening devices between the stones and patches of plaster. Keeping watch on their prey with long-range binoculars, they noticed that Pastoia would often walk outside the ruin with his men to have a private chat. This would be where the most highly charged information was exchanged. As Bloodhound recalls, they were determined to capture these intimate talks.

'We followed Ciccio Pastoia and Nicola Mandalà to a place out in the country. We'd already figured out where they were going, but it was really hard to follow them, along these remote tracks where most cars couldn't even go. It was a terrible road, an awful place to reach – we called it "the devils' arse" – they were crazy to choose it, and we were even crazier to follow them there.

'After we saw where they were going, indicated by the GPS we had planted on their car (although GPS is very unreliable – you have to rely on your intuition), a few of the men had to go back after dark and looked around for a likely place to put a listening device. They found a tree with loads of cigarette butts on the ground around the trunk, and decided that must be where they held their meetings. It was a really difficult job, in the dark, and it's a nightmare if you drop the thing, you have to put it somewhere they won't find it . . .

'Four or five days later we got a break, which told us our intuition had been right. We picked up a conversation between two men, one of whom was evidently in charge. We radioed this fact to the men on the ground, who took down number plates of the cars in the area. We had them.'

While the hidden microphones picked up every word, Ciccio Pastoia held court under his favourite tree. The men smoked, talked and plotted. Pastoia directed them where to take Provenzano's letters. He waxed lyrical about his friendship with the Boss, his affinity for Cosa Nostra. He talked about his loathing for Benedetto Spera and his whole family, about how he wanted to kill Spera's son, if he could do it without Provenzano knowing.

The bugs revealed Pastoia's true similarity to Provenzano: he was capable of plotting behind his back for what he reasoned was the greater good.

On 17 September 2004 police intercepted Pastoia and Mandalà discussing a murder plot, although from the men's conversation they could not figure out who was the target. It later emerged – when he was found lying dead in the street near his home – that the object of their attention was the developer Salvatore Geraci, who had been trying to muscle in on Mafia contracts.

'We'll see about it on Sunday, when we see Uncle', said Mandalà. The agent listening in snatched up a pen and started taking furious notes. He checked his watch: it was already Friday.

'OK, so we'll talk to Uncle on Sunday . . . but we needn't tell him we're going to do it . . . we'll tell him afterwards, because then if we do go ahead . . . when it's done and he knows about it . . .. I'll tell him . . . and he knows why it's got to be done . . . also because he's [Geraci's] not a friend of ours . . .

'We can go ahead and make an appointment because I've already told him . . . we just need to get a reply from No. 25 . . . so between now and Sunday . . . I'll make the appointment.'

When Ciccio Pastoia left his house, driven by his son, at ten past eight that Sunday morning, the unmarked police car was in place up the road. As usual, they would drive ahead of the vehicle they were tracking, rather than follow it. Father and son drove to Baby Luna, a bar beside the main Palermo ring road, all faded silver and glass brick. Its position on the main road and convenient car park once made the Baby Luna a favoured meeting place for mafiosi. Palermo boss Stefano Bontate used to meet Christian Democrat politician Salvo Lima here (before they were both assassinated by the Corleonesi). Mandalà arrived in his Hyundai, and Pastoia got in. As the two men took a circuitous route towards the village of Ficarazzi, near the sea outside Bagheria, the agents in pursuit could barely contain themselves. It really looked as though they were going to catch Bernardo Provenzano after all these years.

'We all kept in touch all that day, waiting by the phone, for the moment . . . it was pretty tense. We realized this trail could take us to Provenzano', said DNA chief Pietro Grasso.

The Hyundai stopped in via Marconi, just outside the village. After a short wait they set off again and drove around the narrow streets before finally stopping at a housing estate, where they left the Hyundai and got into a green Toyota. All morning they carried on driving around Ficarazzi, along narrow residential streets, past the trucking company, along the coast road, revisiting via Marconi several times, and eventually the agents lost track of them.

Back at the operations room an agent picked up a phone call on Mandalà's mobile. It was his wife, and after ticking her off for ringing his mobile, he told her he would be home shortly. Agents drove by Pastoia's house and saw that he was home too. The investigators realized that Provenzano had skipped the appointment, and they had missed their first opportunity in years.

'I got pretty angry with the police who'd been tailing them, saying they must have made a mistake and someone had spotted them', says Grasso. 'But they were adamant this wasn't what had happened, as they would have noticed something was amiss. So we decided to keep an eye on the old farmhouse where we'd had our microphones, but none of the mafiosi ever went back there. So we knew, someone had told them that's where we were getting our information.'

Pastoia and Mandalà had not known they had a tail; their evasive driving was habitual. Provenzano, however, through his own sources, had known that the police would be going to the meeting. He just had not told the others.

The anti–Mafia unit had just missed what seemed to be a golden chance, but they knew they were close. They knew the identities of most of Provenzano's supporters and 'postmen', the routes of his letters and the chain of command. They had kept the whole network under surveillance for months and had built a solid base of evidence against them. No matter how much Provenzano urged his men to be cautious, they continually gave themselves away. Aware of the continual presence of law enforcement agents, they began to feel the pressure. Ciccio Pastoia went to stay with his brother in Emilia, north of Florence. Mandalà invited his friend Campanella to a casino, and when the wives went to the Ladies, confided that he was convinced he was about to get arrested. As the police closed in, he was spending more and more time at casinos, as he considered it a useful alibi.

'I'll be OK', Mandalà said. 'I've booked a flight to South America.' The Boss would find someone else to look after him.

At dawn on 25 January 2005 doors were kicked in all over Palermo, handcuffs snapped on over pyjamas and hundreds of apartments and offices turned over. Over a thousand police and carabinieri were deployed in a massive operation code-named Grande Mandamento, the culmination of three years of investigations by a combined special force, involving hundreds of hours of surveillance. The effect of the raid was to create scorched earth around the Boss of Bosses, picking off his entire support network in Villabate and Bagheria. Pastoia was arrested at his son's house in Emilia, Mandalà in Villabate, with the plane tickets to Venezuela in his wallet.

TV news cameras rolled as, one after another, they were led to police cars, jackets over their heads: Mario Cusimano, who helped set up the trip to Marseille, Nicolò Eucaliptus and Onofrio Morreale, Provenzano's trusted lieutenants in Bagheria.

The news agencies rushed out the first accounts of a major strike against the Boss of Bosses: 'Provenzano ever more alone', 'Back against the Wall', 'Heavy Blow Struck against Provenzano Clan'. Somewhere Provenzano was listening to the headlines on the radio.

A total of forty-six men were arrested on the first sweep. Investigators had Provenzano's inner circle, the men who had seen the Boss just days, even hours, earlier – but they still did not know where the Boss was hiding. They left one of his closest assistants, Stefano Lo Verso, free but followed him closely: they knew he took food to Provenzano regularly and were hoping he would lead them to him. They could not let the old man starve, after all. But after a couple of days of close surveillance, police gave up hope that Lo Verso would take them to his leader and arrested him.

Two days after the arrest Mario Cusimano, claiming he was frightened for his life, asked for protection and started talking. It was something of a record.

Police put Ciccio Pastoia in a cell and left him alone to read a copy of the dossier containing the evidence against him. Pastoia had been warned that his house had been bugged, but he had no idea of the extent to which his words had been immortalized. After all his assiduous attention to detail, his safe house up in the hills, his summits under a tree, he had been careless; he had betrayed everyone. He turned page after page, reading transcripts of his conversations, boasting about breaking the rules of Cosa Nostra, bragging about how he would kill Geraci first and tell the boss later. How he had killed a man in San Giuseppe Iato without asking the Boss's permission: crowing about his own treachery, criticizing the Boss to Mandalà for changing the rules, for failing to follow his own directives.

'Do you have any idea how many times Uncle put me in a difficult situation . . . that's what he's like! He criticizes others for doing something, then he goes ahead and does it himself . . . I've taken care of him for thirty years . . . I know him', he had boasted. 'I know him like the back of my hand . . .'

And there he was, threatening to kill Benedetto Spera's son, the son of a capo mandamento, a made man. 'That bastard . . .'

In other cells in the same prison men of honour were reading the same papers. They would know. And they would go after his own sons: his sons would become the target of vengeance. He had two choices: collaborate and get his family under protection as fast as possible, or kill himself and expiate the vendetta right there, by his own hands.

The old man ripped a sheet off the prison bed, hung it over the bars of the window and tied one end around his neck. When the guards opened the cell door the next morning, they found him dead, the legal dossier open on the bed.

The bank clerk and ex-council leader Francesco Campanella was thrown into panic by the police raid. He told police he wanted to collaborate but then lost his nerve and tried to give them bits of information with no real significance. When news of his arrest on Mafia charges got out, the bank's clients had stormed the building to demand whether they still had their savings. Months later his wife told him she had seen a suspicious-looking person hanging around outside the house. Afraid that his former clients were going to take their revenge against him, Campanella told investigators he had decided to collaborate, this time for real. To prove it, he told them about the forged ID, bearing the name of Gaspare Troia, on which the Boss of Bosses had left the country.

With the latest information detectives composed a new identikit image of the Boss, updating the ancient 1958 black-and-white mugshot that was all they had to go on. Giuffré confirmed the new image was a good likeness, as did others who had seen him recently. Investigators picked up a conversation between two mafiosi sitting in their car, looking at the identikit image in the paper, and discussing the likeness. 'He's not as bald as this picture shows . . .'

The picture was broadcast on *Chi l'ha visto?*, the Italian version of *Crimewatch*, on 7 March 2005 and drew a record audience of

3.6 million. Of the numerous callers to the programme, the producers said a few were convinced they must have seen Provenzano himself.

One sighting had been the previous January at a motorway service station outside Rome, another at a bar outside Florence. Investigators spent the following weeks following up leads all over Italy, and harmless old boys were interviewed in police stations across the country. One man was followed by detectives after he made a number of unexplained journeys from Corleone to Palermo and was seen making nodding contact with an older man at the Palermo railway station. The old man fitted Provenzano's identikit image, and police picked him up half-way down via Maqueda, the long, narrow street lined with stone palazzi that cuts through the heart of Palermo. It turned out the officers had gatecrashed a homosexual assignation.

Cusimano's account of the emergency prostate operation launched a new phase of the hunt for Provenzano. Police visited the old man Gaspare Troia, a retired baker, in Villabate, and inquired about his health. No problems, he told them, no recent operations, nothing wrong with his prostate, and he had never been to France.

In early June prosecutors Pietro Grasso and Michele Prestipino were on their way to Marseille to seize medical notes and question the doctors about their notorious patient. Doctors were a little surprised, somewhat alarmed. They see 2,500 old men every year with similar prostate problems, they said. They did remember one unusual detail: that the fugitive wore three silver crosses on a chain round his neck.

Magistrates Grasso and Prestipino returned from Marseille with a mass of information about Provenzano's state of health, but in reality no nearer to the man himself. They now knew everything about the Boss, including his DNA, his medical history and current condition, diet, scars, blood group. They knew he did not smoke, did not drink, never took sleeping pills, wore a dental plate, was intolerant of wine and allergic to anti-inflammatories. He suffered from stomach-ache but couldn't take antacids. The astonished public had viewed his scratchy signature ('A person with this sort of handwriting is not to be trusted', commented the TV calligraphy experts, instantly earning their appearance fee). They knew him inside out. The only thing they did not know was where to find him.

In the midst of this medical detective hunt came the sudden, mysterious death of a top Sicilian urologist. Dr Attilio Manca, from a small town near Messina, was found dead in his apartment in Viterbo, Lazio, in early 2004. He was discovered with an injection mark in his left arm, and the autopsy said he had died from poisoning.

The cause of death was registered as suicide, but Manca's mother revealed that her son had made a frantic phone call just days before his death, telling her he would shortly be coming home to Sicily. It also emerged that Dr Manca had made an unscheduled visit to France in October 2003, at the same time that Provenzano was having his prostate operation.

His mother is convinced he had been coerced into treating Provenzano and then silenced. Her suspicions had been raised because he had his surgical instruments with him at the apartment when he died, though he did not usually take them out of the clinic. Also the injection of lethal substances had been given in his left arm – but the doctor was left-handed. The inquiry into his death was reopened in October 2006 but has so far reached no conclusion.

Meanwhile Provenzano's options were shrinking fast. He had lost his helpers and supporters, his cover, his health, even his prostate – but somehow he carried on. It showed he had, as one journalist observed, a constitution of steel.

A few months after his death Ciccio Pastoia's grave was ransacked and set on fire. The old man had taken his own life, depriving those he had betrayed of the satisfaction of exacting their revenge. Investigators deduced that the perpetrator was doing Provenzano a courtesy. It was apparently Provenzano's style: to harm Pastoia's widow or his sons would have caused a major row and made the news. This way the signal would be understood by those who needed to know it.

In the calm after the storm 'Alessio', Matteo Messina Denaro, one of the few survivors of the blitz, wrote to the boss: '*Carissimo mio* . . . I'm so sorry to hear about everything that's happened and hope that you are safe and in good hands . . . I don't know how to contact you but I'm hoping you'll get in touch with 121. I'll just have to wait.'

16

The net tightens

'AFTER THE BIG arrests in January 2005 we had to start again from scratch.'

Bloodhound and the rest of the Catturandi group were suddenly victims of their own success. 'We had created scorched earth around Provenzano and burned all our leads, every investigative channel had been blown wide open. We had arrested everyone who had any contact with the Boss. Now we had to find out who had replaced them.'

Grasso announced that his team had 'broken up Provenzano's ministry of post and telecommunications', but this left them with the big question: who were they to follow now? They knew Provenzano would have already built up a new inner circle to function as his personal management and support system. To make life more difficult for the investigators, these would be people with no previous convictions.

'Looking after Provenzano had become a bad business,' said Pietro Grasso, 'a major inconvenience. In the past it was an opportunity, it gave you prestige in the organization – but not any more. With all the police activity it had become a liability. Whoever was looking after him was instantly open to charges of aiding and abetting.'

It was time for a new dynamic, a shake-up of the crack team of investigators who had been working together for eight years. A compact, hand-picked group would work autonomously and exclusively on capturing Provenzano. Renato Cortese, under whose leadership the Catturandi had caught Brusca, Vitale, Aglieri and others, was brought back from the Servizio Centrale Operativo (SCO) in Rome to repeat his success.

Cortese, vastly experienced and softly spoken, with a grizzled beard and dark eyes behind glasses, commanded immense loyalty among his team. Working with Gilberto Caldarozzi, head of the SCO, whose trophies from capturing fugitive mafiosi include the Catania boss Nitto 'the Hunter' Santapaola, Cortese selected seventeen men and one woman from the Catturandi and a further eight men from the SCO in Rome. There were technicians expert in electronic surveillance, dogged, old-fashioned detectives, some with a talent for trailing suspects, and local specialists familiar with the difference in accents from one village to the next.

'We wanted to streamline the investigative group, bringing together police investigating Mafia crime and those searching for fugitives', said Giuseppe Gualtieri, head of the Palermo Flying Squad. 'It's better for the morale of those involved: if you spend ten years looking for a fugitive and you don't find him, it's hard; but if you've successfully rounded up his entire support network, you feel like you've achieved something.'

When picking his team, Cortese favoured single people over those married with children (half the squad, including 'The Cat', the only woman, were single), as they would be on call round the clock, and their work would be a total secret, for the protection of their families. 'You can't live in Palermo if people know who you are', one anonymous member of the group told a TV reporter. 'These people have long memories. They don't forget a face, and they know where your relations are.'[31]

The headquarters of Gruppo Duomo, as it came to be called, were not far from police headquarters, near the cathedral. This separate location meant they could be more autonomous but also helped to build team spirit. They would be working intensive, eighteen-hour days at a dangerous job that no one else knew about, and they needed to trust each other, to create a powerful bond. On their occasional days off they never let the radio out of hearing in case of an urgent recall.

Their headquarters were stripped to the bare essentials. One soundproofed surveillance room was lined with electronic equipment. It was always dark, and agents spent hours staring at screens, viewing and reviewing images from the closed-circuit cameras, following the GPS signals emitted by cars their colleagues had tagged, or glued to the headphones, listening to conversations, playing and replaying sections to catch any hidden meaning. Local knowledge was essential: exchanges were often in dialect and usually in code. This relentless surveillance activity proved essential to the investigation, and at least three men were involved in it continually.

Since people with Mafia connections never say anything of significance on the phone, Cortese's men put bugs in their houses, to pick up private conversations. It was highly dangerous work, but it was the best option open to them.

Meanwhile, of the mafiosi close to Provenzano who had been arrested at the end of January, some were beginning to talk. In April a collaborator claimed that a tunnel underneath a clinic in Bagheria, owned by Provenzano's private health tsar, Michele Aiello, had been used as an escape route by Provenzano. On a rainy night carabinieri closed off the surrounding roads and searched in the dark, using special imaging equipment, for signs of human passage. Eventually, they gave up.

As Easter approached, the prosecutor's office received the usual mysterious tip-offs about where the Boss would be eating his cele-bratory paschal lamb. Because of its connection to family, Church and community, the Mafia boss's celebration of this ritual had taken hold in the public imagination, and, as ever, investigators trekked off to follow up these tenuous leads.

Since Provenzano's Mafia support network had been taken off the streets, the Gruppo Duomo focused on his family. The agents realized that his family were managing to get letters to him; they just needed to figure out how.

Apart from family members, there was another section of the community that Provenzano trusted with his life, and his letters. 'The only people Provenzano ever really trusted were shepherds', said Gualtieri. 'When we got his voice on tape, he was at the sheep farmer Nicola La Barbera's farmhouse. The only place anyone got to meet Provenzano, the few occasions he emerged from hiding, were in rural farmhouses miles from anywhere. He hardly ever went to see

family members, he held very few meetings. We came to the conclusion long ago that he wrote these *pizzini* because he didn't want
to have meetings. But he was forced to have some face-to-face conversations, and those were always held in shepherd's cottages or farm
buildings.'

The shepherds' world is very closed, explained one Corleone resident. 'They feel very much on Cosa Nostra's side. Anyone who is on
the other side, who doesn't do what they're told, is a *sbirro*, a spy. You
would never find a shepherd in these parts who would willingly tell
investigators anything.'

The Boss worked at keeping the rural community onside: a couple
of years earlier he had arranged for a fruit juice factory to offload a
truck full of lemon peel for a cattle farmer in Ciminna (at a certain
time of year, if cows are fed on lemon rind, it gives the milk a particular aroma essential in cheesemaking). Several fugitives had been
lodged in the area, and Provenzano wanted to do this particular farmer
a favour and have the rind delivered free – to build good will among
the local community.

Provenzano had political contacts at the highest level – industrialists, contractors and businessmen – but he never forgot where he came
from. Shepherds had a particular place in his heart. They had a respect
for the old ways, the traditional farming and husbandry, the time-
honoured ways of making ricotta and pecorino: a stake in the status
quo. At some level Provenzano represented the history and traditions
of this community. He may have had contacts at high levels, but now
he was in difficulty, Corleone's shepherds came to his aid.

Arrangements were made for Provenzano to stay at a little farm
cottage belonging to the cheesemaker Giovanni Marino. This old boy
had no previous convictions and was locally famed for his excellent
ricotta, which he made on his little property above Corleone in
Montagna dei Cavalli. He was a traditionalist, respectful of the older
generation, and happy to help.

To prepare for the Boss's arrival, he built a small extension on his
farm cottage, with a toilet, sink and shower. He kept some of his wife's
stuff in storage there and a few bits of farm equipment, but he made
it as presentable as he knew how, with a double bed, a table and chair.

The kitchen had a small stove and some basic cooking equipment. There was also a meat freezer he had used on the farm. He had been given instructions: black out the windows and make sure the door can be securely locked from the inside.

Marino's farm cottage was serviceable and reasonably secure, but we can be fairly certain it was not what the Boss was used to.

Provenzano arrived by night with his sleeping bag and arranged his clothes in an old wardrobe, attire for better times: silk jackets and cashmere jerseys, plaid flannel pyjamas and silk shirts. He was used to pampering himself: his collection of hair and skin products, Armani aftershave and manicure sets, filled four vanity cases, each one packed and ready should he have to make a sudden departure. His corduroys and tartan shirts from the classiest menswear stores in Palermo were arranged in the rickety cupboard. The glossy store bags with ribbon handles that they came in were folded neatly away, ready for the next move.

Provenzano slept in his sleeping bag on top of the bed, dressed and ready for flight. The nights are not very restful if you are always waiting for someone to crash through the door.

The centre of his daily operations was the little table on which he placed his trusty Brother typewriter. On one side, a box for *pizzini* he received – questions, complaints, requests for advice, judgement, adjudication – on the other, letters he had painstakingly typed, folded into half-inch squares and sealed with tape, each addressed with a number, ready for delivery. When he was particularly busy, there were more than a dozen rolls of Sellotape on his desk.

He also had his Bible, in which he slowly and deliberately under-lined passages of particular resonance. He copied out whole tracts of text he wanted to memorize or re-read. He had painstakingly typed out Luke 6: 43–46 ('A good tree does not bear rotten fruit, nor does a rotten tree bear good fruit./For every tree is known by its own fruit. For people do not pick figs from thorn bushes, nor do they gather grapes from brambles./A good person out of the store of goodness in his heart produces good, but an evil person out of a store of evil produces evil; for from the fullness of the heart the mouth speaks.')

He hung his religious pictures – the Last Supper, the Weeping Madonna of Siracuse, Padre Pio. It was not exactly a chapel like his old friend Pietro Aglieri's, but a little shrine, a place of meditation. It was certainly quiet. He was shut in the small, ripe-smelling cottage for most of the day and all night, listening to the sounds of the valley.

His circumstances were sadly reduced, compared with what he was used to, but he was determined to suffer in good cheer. 'Dearest love', he typed, 'I am glad to hear you are well, as I can assure you the same is true of me . . .'

He took care of himself: he brushed his teeth and sterilized his dentures, read up on his symptoms and looked up what foods would suit his condition. He had ordered the complete set of a partwork on health from *La Repubblica* and consulted it regularly, copying out difficult terms. He even wrote out a definition of prostate, to help him remember what was happening to his body. He was particularly concerned that prostate cancer would make him impotent, and copied out a number of different treatments, from psychotherapy to pills to be taken before sex.

His health had become something of an obsession. Cut off from the world and unable to call his doctor when he had any new sensation, he spent hours listening to his body and pondering his symptoms. He copied out the results of his blood tests and took notes on the medicines he had been given.

Shielded from prying eyes by black hospital bin bags taped over the windows, he withdrew more than ever. Sometimes Marino, his host, would drop in for a word, as he delivered fresh ricotta and a bag of clean clothes from Saveria brought up from Corleone, less than a mile away. Other mornings he would not venture in. Whole days would pass when Provenzano would see no one at all. He liked it that way: it gave him more time to focus on his writing. It was his habit to reply to every point in every letter sent to him, and he continually worried that he would forget things. Was his mind going soft in this protective prison? More likely it was a pretext for omitting to respond to difficult points when he wanted to play for time. In some ways, living as a fugitive suited Provenzano's leadership style; the system of *pizzini* gave him time to think about his answer. He often deferred requests for face-to-face meetings, which became increasingly rare – for security reasons, but also because he preferred it that way.

His note-taking had become a compulsion, perhaps a reaction to spending hours alone locked in one room. Occasionally he would listen to music – some hymns, or gentle background crooning: Julio Iglesias. He had the soundtrack to *The Godfather*, an old favourite he had seen in Palermo with his friend Pino Lipari. He set a chair so that he could sit, after his hospitable gaoler opened the door in the mornings, and look out of the crack above the door to enjoy the sunlight without being seen.

Down in Corleone, reactions were mixed at having the Boss back on their doorstep. Tensions were heightened by a subtle increase in police presence.

Those who were recruited to provide material support, security and postal services to the Boss were constantly on call. He did not go out or hold meetings but wrote letters constantly, several a day, and wanted them collected immediately. His presence, though invisible, was keenly felt.

Provenzano's return to Corleone was not an easy time for his family. Saveria and the boys were under more surveillance than ever. Every time they left the house there was a camera monitoring their movements.

Life definitely got more complicated. Saveria was happy to have her man within range so she could attend to his needs on a daily basis, but those needs were becoming more unmanageable. She seldom went out in case someone needed to drop something off or pick something up. The letters between her and her husband during this period were mostly about family business and banal practicalities. He would asked for food, fresh cheese, more coffee; and 'please don't send any more pasta al forno'. She complained of a bad leg keeping her at home; he commiserated with her on having a cold. They also exchanged notes about Angelo's impending wedding. With his continuing prostate problems there was a continual flow of reeking garments to wash.

For the boys, looking after their father was a heavy burden, and he was testing them with his demands, asking to see them all the time.

They had never been involved in Cosa Nostra – their father was most insistent on that – but now that there were fewer old friends to rely on, the immediate family were drawn into his support system.

More than that, after they had moved to Corleone, they had got quite used to living without him, through school and university. They and their mother were a unit. And then, all of a sudden, he was back among them. Francesco Paolo had begun to make a life elsewhere but had to return.

Both young men were fed up. Angelo could not stand the life he was leading. It was not easy being Provenzano's son, organizing meetings and everything he needed. When he summoned them, they arranged to meet him, under considerable stress. 'The whole family was circling around him and his needs', said one investigator. 'He was obsessed with the details and arrangements of his life in hiding and his protection, and he wasn't really paying attention to anyone else's needs. And the boys were tired, tired and fed up with this life.'

The launderette that Angelo had tried to set up with his mother in Corleone had been closed by the authorities after a couple of years, on the basis that the family had failed to prove that it had not been bought and set up with illegally earned capital. When the police came to serve them notice to close the business, Saveria was visibly upset. In all their dealings with her, they had never seen her so emotional, and in their embarrassment they were brisk and businesslike. But this represented a major defeat for Saveria and the boys. Angelo, who saw it as a failure on his part, became withdrawn and depressed, and it was some months before he summoned the determination to challenge the closure in court. Grimly determined not to let his mother down, he got a job as a sales rep for a household goods company, selling electrical appliances. Among all the painfully unglamorous possibilities in the straight world for someone trying to steer away from a life of crime, selling vacuum cleaners door to door has to be high on the list.

Provenzano was always affectionate towards his sons in his letters, and they were warm and respectful in return, but private conversations between the brothers revealed a deep unhappiness.

In the spring of 2005 Paolo graduated with a first-class degree in languages from Palermo University (his dissertation was an ethnic study of the Goths). At his graduation a reporter snapped a picture of him in a mortarboard being congratulated by two female friends, and he ended up on the cover of a magazine.

From Paolo's point of view, he had satisfied his father's wishes by finishing his studies, but his specialism in languages was going to help him get away from the family. While Angelo was stranded, packing bags and phoning for pick-ups, working at his dreary job, Paolo got away: out of 300 candidates he was one of the thirty-six picked to teach in Germany and promote Italian culture. During several trips he and his brother made to Germany, police recorded conversations in which he vented his rage.

By this stage the search for their father had intensified, and their lives were utterly disrupted. There were cameras and microphones everywhere, picking up their every word. When the brothers got a plane to Germany, there was a policeman in the row behind, wearing what looked like an iPod, which was recording their conversation. Angelo's fiancée, who worked in a clothes shop in Corleone, argued with him about his reticence on family matters. Her father worked for a transport agency in Palermo, and she simply was not used to accepting certain things without questioning.

The boys had been brought up to respect their father, but they had developed a critical sense of his world. They had to live with that world but not within it; there was no getting away from it, but no entry either. When Paolo and Angelo packed the car to the roof with Paolo's stuff and set off for Germany in September 2005, the police were with them every step of the way. They booked a cabin on the Palermo–Genoa ferry, and agents stuck microphones in every conceivable spot. Agents listened in to their heart-to-heart.

'Some things have always bothered me', said Paolo, 'when he said we had to leave [to go and live in Corleone], we had to go, because of all our fucking problems, and who ever gave a damn about us? And when I got back on my first Saturday home from Germany, right? And we ended up going over there . . . I don't know why he even wanted us there. I can't see the point of going to see him: he's never even talked to me properly. When I was graduating and I had to take my last exam, no one gave a fuck about whether I might be having any problems, no – I had to go and stand around over at his place. Because that's all I ever do, stand around in his presence. Whether you like it or not, you've always been more involved – at least he talks to you, but I've always stood there saying nothing, since I was a kid.'

'For what it's worth . . . I don't think he planned to come back', Angelo said.

'So what, I'm supposed be happy about it? I'm supposed to be happy that we're rebuilding this weird sort of "family unit" and it wasn't even planned? And then he calls it the will of God.'

'We're all to blame', said Angelo gloomily: their mother was to blame as she had never stood up to him, and they were to blame for putting up with everything. 'If there's personal responsibility, I can take it. We can say it's down to destiny, to God's will . . . but the fact is we have put up with a whole lot of difficult situations and we carry on putting up with them. We can't rebel against it, we can't even shift this cross we bear, to make it easier to carry. I've never said this to anyone, but when you think about the situation we're in, what we've had to go through, could it really be any worse if our father was dead?'

Although some mafiosi have educated their children and allowed them to train for a legitimate profession, most end up getting drawn into the Mafia's weir. Pino Lipari, who counselled his friend to educate his sons and keep them out of the organization, had a son who worked in the family contracting business and a daughter who trained as a lawyer. Whether it was what she originally intended, once she was qualified, and her father got caught up in legal difficulties, Cinzia Lipari specialized in criminal law and became her father's legal representative. She saw it as filial duty, she later explained to investigators, an inescapable obligation to ease her father's burden. It did not mean she shared his choices.

After Lipari's arrest in 1998, his son devoted himself to running messages and painstakingly reconstructing his letters, which were cut up and sewn into the hems of trousers. There was a lot of work and organization involved in rewriting and delivering the messages to the next 'postman'.

In 2002 the whole family was arrested for aiding and abetting a fugitive. In prison, separated from her two small daughters, Cinzia suffered from depression and went into a dramatic decline. Her father professed feeling desperately sorry for what he had done to his family. She later co-operated with the police, admitting she had worked for her father. She agreed that he had ruined her life but said she could not have denied him. The Mafia had ruined him; she just wanted to help.

She blamed not her father, but Provenzano. 'That man has destroyed our family', she told magistrates.

Although the ever-loyal Lipari was evangelical about his friend's good intentions, his family did not share his view. His wife called Provenzano 'Saint Brigit', lacing a code-name with a sharp edge of sarcasm: 'We need Saint Brigit here. If he was a man with enough balls he'd turn up and say, "Here I am" – he's got nothing to lose any more, he's practically dying – he should be locked up, and let fathers with families go home.'

Alone in his farm cottage, the Boss's thoughts were very far from on turning himself in. Night and day he kept working. Whatever happened, the *pizzini* must not ever stop: he had to keep the lines of communication open. If something happened to one of his postmen, he would have him replaced immediately. Any delay, or a pause, and the organization would grind to a halt. Day and night he typed his letters painstakingly, copying out carefully selected sections to send to different people. His careful and profitable management of the organization had become an obsession: he was a sick old man working tirelessly on his legacy.

One of Provenzano's major achievements was to restore the loyalty of the prison population. Men who had been caught in the great sweep following Riina's arrest, most of them from Riina's faction, would be coming out soon, and some of them could be dangerous. To prevent any revenge attacks Provenzano kept the prison population happy: paying into a fund for their legal expenses, seeking their views on major decisions, making sure their families were taken care of. It was an old-fashioned approach, one disapproved of by the young guns, who were overheard wondering why on earth

Provenzano should bother himself about people in prison when there was money to be made. 'We overheard some of the younger mafiosi complaining about Provenzano wasting his time on prisoners', said Alfonso Sabella. 'But he understood that keeping the prison population on your side was vital to prevent Cosa Nostra imploding. He was extremely successful at this – and we don't know quite how he did it.'

Those who had behaved themselves, who had kept a low profile and remained silent, were promoted on their release. 'When I was chief prosecutor in Palermo,' recalls anti-Mafia chief Pietro Grasso, 'I happened to meet two mafiosi whom I had convicted fifteen years before, in the maxi-trial. At that time they were soldiers, on the bottom rung of the organization; now they were regents. I said to them, well done, you've made a career of it. They had done their time, paid their debt to society and proved they were trustworthy. When they'd been released, they got their reward: promotion.'

During the summer of 2005 Provenzano's mediation skills were called on to deal with an increasingly inflammatory situation in Palermo. He had apparently been paving the way for two powerful Palermo bosses, father and son, to run the organization.

Salvatore (Totuccio) Lo Piccolo, the most powerful boss in Palermo, had been in hiding for over twenty years. It was no secret that he expected to be the next Boss of Bosses. He was known as 'the Watch Guy' or simply 'Cartier' after he produced stainless-steel Cartier watches as gifts for Provenzano and Giuffré. An experienced capo who lived modestly and worked hard doing business behind the scenes, he was a dramatic contrast with his son Salvo – a flashy, violent upstart apparently loathed by both investigators and mafiosi.

At the same time Provenzano was dealing with the ambitions of another Palermo boss, Nino Rotolo, a hot-headed capo presently under house arrest, trying to balance the two men's power and influence and avoid a war of succession. It was a lesson he had learned from his mentor Luciano Liggio, who had put him and Riina in harness together, drawing on their different strengths – knowing that there was so much rivalry between them that they would never unite to oust him.

Lo Piccolo had been manoeuvring to build up his power base within Cosa Nostra by linking up with the Inzerillo family – survivors of the Mafia war in the early 1980s and Sicily's foremost drug traffickers, who had been routed by Riina's men and fled to the USA. Lo Piccolo had been working with the Inzerillos, building up a significant income stream with the USA, and now, twenty years after they were banished by decree of the commission, they were beginning to come back. Lo Piccolo was paving the way for their safe return to Palermo and had petitioned Provenzano – who, as ever, heard the economic arguments and tried to find a way to make everyone happy.

In the summer of 2003 police acting on a tip-off staked out a traditional family restaurant, Il Vecchio Mulino, near Palermo, which was hosting a private banquet on a day it was closed to the public. Agents had been told it was a sit-down between Mafia families to settle a row over cattle-rustling. As agents hiding in cars and up trees took photos of the arriving guests, they recognized several old faces: mafiosi from Palermo who had fled for their lives in 1981. This meeting was to do with far more than cattle-rustling.

Rotolo was one of the most senior bosses in Cosa Nostra, with a high degree of autonomy. He was an assiduous disciple of Provenzano, imitating his style in his letters and preaching the Boss's message to his men. 'You have to be loved – it's very different from being feared. Respect, my friends, is one thing. Fear is a different matter: as soon as you turn round . . . and someone gets the chance, they'll put a fist in your face. But if you, as they say, do good, no one's going to touch you.'

Rotolo knew he would be in the front line if the Inzerillos returned seeking revenge, and he was determined to uphold the commission's order of banishment. The men who made that ruling are no longer with us, he argued, so we have no authority to change it. Rotolo lived in fear of the Inzerillos' reprisals, knowing that if anyone came looking for vengeance, they would come to him first. But the *scappati*, the 'escapees', were already slipping back into Sicily, and Provenzano was offering Rotolo no support to hold them back.

Rotolo was serving a life sentence when he was diagnosed with a dangerous heart condition; he was allowed to serve his sentence under house arrest. But police keeping watch at his villa in a residential estate in western Palermo watched as the supposedly ailing capo leaped over his garden fence and held meetings in a corrugated steel builder's hut in an alley behind his villa. Agents who were keeping Rotolo under surveillance knew he had anti-bugging detectors. Shortly before the parties arrived, they would deactivate the devices so that the machine would not pick up their presence. Once the room had been 'swept' for bugs, the devices would be switched back on.

As the agents listened, Rotolo would read Provenzano's letters aloud to his men and comment bitterly on them. Provenzano, realizing he had an explosive situation on his hands, had prevaricated and refused to give Rotolo a free hand. He played for time, telling both sides what they wanted to hear. 'The agreement was made, they have to stay over there', he wrote to Lo Piccolo's man. 'I was wondering if you know anything about this. I don't want to comment as yet', he wrote to Rotolo.

In his little cottage above Corleone, Provenzano was drawing on all his experience and skills as a mediator to diffuse this potential disaster. His letters were masterpieces of neutrality and ambiguity. 'I've talked to everyone from that family, and we're in agreement.'

Rotolo was spitting. 'Everyone from that family? Which family? The Inzerillos, I suppose!'

'I know nothing more about this matter than you have both told me', Provenzano continued, with measured formality. 'I hear you both, but I cannot give my opinion, however much my heart desires it, for several reasons beyond my control. My motto is: may God give us the certainty . . . that we have erred . . . and the strength to come to an agreement, and forgive.'

'Why won't he take responsibility?' Rotolo fumed.

'In Cosa Nostra the tendency is to eliminate the potential danger immediately', says Grasso, 'and not to take any risks. Provenzano took time to prevaricate . . . he said it wasn't his decision, only the people who had given the order could revoke it, and they were all in prison. He didn't resolve the situation, but he bided his time.'

He was avoiding, with admirable skill, conclusive action by one party or the other and successfully keeping both sides convinced that they had his special attention.

Provenzano typed: 'There are only three people left with the power to decide this matter: you, me and Lo Piccolo.' Rotolo was not satisfied. With the hut wired for sound, police heard how the situation in Palermo was hurtling towards war.

'One shot, here, that's all it'll take', Rotolo instructed his men. The agent listening at the end of the wire realized he was planning to murder Lo Piccolo and his son.

But while Provenzano had played for time, the Inzerillos were coming home, and the question of the *scappati* became academic. Rotolo did not have anyone shot, but he did have the satisfaction of kicking one of Lo Piccolo's men out of the organization. The Boss's tactics had angered him, but they had, for the moment, held him at bay.

Provenzano's talents as a mediator were required in family life as well, where a quarrel over money had blown up into a feud between the three brothers.

On 8 June, Falco, 'Hawk', was on duty in the Palermo HQ, listening to a conversation between Provenzano's two brothers, Simone and Salvatore, via a device planted in Salvatore's home in Corleone. The three-storey corner house was wedged into the end of a cul-de-sac, opposite his mother's family home. It was almost impossible for anyone to drop into the narrow street unobserved, but one of the agents had managed to break into the house and install a bug.

The brothers were moaning about Binnu, the famous outlaw. A long-standing row about an inheritance was rumbling on, despite the Boss's immense wealth and the good offices of his nephew Carmelo Gariffo, who was trying to smooth things over. They complained that Bernardo's sons were getting unfair advantages.

'What the hell did he contact me for', grumbled Salvatore. 'Did he really send for me after eight years to have an argument?'

In the police operations room Hawk strained to hear every word. The brothers' bitterness was palpable. Binnu's status as Italy's most wanted man was apparently becoming an intolerable burden.

'So he's still here then.'

After hours of listening to rambling, irritable conversations Hawk was not sure he had heard right. But when he cleaned up the tape and played it back without the background noise and interference, there it was. 'Iddu', they called him: 'Himself'. There was no doubt who they were talking about. Hawk got straight on the phone to the chief, and told him to come in right away: 'You've got to hear this.'

These few ill-tempered words by Provenzano's brother had let the Catturandi know their prey had come home to roost and was living in Corleone.

17

The arrest

THE FAMILY: IT was the last refuge, a natural network when all else failed. Provenzano had gone home to Corleone, where he could be cared for and protected by people he trusted. He had quarrelled with his brothers, it was true, but now he was in difficulties and needed their help.

The investigation initially focused on the Boss's favourite nephew, Carmelo Gariffo, who had recently come out of prison and was living just around the corner from Saveria in Corleone. He had evidently lost no time getting back in contact with his uncle, but the police couldn't follow him without being spotted. Conducting surveillance on foot within Corleone was almost impossible. An agent wandering about the narrow streets would be noticed within minutes, and asking for the neighbours' co-operation was out of the question. A tiny camera was planted on a street light outside Saveria Palazzolo's house to record every visitor, every movement to and from the house. Cameras were fixed on Gariffo's door, just around the corner. Listening devices inside the houses relayed their every word, but no one ever mentioned Provenzano.

Investigators turned up other interesting links. Gariffo's daughter Mariangela was married to Giuseppe Lo Bue, an ambitious young mafioso living in Corleone and working with Provenzano's older son, Angelo, in the domestic appliance firm. Angelo in general kept himself to himself and spent his time with his mother or his fiancée, but over the winter of 2005 he was seeing a lot of Lo Bue. The cousins were the same age and had a fair amount in common; they spoke on the phone a lot, and Lo Bue dropped by the house most days. In fact, as the police intensified their surveillance on Palazzolo's house, they noticed that he dropped in on 'Aunt Saveria' with surprising regularity, not always staying long enough for a meal or a chat. Sometimes he dropped by even when he had called ahead and had been told Angelo was not there. This pushiness was odd, and aroused agents' suspicion; could he have had an ulterior motive for his visits?

Police observers began to notice a pattern: the same people coming and going, the same habits repeated. Gariffo, although active in the family business and in contact with Provenzano, never visited his aunt, although she occasionally went to see him, usually with Angelo in tow.

Numerous phone conversations between Angelo and Giuseppe, monitored around the clock by agents in the darkened operations room, revealed nothing of interest to the investigation until they started talking about 'stuff' that needed to be delivered.

Whenever Lo Bue called by, he would leave with a blue or white plastic bag. It looked, to the agents studying the images, as though he was taking out the rubbish, but he walked right past the street bins outside the house and took the bags with him in his car.

'We see him go in to the house with bags, or packages, and when he comes out he's almost always got a bag with him', recalled Giuseppe Gualtieri, head of the flying squad. 'It looks like he's got clothing in those bags, but it's puzzling, because why should he take his washing for Angelo's mother to do . . . Another thing we notice is that, whenever Giuseppe Lo Bue leaves Saveria Palazzolo's house, he always, without exception, goes to see his father, on the outskirts of Corleone. When he leaves his father's house, he hasn't got the packages any more, or else he's carrying something small. He is leaving those bags at his father's.

'It's an unbelievable job, trying to carry out surveillance in a town like Corleone. It's a perfectly normal town, but it's in the mountains, which means you're always overlooked, and any novelty, anything that looks out of the ordinary, is immediately noticed and instantly reaches the ears of those few criminal members of the community. So the micro-cameras we use have to be extremely well placed. We can't have them all over the town, as someone will inevitably spot one, and then they'll go looking for the rest. We have to operate in and around Corleone without being spotted, which is no mean feat. People talk about Provenzano as the Phantom of Corleone, but it's our boys who were the real phantoms.

'We posted look-outs all around the area, using high-powered binoculars, to cover whoever was putting the cameras in place: that way we could warn them that someone was coming, that an old guy seemed to have noticed them, that the cattle herdsman was on his way through.'

The police logged constant trips by Lo Bue to pick up packages or drop something off. During this time officers listening in on the couple's phone line late one February night heard his wife complaining that she barely saw him any more. Mariangela had an immaculate Mafia pedigree, but just recently Giuseppe had got far more involved than she expected. She was at home with the baby, and he was never around.

> Mariangela: This isn't like being a family, I'm sick of only ever seeing you when you've got a gap in your schedule.
> Giuseppe: For the moment, there are more important things, like making sure the children lack for nothing. Of course it's better when we can spend time together, but you know there are times when there are other demands on us, and we've got to put up with it.
> M: But we've been living like this for eight months now . . .
> G: Yeah, I've been doing this for eight months, but at least, when you want to sit down and have a rest for five minutes, you can. I can't even do that.
> M: OK, go ahead, you carry on and let's see where it gets you . . . as far as I can see, you do things because you've made commitments to other people and you don't want to look bad.
> G: Well then, you should be proud of your husband if he doesn't look bad . . . you know you should be proud to say, if my husband makes a commitment he sticks to it.
> M: I don't need you to tell me why I should be proud of my husband, thanks. But I do know I've got a virtual husband – he only ever talks to me on the phone.
> G: But I've taken this on for everyone's sake.
> M: We'll see, one day, when you're on your own . . . [in prison]
> G: Mariangela, listen: I could be on my own for three or four years, then I'd be back with you . . . and I would do the same thing again, to make sure, like I said, the children don't miss out. Maybe you haven't understood that.

To the police this tragic little late-night conversation provided a strong clue that Lo Bue was involved in something important within the organization, and had been for several months. If their instinct was right, that those bags were on their way to Provenzano, the Boss could not be far away.

Police surveillance later revealed there were other pressures on Mariangela. Her husband talked on the phone with his mistress and made arrangements to go and see her in Trapani, over an hour's drive away. One late afternoon there was a frenzied volley of calls as he tried to drop off a package before heading out to see his mistress, and found no one home in Corleone.

By the end of January it was clear that Giuseppe Lo Bue was collecting packages from Angelo and Saveria and taking them to his father. But where did they go next?

Bloodhound was one of the most senior members of the Gruppo Duomo. He described the intense period leading up to the arrest. 'We start watching Giuseppe Lo Bue's father. After his son's visits he takes boxes or containers out to his car. We set up look-outs along the roads to see if we can spot where he's taking them. This is a slow process: he seems very wary and spends a lot of time watching out of the door of his workshop. We can't tell if he's seen something, if he's looking for us, or something else. To avoid being spotted we have to follow him just a short way on one trip, then another short distance the next. Finally we get a break: the father is seen meeting a man, and we manage to get down the number plate.

'This car turns out to be registered to the wife of Bernardo Riina [no relation to the former Boss], who has a criminal record for Mafia association. He lives just by the junction above Corleone.

'At this point it feels like we're getting somewhere. We decide to focus our investigation on Riina.'

Throughout those early months of 2006 Bloodhound and the other special agents were working night and day, tracking their suspects around Corleone without being seen. 'Following these guys with bags was incredibly difficult', he recalls. 'We had just one agent in a car – two agents and you'd attract attention instantly. They'd drive around, sometimes right into a garage, so you wouldn't see them taking the bag out of the car. Lo Bue drives incredibly fast and takes evasive action, so it was extremely hard for us to follow him and find out where he goes. There were times we thought we'd never get to the end of the trail, or that we'd made a mistake and were following the wrong man.'

It was an increasingly difficult and demanding job the unit was doing: progress was excruciatingly slow, but they could not take their eyes off the monitors for a second in case they missed something that might be important. There was also the strain on family life: they couldn't tell anyone – including their families – they were doing this job, because they were all from this area.

'It was about the end of January when we started following these blessed plastic bags,' Bloodhound takes up the tale, 'and we were still following them at the end of March, trying to figure out where they led. Fortunately for us, they got into a routine. Their movements started to look too regular. Once they got into a routine, they were in trouble – as we would have been. Once your movements become predictable, you've had it.'

One early morning towards the end of March the surveillance operation managed to keep track of the packages going from Saveria's house to Lo Bue's father and other bags coming back via the same route within an hour. Provenzano must be very near.

'One time one of our guys managed to follow Lo Bue's father in his car through the narrow streets of Corleone. He got out of his son's car and into Riina's silver Golf, then headed towards the edge of town. Our guy overtook him, and as he carried on the main road, he could see Riina's car behind him, turning off towards the old main road. We closed off two of the upper roads to see which way he came back, but he came back by another route – that's when we discovered he was coming back from Montagna dei Cavalli.'

The valley above Corleone, overlooked by the massive Rocca Busambra, is approached along a winding mountain road. As you enter the valley, it opens up like a secret garden. Following a gentle slope, there are fruit trees and palms, villas and farm cottages. Horses graze in small paddocks. Its exposed sloping sides and beguiling open landscape made surveillance extremely difficult without being seen.

'As we stepped up the surveillance on Bernardo Riina,' Bloodhound
went on, 'we had to dress to fit in with the surroundings; we all have
our own wardrobe at home for different surveillance jobs, I've got a
hat that looks pretty rustic: it did fine for this job.

'We discover Riina's going up to this place every few days, even
though he hasn't got any property up there. We set up a watch from
the mountain behind Corleone, 8 km away, to see if he's visiting relatives who live on the other side of the valley, but he doesn't appear.
We're mystified. Where is he going?'

To find out, the group had to change their surveillance position, to
a much riskier spot just 1.5 km away. This would give them an open
view of the other side of the valley. On 3 April they watched Riina's
Land Cruiser turn off the main road through the valley on to a track
leading to a sheep farmer's yard. Riina left again shortly afterwards.

The group had, perhaps, found the packages' ultimate destination.
The farm was visited by several people in the mornings, who stopped
to get fresh water from the spring and buy the farmer's ricotta cheese.
It seemed an unlikely place for the Boss of Bosses to remain undis-
covered, but they had taken so long to get this far, it had to be worth
the effort to keep it under surveillance.

'He seemed to have chosen a place that was so obvious it was completely overlooked', said Gualtieri. 'No one believed it possible that
he could be there. Certainly, if he was there, he never went out.'

Bloodhound and his colleague Lynx set up watch on the higher
slope of Montagna dei Cavalli. 'We went up there before dawn,
dressed in black, climbing rocks in the dark, watching constantly for
anyone who might have seen us. We had to stay so still, lizards were
crawling over us. After a few days we requisitioned a hut from main-
tenance staff working on radio masts on top of the mountain, keeping
the farm cottage under surveillance through our long-range camera
and watching the monitor, for eighteen hours a day. Instead of
filming the cottage, we relayed the images directly to Palermo. We
didn't leave the hide during daylight hours, unless absolutely necessary, and we'd go down after dark. I'd get home for two hours, for a
quick rest. I didn't see my wife for the whole time. We took a bottle
of water and some biscuits or panini with us, but we had to be

absolutely sure not to leave any trace behind: not a wrapper or a tissue or a plastic cup, not even a cigarette butt, or the game would be up. The same pair of us did the trip every day; we got to know the terrain, what time the shepherd would go past, what movements were usual and what was unexpected. If anyone came near while we were walking up, we crouched down and covered ourselves with a camouflage net.'

A short track led past a little house and into the yard, where the people who came to buy ricotta parked their cars. Two large concrete sheds, where Marino made his cheese, opened on to the yard. The little house had a rough concrete porch with a straggling vine growing up it, a small window and door covered with plastic strips to keep flies out. At seven in the morning Marino arrived and opened the door, but no one ever came out.

Officers on surveillance followed the journey of packages from Palazzolo's house to the cheesemaker's yard on 3 April, then again the following day and the next. By the fourth trip the group could see the postmen had got into a routine: they had got lazy. On 9 April the same Spar carrier bag was used for the whole trip. The operations room was at fever pitch.

'On 10 April we were pinned to the monitor the whole day', recalls Bloodhound. 'But no one came. We were pretty discouraged: it had been a year since we started this new phase, and we felt that probably no one would put any money on our investigation. We had no certainty that we were on the right track. We'd been staring at the monitor for the whole day without seeing any movement.'

The group's moment of dismay didn't last long. Meticulous police work had led them to this place. All that was missing was a positive sighting that someone, in all probability Provenzano, was hiding in that farm cottage. The following morning they got it.

'On the morning of 11 April we saw Marino take a container of ricotta into the house and come out again. Then, suddenly, we got our break: just for a moment we caught sight of an arm reaching out through the door.'

The two agents had been watching the hut for ten days. Riina and Marino had gone into the cottage for brief moments, but no one had come out. That arm, passing out a container, showed there was indeed someone inside. It appeared just for an instant, on their screen.

'I do manage to stay pretty calm on the outside, but it was an incredibly exciting moment', said Bloodhound. 'I called Cortese back at the base. We didn't know it was definitely him, but whoever it was, we were going to go in. As soon as I let them know there was someone in the hut, the whole group mobilized. Lynx and I stayed up there, to watch what was happening and give the signal. I told them it would be best to wait for two hours, till Marino closed up shop and all the people had left. It was crucial for Renato's men to get there when everyone had gone but before Marino left. He would be closing up the cottage, and we didn't know if it had a metal door; it might have a security bar behind it as well. If we were forced to use acetylene torches to break in, it could take fifteen minutes, in which time he could escape down a tunnel or destroy any documents. It wouldn't be the first time.

'As the last car was leaving, I called Renato, and shouted: Go!'

The units had sped over from Palermo and were close by at this point; the first car drove up the little track moments later. When he heard the car, Marino ran towards the door, then relaxed when he saw what he thought was Riina's white jeep.

As Renato Cortese flew out of the car, the old shepherd tried to reach the cottage, but Cortese caught up with him, threw him to the ground and dashed for the door. Bloodhound and Lynx watched intently as their commander disappeared inside, followed by two others. Within moments they had a call.

'It's him!'

'The first call I made was to my wife', says Bloodhound. 'I told her, "Everything's gone according to plan, it's good news. I probably won't be seeing you for a few days."'

'"That'll make a change, then." She laughed.

'By the time we got down to the farmyard, it was crazy. Everyone was hugging each other and crying, slapping each other on the back. I went inside, to take a look at Provenzano, and introduced myself. He shook my hand and congratulated me. He asked us if we'd had any help in finding him, from informers. We told him no one had helped us, we'd just followed the packages. What made me realize he was really intelligent was the way he never answered a question. He waited till you had answered your own question, then he would give the merest sign of assent or else say nothing.

'I asked him what he'd have done if he'd seen us up there.

'"I would have exercised my right to escape", he said.'

Caldarozzi and Bloodhound put Provenzano in an unmarked car and drove him down to Boccadifalco, an airport near Palermo. They drove without sirens or escorts so as not to attract attention. Marino, the old shepherd, was arrested.

From Boccadifalco, Provenzano was taken to police headquarters in Palermo, where an angry crowd had gathered in the spring rain. As he was bundled from the car into the building, he was jostled and pushed, as the crowd surged forward shouting 'Bastard! Murderer!' as he was ushered through the gateway and escorted inside. News of the Boss's capture had been released almost instantaneously on the wires, and TV trucks were already pulling up outside police HQ.

Provenzano was dwarfed in the jostling, baying crowd of police officers in balaclavas and bulletproof vests. With his spectacles on a string and an enigmatic smile, he looked like a simple, harmless old man.

Prosecutors Marzia Sabella, Michele Prestipino and Pietro Grasso left their offices in the court-house and roared straight round to police HQ to meet their prisoner and make sure everything was in order before he was transferred to the maximum-security unit at Terni, in Umbria. After trailing him for so long, it was an emotional moment.

'As the investigation intensified, I had started thinking I saw him everywhere', Sabella recalls. 'But when it came to it, I would never have recognized him. He didn't look like the Boss.

'He was a bit bewildered by finding himself in the midst of a noisy crowd and so much confusion after spending all that time alone. Not that he made a scene, he was perfectly dignified. We tried to create a bit of order, asked the police – who were jostling to get a glimpse of the Boss – to clear out and leave only essential personnel. We made sure he had what he needed. He asked for some medicine, a nurse was called, but I think he had it in a pocket.'

They introduced themselves, though she was aware no introductions were necessary – as the only female member of the team, it was obvious who she was. When Provenzano offered his hand, it was a great moment, something like a diplomatic encounter. 'It was only a cease-fire', Sabella says. 'The next time we saw him he was uncommunicative. But that day I felt sorry for him. He just looked like a sick, old man. He looked beaten.

'It was hard to register that what we had waited for so long was actually happening . . . that he was there in front of us.'

After Provenzano was escorted out for the short drive to the airfield Sabella and her colleagues drove up to the farm, to examine for themselves the conditions in which he had been living. After months of concentrated detective work it was a strange experience.

'Going into the hideout, I had a moment of *déjà vu*. We had studied his habits and methods in such depth, I felt like I already knew everything that was there', says Sabella. 'I had the feeling of having been there many times: everything was strangely familiar. Through the *pizzini* and the *pentiti*'s reports we were aware of a lot of his habits and needs, and we recognized many things from descriptions. We found exactly what we expected to find.'

Sabella was, however, shocked by the Boss's living conditions. 'It was a rustic cottage kept in the most appalling state', she said. 'The standards of hygiene in the kitchen left a lot to be desired – the stove was filthy with baked-on food.' However, a new bathroom had obviously been built on the side of the cottage, with a shower, lavatory and sink, and that was clean.

'He was quite well organized: he had sent his dirty laundry to be washed just about every day, and the freezer was full of meat. There had been a problem with the television, and there were written instructions from his son on how to make it work.'

The police had been instructed to seal off Marino's farmyard and make a thorough and detailed search or the contents of the Boss's last hideout. After the fiasco of Riina's hideout, which the carabinieri had not only failed to search but did not guard, leaving mafiosi free to go in and remove important evidence, it was vital that no such omissions were repeated. It was hoped that the contents of Provenzano's hideout would give important clues as to how he had remained hidden for so long, and over the following days an exhaustive inventory was made, of everything from thirty rolls of Sellotape to incontinence pads for his prostate problem. Outside the cottage two handguns were found hidden under a large stone. There were bundles of cash, each one counted, tied and systematically labelled with the name of the person it was going to. It was an orderly, centralized financial system. There was a calculator with a bit of cardboard taped to the back giving the conversion rate of old lire to Euros.

In his typewriter there was a letter he was writing to his wife; on one side there were the *pizzini* he had to reply to, on the other, the ones he had already answered. 'He apparently worked with an in-box and out-box, like any normal office worker', remarked Gualtieri. 'Obviously this is how he spent all his days; it was slow and arduous work. He had to answer the letters straight away, otherwise the Mafia machine would grind to a halt.'

Like his colleague, Michele Prestipino found the boss's hideout gratifyingly familiar: 'We had been told by several *pentiti* that Provenzano always carried with him a blue backpack, a sleeping bag and an electronic wand for detecting listening devices', he said. 'When we got to the hideout, there they were: the backpack, the sleeping bag, the wand.'

'Everything was arranged for him to stay shut inside', Sabella observed. 'In a way, he was buried alive.'

'He is a peasant at heart. The other bosses, like Brusca, loved buying expensive stuff, they had Rolexes and Ferraris . . . if Provenzano had wanted a Rolex, he could have had one; his followers would have trampled each other to get him one. What he wanted was power.'

From all the stuff he had collected, it appeared Provenzano had been at the cottage for at least a year, and he may not have been planning to stay long. 'I had the impression he was about to leave this place', said Sabella. 'He had a suitcase packed and ready, and he'd written an inventory of everything in it. And there was something in one of the letters from his son, which said: "If you're still there. . .".'

He never managed to move on to the next hiding place. There in the little farm cottage stinking of cheese, cupboards stuffed with someone else's old clothes, bags full of rotting vegetables, the Boss of Bosses, the man who had saved Cosa Nostra from self-destructing, saw his Mafia career brought to a sudden, non-violent end.

Epilogue

SINCE THE PRISON door swung shut behind the Boss of Bosses a series of trials has opened, reopened and gathered pace. At the time of writing, eight trials are currently ongoing.[32] These days Provenzano, for so many years the absent star defendant, attends court proceedings via video link. Sitting in front of a camera in the prison's specially equipped witness room, he endures the tortures of the damned listening to his former friend Nino Giuffré.

Giuffré is led into court, tall and imposing, his grey hair cropped short, his face expressionless. At times it seems as though his infernal punishment will never end: he must keep returning to courtrooms all over the country, answering the same questions again and again. He takes his position behind a hospital screen. From the public benches one can just see a foot punctuating his cadences, tapping rhythmically in a slip-on shoe.

Once the witness is in place, the screen lights up as the video link is activated. The Boss is at his post, sitting at a prison table with the camera trained on him. He answers to confirm his name, but nothing more. Occasionally he makes a phone call to his lawyer, to ask a question or locate a document. Much of the time he takes notes or reads the papers laid out meticulously in front of him. Years of keeping tabs on many complex deals have given him the habit of fastidious note-taking.

Who knew Giuffré could talk so much? *Manuzza*, with his crippled hand, so hard-faced, taciturn and closed – when did he get so chatty? In a low growl, full of deference to the prosecutors and the judges, reserving his withering scorn for Provenzano's lawyers, Giuffré talks and talks. He asks permission to embark on digressions to explain the meaning of some incident or to express his judgement on a particular individual. Sometimes even the judge wishes he would shut up and begs the prosecutor to stop him. 'Do please interrupt the collaborator when you can see he is setting off on a tangent that doesn't concern us.' At times he seems to enjoy retelling the more extreme episodes of his life in crime, beginning long parentheses with phrases like 'One fine day . . .'. When he finishes his answers, he gives a courteous signal: 'Prego'. Next question. Ask me anything. Provenzano, framed on the screen mounted over the judges' table, takes notes, ponders and reads his legal papers. Occasionally, when the litany of betrayal gets too much, he gets up in disgust and walks out of shot. He would rather sit in his cell than listen to this.

Since his arrest Provenzano has admitted little more than his name. Much about his long period in hiding is still a mystery. The contents of his last refuge were exhaustively catalogued ('One plastic fly swat with metal handle. One small white plastic plug for a handbasin, attached to a metal chain. One set of bathroom scales. One transparent container with lid labelled Nestlé containing foul-smelling vegetables . . .'). They revealed his lifestyle, his tastes, his health and sanitary problems, his religion, musical tastes, preferred brand of toothpaste, mania for writing things down. They did not reveal one detail about his business affairs, or about the political connections that had kept him out of gaol for so long.

Conspiracy theorists claimed Provenzano had been expecting the police any day, and that he had made sure to dispose of any important document. The supergrass Tommaso Buscetta, who died in April 2000, had a theory that for Provenzano to survive the years of Riina's bloody assault on the rest of the world he must have had a powerful protector. The anti-Mafia chief Pietro Grasso believes that the Boss was protected not by one individual politician but by an entire system, from the grassroots to the height of political influence, colluding with Cosa Nostra. The acquittal of the two carabinieri who had failed to search Riina's hideout brought us no closer to the truth about who was protecting the Mafia's secrets.

According to some, renewed negotiations between the Mafia and certain authorities may well have begun in 2001. Assistant prosecutor

Alfonso Sabella was at the ministry of justice. 'There were strange things going on among the prisoners. One of the more senior Mafia figures had volunteered for a cleaning job that gave him access to different floors. Now no mafioso of this man's rank would have taken a cleaning job, out of principle. It would have been beneath him. So it was clear to me that something was going on. I realized there was a negotiation in progress, and I wrote a report to that effect.

'As soon as I delivered my memo, the very next day, my office at the ministry was closed, and I lost my job.'

Provenzano still has some power: he is master of his secrets. Every request he granted, every recommendation for an employee or a polit-ical candidate, every guarantee he made, is logged somewhere. Up to now his lawyers have played down his role in the last two decades of Mafia history, but like his first master, Luciano Liggio, he may end up dragging others down with him.

Prosecutors suspect that, like Liggio, Provenzano has successfully hidden his fortune behind a complex trail of foreign investments and property deals, private health companies and shares in construction companies. After Riina's arrest, land and assets worth £200 million were confiscated in the first couple of years. Nothing like that amount has been traced to Provenzano. Eighteen months after the arrest the authorities seized properties in the tourist resort of San Vito Lo Capo to the value of €1 million.

However, the state is exacting its meticulous revenge. When mag-istrates asked Provenzano if he was married, he replied, 'In my heart'. He would like to be married on paper too – but the terms of his incar-ceration are harsh: he may receive visitors only behind a Perspex screen, and if he wanted to get married, that screen would stand between him and Saveria. They would not be able to touch or kiss. It is inhuman, they insist, but so far the authorities have not relented: the law denies any expression of human tenderness to convicted mafiosi. The authorities may decide that Bernardo Provenzano and his long-time companion have already enjoyed enough privileges.

Saveria clearly longs to be married to her man. When a friend recently told her she was marrying the father of her children, Saveria said she was very happy for her. The friend said she wasn't that hung up on the idea of marriage, after all these years. Saveria took her friend's hand in hers, and gave her an earnest look. 'If you can do it,' she said solemnly, 'you should.'

Provenzano's health is not improving; he's receiving hormone treatment, but according to his lawyer, his thyroid is swelling and he's increasingly uncomfortable. His state of health is not improved by his fastidious temperament and having hours of the day to worry about his physical symptoms, as is his wont, with nothing to distract him. He recently wrote to his lawyer complaining that he felt the doctors had 'abandoned him'. He is not allowed a typewriter and takes a long time to write by hand, so his deeply ingrained epistolary habits of the last decade have been effectively denied him.

Saveria's letters take a month to arrive, and each one is opened, read and censored. Lawyers and clients who want to have face-to-face meetings must submit to invasive body searches before and after the meetings. Even with his incontinence problems, Provenzano is not allowed to keep more than one spare pair of trousers in his cell. Although prison conditions are grim, he does not complain. According to his legal team, he suffers in silence, but they can tell. Some weeks he has two or more court appearances, in trials for crimes that date as far back as 1969. It is scarcely surprising he sometimes gets confused.

His sons, Angelo and Paolo, can breathe a bit easier now their father's in prison; they don't have to worry about his health or answer his incessant demands. Once a month they accompany their mother on the ferry to Genoa, then the long drive to the prison for the visiting hour. Saveria has spent so long confined to a small area that she can't cope with these gruelling trips alone. Then, as soon as they had got the routine of the trip to Umbria down pat, their father was moved to Novara.

Paolo, who seemed to have made his escape from Corleone, has come back from Germany, having lost his college job. Pressure from the media was extremely embarrassing for a young man hired to improve the image of Italians abroad. The college authorities were understanding, but Paolo did not want to put them under that sort of strain and packed his bags. He is currently looking at courses to get some other qualification.

The two brothers gave their first interview, to the BBC, in 2007, in which they were filmed in their lawyer's office in Palermo. Speaking on camera for the first time, they seemed very tense, staring, presumably as instructed, fixedly at their lawyer, the exuberant Rosalba de Gregorio. Angelo was fiddling nervously, entwining his delicate fingers around each other and smoking. Physically he is much lighter than his brother, with chestnut hair, like his father, and the same green eyes and glasses. His expression changes from laughter to deadly seriousness in a moment, and, like his brother, his emotions seem very close to the surface. Paolo is taller, a little heavier and dark, with brown eyes and thick, curly black hair. They talked in bursts, as though they have so much to say that they will never let out.

'Physically he's not doing too badly', Angelo says in response to the lawyer's question.

'He is a bit better,' Paolo goes on, 'but he's still disoriented. He's going to need a bit of time to get used to being in solitary. The only people he talks to are the guards, so you can imagine . . .

'He got the bag of laundry OK this time, but there's still a problem with sending him books.'

Asked about his relationship with his father, Angelo said he had given him sound advice such as 'Get up early in the morning,' and 'Do unto others as you would like them to do unto you.'

'They may be small phrases, but they are the things that stay with you for your whole life.'

Paolo spoke up. 'I can't say that my memories of my father correspond in any way with what the papers or the police say about him.'

On the subject of their father's guilt the two men seem to have no way of grasping what he may have done. They make it clear they could never accept the evidence, as that would mean they would have to judge him, and this they would never do. 'I don't believe, I don't want to believe any of it, in the sense that he is my father, and he is a man', says Angelo. 'He may have made mistakes. He may have made choices that I know nothing about. But that is basically his business, those are his choices. As far as I'm concerned, he will always be my father.'

'Everyone who says he is the godfather of Cosa Nostra has to accept that there are many godfathers', Paolo says, doing his best to minimize his father's reputation. 'If you take one out, another one pops up. There's always another one coming along.'

The brothers may have decided it is time they did a little positive PR. After years of being left out of any Mafia inquiry, in 2007 Angelo's name came up in an investigation into protection rackets. Police taping conversations between a Palermo capo and one of his men heard them discussing how a victim of extortion said he was going to appeal to Angelo for help. Palermo's chief prosecutor was quick to announce that Angelo would not be subject to a criminal investigation, but clearly he needs to do more than simply lead a law-abiding life. Giovanni Impastato, whose brother was murdered for campaigning against the Mafia (of which their father was a member), believes the Provenzano boys should publicly renounce Cosa Nostra.

Will Angelo ever make a clean break from his father? Historian Salvatore Lupo says, 'Any boss who has accumulated enough capital can get away and make a new start somewhere far away. In another country his sons can become part of the middle classes like anyone else. But if he doesn't move away, the Mafia is always ready to pull him back in.'

Provenzano's careful stalling and sustained negotiation had avoided a war between the Palermo clans led by Salvatore Lo Piccolo and Nino Rotolo, but after his arrest there was a very real danger that the conflict could be re-ignited in a contest for the leadership of Cosa Nostra. But in June 2006, in an operation code-named Gotha (Ruling Class), Rotolo and several of his closest supporters were arrested.

Once Rotolo was behind bars, the American *scappati* - members of the Inzerillo family driven into exile in the 1980s - met no further opposition to their return. At the point Salvatore Lo Piccolo was considered to be the boss, and still faithful to Bernardo Provenzano. Investigators believed he and his son were rebuilding the transatlantic partnership that created a massive international heroin trade. There are those who believe the Inzerillos are planning to take revenge on the Corleonesi.

'There was a battle for power in which one side was cut out, almost eliminated, and now the heirs of those people are coming back', says Lupo. 'It's possible that the power struggle will start again.

'This conflict was not resolved in the usual way. In most circumstances, if there is a conflict, it explodes in violence, then the two sides come to terms. But this was different: it involved the annihilation of one side. We haven't figured out why, and we have yet to see how the whole story turns out. There's a group of mafiosi today who are very worried about the return of the Inzerillos, that they might take their revenge – which is unusual, because the Mafia in general is nothing if not pragmatic, and long violent feuds are disadvantageous in every way. There has to be a reason why this violent conflict is impossible to resolve.'

Another insider says: 'If they don't stop the *scappati* coming back, there's going to be another war. We live in very dangerous times. One side could be planning another massive crime against the state, to prove their strength.' But before any massive crime could be carried out, police raided a farmhouse near Palermo and arrested Salvatore Lo Piccolo and his son. 'I love you Dad!' called out Sandro as they were bundled into squad cars.

In Lo Piccolo's hideout police found a letter saying, 'Uncle [Provenzano] agreed we should let them [the *scappati*] come back because that way we'd be in a much better position to see what they were up to.'

The capture of a Mafia boss does not mean the Mafia is defeated – or even that *he* is defeated. Lirio Abbate, reporter for the ANSA news agency in Palermo and author of a book on Bernardo Provenzano's accomplices, was recently given police protection and left Palermo in a hurry. Police investigating the Brancaccio clan had listening devices planted in a mafioso's house. While monitoring their conversations, they heard detailed discussions of Abbate's movements and habits that could only mean Cosa Nostra was planning to kill him.

One of the first public figures to express support for the journalist was the president of the region, Salvatore Cuffaro, who at the time was on trial. After he was sentenced to five years for revealing official secrets, Cuffaro refused to step down until public protests and political pressure forced him to reisign.

Although Provenzano is in solitary confinement, with limited access to a very few individuals, others are still working on his behalf. In September 2007 Giuseppe Lipari, Provenzano's consigliere and front man for many of his investments, was arrested, accused of Mafia association, after arranging the sale of property worth €3 million belonging to Provenzano. The magistrates claimed that Lipari's work as business manager for Cosa Nostra had gone on uninterrupted for over twenty years.

Lipari had been released just two days after Provenzano's arrest and had set to work straight away, trying to convert some of the Boss's extensive property holdings into hard cash. On the day of his arrest officials confiscated papers, letters and notes from Provenzano's cell in the Novara maximum-security prison, hoping to find documents relating to the sale. The former Boss, always an assiduous note-taker, would have accumulated a mass of paperwork to while away the hours in solitary confinement and will be quite bereft without it.

While there has been unprecedented international interest in Bernardo Provenzano's arrest, it remains to be seen if anything has really changed. Grasso says that the culture in Sicily, even in Corleone, is changing. He claims that with Provenzano a figure of fear and oppression has been removed, and points to the fact that many young people from the Corleone area have been applying to work in farming co-operatives on land confiscated from the Mafia. 'This means that Provenzano, while he was outside prison, inspired fear – not direct intimidation but an underlying fear that prevented them setting foot on Mafia property.'

On a hot July day in 2007 a bus load of Tuscan youths from a church group arrived in Corleone, full of excitement about spending time in the capital of organized crime. They had come to work for a fortnight in the fields and vineyards confiscated from the Mafia and to meet young people from the legendary Italian crime capital. They were full of missionary zeal, hoping to befriend young people from this benighted land and make a difference by offering solidarity.

They were staying in what used to be the Provenzano family home, a simple three-storey house where Provenzano's mother lived until her death a few years ago. The house had been confiscated and turned over to a church group. While the students unpacked and talked excit-edly about their expectations, Provenzano's brother Salvatore drove up in his Fiat Panda and demanded that the Tuscan driver move his minibus. 'I park here, it's my right', the old man muttered, and walked past the chattering students, heading for his house at the corner.

Grasso's optimism may have been premature: one of the organizers of the youth group revealed that some of the vineyards confiscated from mafiosi had been expertly vandalized by an unknown hand. But Grasso is determined to stay positive: 'We must continue to hope, to give the impression that we believe in what we're doing', he says. 'We must show that we believe in this fight, which is the fight not just against organized crime, but for freedom, for the democratic future of a people that has been oppressed by the Mafia. We have got Provenzano, but when you cut off the lizard's tail, it grows another one.'

In December 2007 Provenzano's security status was increased after the authorities discovered that he had been communicating with other mafiosi inside the prison. Conditions in the maximum-security were already harsh, but the governor is taking no chances. Provenzano was banned for six months from further communication with the outside world and deprived of his television and radio. Signs that he was man-aging to get messages to Mafia associates were described as 'exceed-ingly alarming': they indicated that, with all the deprivations inflicted by several life sentences, Bernardo Provenzano is still the Boss of Bosses.

Sources and notes

For each chapter the reader will find here the main sources, and also end-notes where relevant or possibly of interest.

Introduction

My main sources on the last stages of the investigation leading up to the arrest of Provenzano were interviews with police chief Giuseppe Gualtieri, now based in Trapani but formerly head of the Palermo flying squad, and with one of his agents, code-named Bloodhound.

Much of my information for this chapter came from interviews with the following: assistant prosecutor Michele Prestipino, the driving force behind several investigations into Provenzano and his supporters, who was inter-viewed in Palermo; chief anti-Mafia prosecutor Pietro Grasso, now based in Rome but formerly chief prosecutor in Palermo; Alfonso Sabella, formerly assistant anti-Mafia prosecutor in Palermo; Marzia Sabella, currently assistant prosecutor in Palermo; General Angiolo Pellegrini, a long-serving officer with the carabinieri, now retired; and historian Salvatore Lupo, who teaches at Palermo University, author of the definitive *History of the Mafia*.

The testimony of Nino Giuffré, Provenzano's associate and former friend, provided the basis of this book. The witness statements reproduced in this chapter are from: the trial of Provenzano's alleged moles, known as 'Talpe' (Michele Aiello and others), delivered on 8 March 2005; the trial of Provenzano's supporters, Grande Mandamento, delivered on 9 February 2007; and the trial of Giuseppe Biondolillo and others, dated 16 October 2002.

I have also drawn on the following books: *Il gioco grande*, by Giuseppe Lo Bianco and Sandra Rizza, an account of the conspiracy theories behind Provenzano's career and his arrest; and *Il codice Provenzano*, by Michele

Prestipino and Salvo Palazzolo, based on the letters between Provenzano and his men. *Bernardo Provenzano, il ragioniere di Cosa Nostra*, by Salvo Palazzolo and Ernesto Oliva, contains a prologue by Umberto Santino, director of the Centro Siciliano di Documentazione Giuseppe Impastato, which lays bare the myths surrounding Provenzano's status.

1 Saverio Lodato, *Trent' anni di Mafia*, p. 558. Camilleri has since published a book based on Provenzano's *pizzini*, called *Voi non sapete* (Mondadori, Milan, 2007).
2 *La Repubblica* (31 March 2006).
3 Michele Prestipino and Salvo Palazzolo, *Il codice Provenzano*.

Chapter 1: Corleone bandits

The most useful historical document of this period is *Michele Navarra e la Mafia del Corleonese*, by Carlo Alberto Dalla Chiesa, a report on the criminal activities of Liggio and his clan, detailing the violent feud between Navarra and Liggio.

Legal documents

Tribunale di Palermo, sentence in the trial of Marcello dell'Utri and Gaetano Cinà, 11 December 2004.

Corte d'appello di Bari, sentence against Luciano Liggio and others, 24 September 1970.

I also draw on the following books: *Nel segno della Mafia*, by Marco Nese, a colourful biography of Luciano Liggio; *Excellent Cadavers*, by journalist Alessandro Stille, which gives a vivid account of the Corleonesi's rise to power; *Bernardo Provenzano: il ragioniere di Cosa Nostra*, by Salvo Palazzolo and Ernesto Oliva, which uncovers some extraordinary documentation of Provenzano's early career; *Il codice Provenzano*, by Michele Prestipino and Salvo Palazzolo; and *Gli uomini del disonore*, by Nino Calderone with Pino Arlacchi, which gives a vivid account of Provenzano and Riina's early careers.

4 Pino Arlacchi, *Gli uomini del disonore*. The *pentito* was Catania boss Nino Calderone.

5   Salvatore Lupo, *Storia della Mafia*, p. 201.
6   Ibid., p. 205. The mafioso was Rosario di Maggio.

Chapter 2: Palermo ambitions

The greatest documents of the historic 'maxi-trial' of 1986–7 are: *L'atto d'accusa dei giudici di Palermo*, edited by Corrado Stajano, a synthesis of the case against the more than 400 mafiosi; and *Excellent Cadavers*, by Alessandro Stille, which gives the inside story of the investigations leading up to the trial. *Mafia Business*, by Pino Arlacchi, builds up a picture of how Cosa Nostra constructed its financial empire.

This chapter draws on author interviews with the historian Salvatore Lupo, assistant prosecutor Alfonso Sabella and chief anti-Mafia prosecutor Pietro Grasso.

I also draw on the following: John Dickie, *Cosa Nostra*; Saverio Lodato, *Trent' anni di Mafia*; Salvatore Lupo, *Storia della Mafia*; Michele Prestipino and Salvo Palazzolo, *Il codice Provenzano*; Lirio Abbate and Peter Gomez, *I complici*; Giovanni Brusca, interviewed by Saverio Lodato, *Ho ucciso Giovanni Falcone*; and Salvo Palazzolo and Ernesto Oliva, *Bernardo Provenzano: il ragioniere di Cosa Nostra*.

7   Tullio Pironti, *La vera storia d'Italia*, p. 833. The collaborator was Dr Gioacchino Pennino.
8   Michele Prestipino and Salvo Palazzolo, *Il codice Provenzano*, p. 68. The mafioso was Carmelo Amato.
9   Sentence against Marcello dell' Utri. The collaborator was Altofonte boss Francesco Di Carlo.
10 Alessandro Stille, *Excellent Cadavers*, p. 82. The insider was the drug trafficker Bou Ghebel Ghassan, who was arrested for providing morphine base to the Greco family.

Chapter 3: Love and title deeds

Background descriptions of the Palazzolo family status in Cinisi are based on an author interview with Giovanni Impastato, who grew up with a mafioso father.

Palazzolo and Oliva, *Bernardo Provenzano: il ragioniere di Cosa Nostra*, gives a detailed account of how Provenzano built up an illegal empire using front-men and -women to cover his tracks. Also useful for background was Enrico Bellavia and Silvana Mazzocchi, *Iddu*. The position and status of women is described in: Liliana Madeo, *Donne di Mafia*, Teresa Principato and Alessandra Dino, *Mafia Donna*; and Clare Longrigg, *Mafia Women* (Chatto & Windus, London, 1997).

Legal documents

Tribunale di Palermo, testimony of Giovanni Brusca in the trial of Simone Castello and others, 12 December 2000.

Report by the Partinico company of carabinieri, 27 November 1983, in the trial of Bernardo Provenzano and eighteen others.

Tribunale di Palermo, fifth session, evidence admitted in the trial of Filippa La Fiura, Saveria Palazzolo and others. The sentence was given on 18 December 1990.

11   Ordinanza di custodia cautelare emessa dal gip di Palermo nell' ambito dell' inchiesta Grande Oriente, 6 November 1998.

Chapter 4: Bagheria's feudal lord

Much of the detailed information on Provenzano's business dealings comes from an interview with General Angiolo Pellegrini, who investigated Provenzano's activities in the early 1980s. Another rich source on the early days in Bagheria was the testimony of Nino Giuffré in the trial of Giuseppe Biondolillo and others, before the court of Termini Imerese (temporarily relocated to Padua's maximum-security facility), 16 October 2002.

Legal documents

Procura di Palermo, deposition of the collaborator Angelo Siino, known as the Mafia's 'minister of works', 10 June 1998.

Report on the collaboration between mafioso Gino Ilardo and Colonel Michele Riccio of the carabinieri special organized crime division (Raggruppamento Operativo Speciale, or ROS), Rome, 30 July 1996.

Tribunale di Palermo: examination of Nino Giuffré in the trial of Michele Aiello and others known as Talpe ('Moles'), Milan, 8–9 March 2005.

Tribunale di Palermo: judicial report no 3033/16 1983 in the case of Gariffo Carmelo and twenty-nine others.

Also cited are: Palazzolo and Oliva, *Bernardo Provenzano: il ragioniere di Cosa Nostra*; Prestipino and Palazzolo, *Il codice Provenzano*; and Stille, *Excellent Cadavers*.

12 This description was given by the collaborator Gino Ilardo to Colonel Michele Riccio of the carabinieri special organized crime division.

Chapter 5: The split

My most valuable source for this and the following chapter is assistant prosecutor Alfonso Sabella, who was at the centre of an extraordinary series of investigations in Palermo throughout the 1990s. Sabella was instrumental in the collaboration of Giovanni Brusca, whose testimony in the trial of Simone Castello and five others, dated 12 December 2000, is the other principal source.

Legal documents

Also important is Nino Giuffré's testimony in the trial of Giuseppe Biondolillo and others, before the court of Termini Imerese, 16 October 2002.

The Mafia collaborator Salvatore Cancemi's testimony was reported in the arrest warrants for those responsible for the murder of judge Falcone, his wife and escort, issued by the Procura distrettuale antimafia di Caltanissetta.

Trial of Simone Castello and five others, Tribunale di Palermo, deposition of Salvatore Barbagallo, 11 December 2000.

The extraordinary revelations of supergrass Tommaso Buscetta are contained in *La Mafia ha vinto*, by Sicilian journalist Saverio Lodato. Other revelations by collaborators about the relationship between Riina and Provenzano are contained in: Palazzolo and Oliva, *Bernardo Provenzano: il ragioniere di Cosa Nostra*; Giovanni Brusca, interviewed by Saverio Lodato, *Ho ucciso Giovanni*

Falcone; Alessandro Stille, *Excellent Cadavers*; Sandra Rizza and Giuseppe Lo Bianco, *Il gioco grande*; Lirio Abbate and Peter Gomez, *I complici*; and Prestipino and Palazzolo, *Il codice Provenzano*.

13 Carnevale was suspended for five years, but was eventually acquitted of any wrongdoing.
14 Prestipino and Palazzolo, *Il codice Provenzano*, p. 138. The mafioso was Ino Corso.
15 Trial of Simone Castello and five others, Tribunale di Palermo. The mafioso was Salvatore Barbagallo.

Chapter 6: Family matters

The details of Saveria Palazzolo's move to Corleone, and her life there, are based on author interviews with the former mayor of Corleone, Pippo Cipriani, and with Provenzano's lawyers past and present, as well as police on surveillance duty. I have also drawn on details contained in Palazzolo and Oliva, *Bernardo Provenzano: il ragioniere di Cosa Nostra*.

Provenzano's sons spoke to the BBC in an interview broadcast in September 2007 (*The Real Godfather*). Details of Provenzano's sons' lives, and their conversations secretly recorded by the police, are reported in Abbate and Gomez, *I complici*.

Giovanni Brusca and Tommaso Buscetta's interpretations of the family's return to Corleone are contained in Saverio Lodato's interviews (*Ho ucciso Giovanni Falcone* and *La Mafia ha vinto*).

Lipari's correspondence with Provenzano about his sons' careers is taken from Palazzolo and Bellavia, *Voglia di Mafia* (Carocci, Rome, 2005).

The full story of Provenzano's consigliere Pino Lipari and his unfortunate family is given in Prestipino and Palazzolo, *Il codice Provenzano*. The story of the Provenzano family Christmas in Germany is drawn from an account in Enrico Bellavia and Silvana Mazzocchi, *Iddu*. Further details of the mafiosi's disaffection with Riina's excesses are contained in Alessandro Stille, *Excellent Cadavers*.

16 *L'Espresso* (22 June 2000).
17 Letter from Lipari to Bernardo Provenzano, cited in Abbate and Gomez, *I complici*, p. 282.
18 Conversation between Angelo and Paolo Francesco recorded by police investigators on 28 September 2005, quoted in Abbate and Gomez, *I complici*.

Chapter 7: Goodbye Totò

The analysis and background of Provenzano's position in the lead-up to the murder of judge Falcone are based on an author interview with assistant prosecutor Nino Di Matteo in Palermo. The account of the plot to murder the anti-Mafia prosecutor Pietro Grasso is based on an author interview with Dr Grasso.

Much of the description of the dynamic between Riina and Provenzano in the lead-up to Riina's arrest, including the detail of meetings to discuss strategy, comes from the testimony of Nino Giuffré. This chapter draws on testimony given on 14 May 2003 to the judges of the Palermo court of assizes, during the trial, named 'Golden Market', of Riina and members of the commission of Cosa Nostra. Giuffré also described the threat Falcone's investigations posed to Cosa Nostra.

Giovanni Brusca's views on Provenzano's role before the assassination of judge Falcone are taken from his interview with Saverio Lodato (*Io ho ucciso Giovanni Falcone*). Lodato's book *Trent' anni di Mafia* contains Brusca's account of Riina's alleged negotiations with the authorities. The analysis by former Palermo boss and supergrass Tommaso Buscetta comes from Lodato's interview (*La Mafia ha vinto*).

The collaborator Angelo Siino's description of the events leading up to judge Borsellino's death was given in the trial of his alleged killers, September 1998.

Excellent Cadavers, by Alessandro Stille, details the mounting corruption scandals that contributed to the death of the first Italian Republic, and the disaffection of senior Mafia figures with Riina's violent strategy. Stille also reports the Mafia's threats against politicians.

This version of the alleged 'negotiations' between Mori and Cosa Nostra is based on the motivation for the sentence for the 1993 bombings, Tribunale di Firenze, and on an interview with assistant prosecutor Antonio Ingroia. I also draw on the account in *Il gioco grande*, by Sandra Rizza and Giuseppe Lo Bianco. Anti-Mafia chief Pietro Grasso's views about Riina's strategy are reported in the same book.

Provenzano's line about putting his hands up to stop Lima banging his head is quoted in *I complici*, by Lirio Abbate and Peter Gomez. Giusy Vitale's testimony about the extraordinary meeting of Mafia capos was reported in *La Repubblica* (19 November 2005).

19 Liliana Ferrara, who worked with Falcone at the Ministry of Justice and took his job after his death, quoted in Stille, *Excellent Cadavers*, p. 350.

Chapter 8: The regent

Much of the material in this chapter is drawn from an author interview with assistant prosecutor Alfonso Sabella, who conducted a series of successful investigations against the Corleonesi during this period.

Brusca's accounts of the meetings and political manoeuvring that followed Riina's arrest are based on his testimony in the trial of Simone Castello and others, Tribunale di Palermo, 12 December 2000, and on his interview with Saverio Lodato (*Ho ucciso Giovanni Falcone*).

I have drawn heavily on Nino Giuffré's sensational testimony in the trial of Giuseppe Biondolillo and others, Tribunale di Termini Imerese, 16 October 2002. Mafia plots to blow up monuments, and to poison and maim ordinary people, were revealed by the *pentito* Vincenzo di Sinacori testifying in the trial of the 1993 bombers, in Florence. John Dickie, *Cosa Nostra*, gives an account of the bombings on the mainland in 1993.

The account of Vincenzina Marchese's tragic end is recounted in Teresa Principato and Alessandra Dino, *Mafia donna*, and Clare Longrigg, *Mafia Women*. The account of the war between the Di Peris and the Montaltos is based on the author interview with Alfonso Sabella, and is also described in Prestipino and Palazzolo, *Il codice Provenzano*.

20 Alfonso Sabella heard this account direct from Brusca.
21 The *pentito* Salvatore Cancemi quoted Riina's order.
22 Teresa Principato and Alessandra Dino, *Mafia donna*, p. 86. Bagarella's driver and friend Tony Calvaruso later testified about this whole period.

Chapter 9: A new strategy

The main source of this chapter is the report on the collaboration between the mafioso Gino Ilardo and Colonel Michele Riccio of the carabinieri special organized crime division (Raggruppamento Operativo Speciale or ROS), Rome 30 July 1996, filed in the Grande Oriente investigation. This report contains Riccio's account of the fateful meeting at the farmhouse near the Mezzojuso junction in 1995.

Other legal documents

Arrest warrant in the trial of Bernardo Provenzano and his aides, known as Grande Mandamento, issued 5 October 2004, Tribunale di Palermo.

Nino Giuffré's testimony in the trial of Giuseppe Biondolillo and others, Tribunale di Termini Imerese, 16 October 2002.

Trial of Simone Castello and five others, Tribunale di Palermo, deposition of Salvatore Barbagallo, 11 December 2000.

Testimony of Giovanni Brusca in the trial of Simone Castello and others, Tribunale di Palermo, 12 December 2000.

The major source on Provenzano's strategy is an author interview with assistant prosecutor Nino Di Matteo, Palermo. Also useful were *Iddu*, by Enrico Bellavia and Silvana Mazzocchi, and *Bernardo Provenzano: il ragioniere di Cosa Nostra*, by Salvo Palazzolo and Ernesto Oliva. I also draw on news stories from ANSA and *La Repubblica*.

23 *Il fantasma di Corleone*, TV documentary directed by Marco Amenta, 2006. Riccio himself was subsequently convicted of colluding in a drugs operation and is now in prison.

Chapter 10: A management handbook for the aspiring Mafia boss

This chapter is based largely on the letters from Provenzano to his lieutenants. Some of these letters were explained by Giuffré and admitted as evidence in the trial known as Grande Mandamento, Milan, 8–9 February 2007. Prestipino and Palazzolo, *Il codice Provenzano*, offers a valuable interpretation of the letters between Provenzano and his closest advisers. Lipari's letters to Provenzano are filed with the investigation into Lipari's role, Tribunale di Palermo.

Other letters are contained in the report on the collaboration between the *mafioso* Gino Ilardo and Colonel Michele Riccio of the carabinieri special organized crime division (Raggruppamento Operativo Speciale or ROS), Rome, 30 July 1996. The letter to Salvatore Genovese is filed with the Grande Oriente investigation, Tribunale di Palermo.

Salvo Palazzolo and Ernesto Oliva, *Bernardo Provenzano: il ragioniere di Cosa Nostra*, offers a fascinating account of Provenzano's new strategy. Another account of Provenzano's *modus operandi* is contained in the testimony of the collaborator Nino Giuffré, reported in the arrest warrant for Angelo

Tolentino and forty-nine others, operation Grande Mandamento, Tribunale di Palermo, 2004. For more detail on Provenzano's leadership style and tactics I have also drawn on Nino Giuffré's testimony in the trial of Giuseppe Biondolillo and others, 16 October 2002.

Provenzano's security preoccupation was described in the testimony of Nino Giuffré in the Talpe or 'Moles' trial (Michele Aiello and others), Tribunale di Palermo, 8 March 2005. Letters demonstrating Provenzano's humble rhetoric are contained in the testimony of Nino Giuffré, trial of Salvatore Umina and others, application for arrest warrant, Tribunale di Palermo.

Provenzano's leadership strategy was discussed in author interviews with anti-Mafia chief Pietro Grasso in Rome, assistant prosecutor Nino Di Matteo in Palermo, and with assistant prosecutor Michele Prestipino, who has worked closely on Nino Giuffré's collaboration, basing much of his prosecutorial work on the *pizzini*. Provenzano's revolutionary use of pen and paper to communicate with his captains was described in an author interview with carabinieri general Angiolo Pellegrini, Rome.

Provenzano's extreme caution was described in the testimony of Giovanni Brusca in the trial of Castello Simone and five others, Tribunale di Palermo, and in Giovanni Brusca, interviewed by Saverio Lodato, *Ho ucciso Giovanni Falcone*. Teresa Principato and Alessandra Dino, *Mafia Donna*, contains an illuminating account of the mafioso's religion.

Salvo Lima's attitude to Cosa Nostra was revealed in Siino's testimony to the trial of former prime minister Giulio Andreotti, reported by ANSA on 18 December 1997.

24 Thus Villabate boss Nicola Mandalà explained Provenzano's orders to his friend Francesco Campanella (*Il codice Provenzano*, p. 214).
25 The murder of Salvatore Geraci is described in detail in the arrest warrant in the Grande Mandamento investigation.

Chapter 11: Politics for Pragmatists

The substance of the alleged support for Forza Italia by Provenzano and Cosa Nostra families across Sicily is contained in the sentence against Marcello dell'Utri and Gaetano Cinà, in a chapter titled. 'La stagione politica', Tribunale di Palermo, December 2004. These allegations are substantially repeated and expanded in the testimony of Nino Giuffré in the 'Talpe' trial

(Michele Aiello and others), Milan, 8 March 2005, and in the arrest warrant for Onofrio Morreale, as well as in the trial named Grande Mandamento, Milan, 9 February 2007.

Accounts of meetings and alleged promises are based on the report on the collaboration between the mafioso Gino Ilardo and Colonel Michele Riccio of the carabinieri special organized crime division (Raggruppamento Operativo Speciale or ROS), Rome, 30 July 1996.

The most comprehensive work on the collaboration between politicians and Cosa Nostra is contained in Lirio Abbate and Peter Gomez, *I complici*. The account of the corruption behind the development of the commercial centre in Villabate is based on an author interview with Nino Di Matteo, Palermo, as well as details in *I complici*, as above.

The Sicilian separatist movement is described in Sandra Rizza and Giuseppe Lo Bianco, *Il gioco grande*. Giuffré's sensational revelations about meetings with representatives of Forza Italia were reported in *La Repubblica* (4 December 2002). Alessandro Stille, *Excellent Cadavers*, describes the way Cosa Nostra replaced 'tame' politicians with their own people. The descriptions of Mandalà's indiscretions are based on Prestipino and Palazzolo, *Il codice Provenzano*. The Sicilian public health crisis was reported in *The Guardian* (1 January 2007).

26 Sentence against dell'Utri. The speaker was the mafioso Gaetano Cinà.
27 Ibid. The collaborator was Salvatore Cucuzza.
28 Alessandro Stille, *Excellent Cadavers*, p. 315. The magistrate was Francesco Misiani.

Chapter 12: Treacherous friends

The account of Spera's arrest is based on an author interview with police agent Bloodhound, who was one of the arresting officers. The search of the surrounding area was discussed in an interview with General Angiolo Pellegrini.

Tolentino and Episcopo's conversations, recorded by the police, are reported in Enrico Bellavia and Silvana Mazzocchi, *Iddu*.

The battle for control of Belmonte Mezzagno is described in Prestipino and Palazzolo, *Il codice Provenzano*, and in Palazzolo and Oliva, *Bernardo*

Provenzano: il ragionere di Cosa Nostra. Prestipino and Palazzolo also give an account of the battle for Agrigento.

Legal documents

Testimony of Nino Giuffré, in the Grande Mandamento trial, Milan, 8–9 February 2007.

Testimony of Nino Giuffré, 'Talpe' trial (Michele Aiello and others) Milan, 8 March 2005.

Letter from Provenzano admitted in evidence in the trial of Bernardo Provenzano and others, Milan, 10 February 2007.

Letter from Provenzano to Brusca filed with Grande Oriente investigation, Tribunale di Palermo.

Press reports

Interview with Simone Provenzano in *L'Espresso* magazine (22 June 2000). *La Stampa* (1 February 2001).

Chapter 13: Letters home

The letters from Saveria to her husband, and from Angelo and Paolo Provenzano to their father, were confiscated during the arrest of Benedetto Spera and filed with prosecution papers in Palermo (corte di assise di Palermo, processo contro Benedetto Spera ed altri).

The account of the relationship between Provenzano and his family members is based on an author interview with police chief Giuseppe Gualtieri, Trapani. Angelo Provenzano was interviewed by a reporter from the ANSA news agency, 31 May 2002.

The account of life in Corleone is based on an author interview with Pippo Cipriani, former mayor of Corleone.

Legal documents containing background on the families include Giuffré's testimony in the Grande Mandamento trial, 8–9 February 2007. The police interception of Salvo Riina's conversation is transcribed in the Richiesta per l'applicazione di misure cautelari nei confronti di Riina Giuseppe Salvatore ed altri, DDA Palermo.

Accounts of the Provenzano family's life were given in *La Repubblica* (23 June 1996, 13 December 2000, 14 February 2001).

Analyses of family life are contained in Tommaso Buscetta, interviewed by Saverio Lodato, *La mafia ha vinto*, and Teresa Principato and Alessandra Dino, *Mafia donna*. Provenzano's letter to Brusca is filed with the Grande Oriente investigation, Palermo.

29 Ninetta Bagarella's letter was reproduced in full in *La Repubblica* (23 June 1996).
30 Giovanni Impastato, brother of the murdered anti-Mafia campaigner Giuseppe Impastato, wrote an open letter to Provenzano's sons after the boss's arrest, asking them to disown the Mafia, published in *L'Unità* (19 April 2006).

Chapter 14: Spies and leaks

The events described in this chapter are based on Giuffré's testimony and letters from Provenzano submitted as evidence in the 'Talpe' trial of Michele Aiello and others, Tribunale di Palermo, 8–9 March 2005. The memorandum of the chief prosecutor in the same trial was also very useful.

I draw extensively on Nino Giuffré's testimony in the trial of Giuseppe Biondolillo and others, Tribunale di Termini Imerese, 16 October 2002. The descriptions of Provenzano's secret meetings and security measures come from Giuffré's testimony in the trial of Carmelo Umina and others, Tribunale di Palermo, and from the introduction to the arrest warrant in the trial of Bernardo Provenzano and others (Grande Mandamento), Tribunale di Palermo. From the same document I draw on the chapter on 'The Position of Benedetto Spera and Bernardo Provenzano'.

The police's near-miss with Provenzano is based on police records contained in an account in *Iddu*, by Enrico Bellavia and Silvana Mazzocchi. The conversation between Lipari and his family members is contained in Prestipino and Palazzolo, *Il codice Provenzano*. The account of the bugging of Guttadauro's house is contained in Lirio Abbate and Peter Gomez, *I complici*.

Chief anti-Mafia prosecutor Pietro Grasso gave an interview to the author about the political significance of these events.

Chapter 15: Prostate trouble

Chief prosecutor Pietro Grasso and assistant prosecutor Michele Prestipino travelled together to Marseille on the trail of Provenzano. They both talked to the author about this part of the investigation.

Ciccio Pastoia's assertions about his relationship with Provenzano are contained in the 'Grounds for Arrest' in the Grande Mandamento investigation, Tribunale di Palermo.

Francesco Campanella's account of his work on the faked ID card, with other details of his friendship with Nicola Mandalà, is contained in Ordinanza Applicativa della Custodia Cautelare for Onofrio Morreale and others, Tribunale di Palermo, June 2006.

The request for chicory and other matters are contained in letters from Provenzano to Giuffré, Grande Mandamento trial.

The plot to kill Geraci is also recounted in detail in papers relating to the Grande Mandamento investigation, and was also described in an author interview with chief prosecutor Pietro Grasso.

Lipari's arrangements are found in Prestipino and Palazzolo, *Il codice Provenzano*. The letter from Matteo Messina Denaro to Provenzano of 6 February 2005 is also quoted in *Il codice Provenzano*. Buscetta's account of the stress of life on the run comes from Saverio Lodato, *La Mafia ha vinto*. An article in *La Repubblica* (30 January 2003) describes Provenzano's compulsive behaviour, based on his letters.

A full account of the Villabate Mafia's activities can be found in Lirio Abbate and Peter Gomez, *I complici*. Salvo Palazzolo and Ernesto Oliva, *Bernardo Provenzano: il ragioniere di Cosa Nostra*, also contains documentation of Michele Aiello's activities in private health. The police transcripts of conversations about the identikit image are reported in Enrico Bellavia and Silvana Mazzocchi, *Iddu*.

Chapter 16: The net tightens

The last major push to capture Provenzano was described to the author by the agent Bloodhound, by chief anti-Mafia prosecutor Pietro Grasso and by police chief Giuseppe Gualtieri. I also interviewed assistant prosecutor Marzia Sabella about the investigation. Alfonso Sabella talked to the author about Provenzano's record as Mafia boss in the latter stages.

Renato Cortese's account of the investigation and arrest are contained in Enrico Bellavia and Silvana Mazzocchi, *Iddu*. The police record of the conversation between Provenzano's brothers is also reported in *Iddu*. The Lipari family's troubles are reported in Prestipino and Palazzolo, *Il codice Provenzano*. Rotolo's conversations secretly recorded by police and Provenzano's correspondence about the return of the *scappati* are also contained in *Il codice Provenzano*. The conversation between Angelo and Paolo Provenzano intercepted by the police is reported in Lirio Abbate and Peter Gomez, *I complici*. The transcripts are filed with the inquiry into Riina's capture, Tribunale di Palermo.

31 A member of the Gruppo Duomo speaking on *Scacco al re*, documentary broadcast in 2007 on Rai Tre television.

Chapter 17: The arrest

This account of Provenzano's arrest is based on an author interview with the agent Bloodhound.

Further details of the last stages of the investigation come from an interview with police chief Giuseppe Gualtieri and author interviews with assistant prosecutors Michele Prestipino and Marzia Sabella.

An hour-by-hour progress report is contained in the police report, Gruppo Duomo, 12 June 2006. The phone conversation between Mariangela and Giuseppe Lo Bue was recorded by police on 3 Febuary 2006 at 22.27, and contained in the same report.

Police chief Renato Cortese's account of his part in Provenzano's arrest is contained in Enrico Bellavia and Silvana Mazzocchi, *Iddu*.

Epilogue

This chapter is largely based on interviews with the assistant prosecutor Alfonso Sabella, the historian Salvatore Lupo and the anti-Mafia chief prosecutor Pietro Grasso, as well as Provenzano's lawyer, Rosalba de Gregorio.

Angelo and Paolo Provenzano talked about their lives in the BBC documentary *The Real Godfather*, broadcast in September 2007. Angelo's alleged mediation was revealed in the course of an investigation by the carabinieri, reported by the ANSA news agency, 30 May 2007.

Details of Lipari's arrest are contained in the *Richiesta di applicazione di misure cautelari a carico di Lipari Giuseppe ed altri*, Tribunale di Palermo, September 2007.

32 The vast operation Grande Mandamento, which scooped up Provenzano's supporters in Villabate and Bagheria, concluded in November 2006 with the conviction of all Provenzano's former supporters. Spera got twenty-eight years; Onofrio Morreale, the youngblood secretly initiated and promoted by his master, got eighteen. Nicola Mandalà was sentenced to thirteen years.

Bibliography

LEGAL DOCUMENTS

Nino Giuffré's testimony in a series of trials:
  Verbale dell'interrogazione del collaboratore Nino Giuffré nel procedimento contro Giuseppe Biondolillo + altri, Termini Imerese, 16 October 2002
  Richiesta di misura cautelare per Umina Salvatore + 9, 14 July 2004
  Processo Talpe (Michele Aiello + altri) Tribunale di Palermo, 8 March 2005
  Processo a carico di Bernardo Provenzano + altri, Tribunale di Palermo, 8–10 February 2007
Sentence in the trial of Marcello dell'Utri and Gaetano Cinà, Tribunale di Palermo, 11 December 2004
Corte d'appello di Bari, 24 September 1970, sentenza
Pellegrini's report on Provenzano's early business expansion: Rapporto della Compagnia dei Carabinieri di Partinico alla Procura di Palermo, concerning Bernardo Provenzano and eighteen others, 27 November 1983
Colonel Michele Riccio's report on the collaboration of Gino Ilardo: Rapporto dei carabinieri del ROS (Raggruppamento Operativo Speciale) alle direzioni distrettuali antimafia di Caltanissetta, Catania, Palermo, Messina e Genova, 30 July 1996
Ordinanza di custodia cautelare emessa dal gip di Palermo nell'ambito dell'inchiesta Grande Oriente, nei confronti di Bernardo Provenzano + 20, 6 November 1998
Procura di Palermo, verbale di interrogatorio del collaboratore Angelo Siino, 10 June 1998
Introduction by chief prosecutor Nino Di Matteo in the trial known as 'Grande Oriente', Tribunale di Palermo, 13 October 2000
Verbale di interrogatorio del collaboratore Giovanni Brusca davanti

al Tribunale di Palermo, nel processo Simone Castello, 12 December 2000

Atti del procedimento penale nei confronti di Saveria Benedetta Palazzolo + altri, Tribunale di Palermo, 1983. Sentence, 18 December 1990

Memoria della Procura di Palermo nel Processo Talpe (Aiello Michele + altri), 1 October 2005

Fermo disposto dalla Procura di Palermo nei confronti di Angelo Tolentino + 49, nell'ambito dell'operazione Grande Mandamento sulla mafia di Villabate, 25 January 2005

Ordinanza applicativa della custodia cautelare nei confronti di Giuseppe Morreale + altri, Tribunale di Palermo, 21 September 2006

Ordinanza applicativa della custodia cautelare nei confronti di Riina Giuseppe Salvatore + altri, Tribunale di Palermo, 2000

Processo Trash (mafia e appalti) Tribunale di Palermo, interrogazione del collaboratore Giovanni Brusca 30 May 1998

Provvedimento di fermo di indiziato di reato nei confronti di Rotolo + 51, part of investigation 'Gotha' into Palermo families, Tribunale di Palermo, 20 June 2006

Richiesta di applicazione di misure cautelari a carico di Lipari Giuseppe + altri, Tribunale di Palermo, September 2007

Sentenza della corte d'assise di Palermo nei confronti di Benedetto Spera, 15 June 2002

Ordinanza di custodia cautelare nel procedimento a carico di Gariffo Carmelo, 3 May 2006

Police report, Gruppo Duomo, 12 June 2006

Books

Lirio Abbate and Peter Gomez, *I complici* (Fazi Editore, Rome, 2007)

Pino Arlacchi, *Mafia Business* (Verso, London, 1986)

Enrico Bellavia and Silvana Mazzocchi, *Iddu* (Baldini Castoldi Dalai, Milan, 2006)

Nino Calderone with Pino Arlacchi, *Gli uomini del disonore* (Mondadori, Milan, 1992)

Carlo Alberto Dalla Chiesa, *Michele Navarra e la Mafia del Corleonese* (La Zisa, Palermo, 1990)

John Dickie, *Cosa Nostra* (Hodder & Stoughton, London, 2004)

Giovanni Falcone with Marcelle Padovani, *Cose di Cosa Nostra* (Rizzoli, Milan, 1991)

Pietro Grasso and Francesco la Licata, *Pizzini, veleni e cicoria* (Feltrinelli, Milan, 2007)

Felicia Impastato, interviewed by Anna Puglisi and Umberto Santino, *La Mafia in casa mia* (La Luna, Palermo, 1987)

Giuseppe Lo Bianco and Sandra Rizza, *Il gioco grande* (Editori Riuniti, Rome, 2006)

Saverio Lodato, *Ho ucciso Giovanni Falcone* (Mondadori, Milan, 1999) [interview with Giovanni Brusca]

Saverio Lodato, *La Mafia ha vinto*, (Mondadori, Milan, 1999) [interview with Tommaso Buscetta]

Saverio Lodato, *Trent'anni di Mafia* (BUR, Milan, 2006)

Salvatore Lupo, *Storia della Mafia* (Donzelli, Rome, 1993)

Liliana Madeo, *Donne di Mafia* (Mondadori, Milan, 1994)

Marco Nese, *Nel segno della Mafia* (Rizzoli, Milan, 1975)

Salvo Palazzolo and Ernesto Oliva, *Bernardo Provenzano: il ragioniere di Cosa Nostra* (Rubbettino, Catanzaro, 2006)

Michele Pantaleone, *Mafia e politica* (Einaudi, Turin, 1978)

Tullio Pironti (ed.), *La vera storia d'Italia* (Naples, 1995)

Michele Prestipino and Salvo Palazzolo, *Il codice Provenzano* (Editori Laterza, Rome and Bari, 2007)

Teresa Principato and Alessandra Dino, *Mafia donna* (Flaccovio, Palermo, 1997)

Corrado Stajano (ed.), *L'atto d'accusa dei giudici di Palermo* (Editori Riuniti, Rome, 1986)

Alessandro Stille, *Excellent Cadavers* (Pantheon, New York, 1995)

Index

Index

Villages, towns and cities are in Sicily or on the Italian mainland unless otherwise stated.

Abbate, Lirio, 267
'Accountant, the' *see* Provenzano, Bernardo
Aglieri, Pietro, 75, 80, 118, 123–4
Agrigento (town), 22, 55, 185–7
Aiello, Michele ('the Engineer'), 172–3, 206, 210–13, 235
Altofonte (town), 41
Amato, Carmelo, 203
Andreotti, Giulio, 28, 77, 100, 106, 162
Asinara (prison island), 65
Asset Development (commercial development company), 171, 172

Badalamenti, Gaetano, 25, 26, 32, 40, 43, 46, 60
Bagarella, Calogero, 13, 18, 21, 24, 47
Bagarella, Giovanni, 198
Bagarella, Leoluca:
    and Luciano Liggio, 13
    and trial acquittals, 20–1
    and Salvatore Riina, 47, 113
    anger at Riina's harsh rule, 79
    character and personality, 116
    promotes bombing strategy against state, 118–21
    murder of Giuseppe Di Matteo, 122–3
    feud in Villabate, 124–6

final arrest, 126
involvement in separatist politics, 162–3
Bagarella, Ninetta (wife of Salvatore Riina), 47–8, 118–19, 151, 193–6
Bagheria (town):
    as Mafia base, 48–9, 56–9, 79, 140, 156, 169
    description, 53
Barbagallo, Salvatore, 125, 130, 155
Bari (town), 21, 27
Basile, Emanuele, 37, 70
Belmonte Mezzagno (town), 123, 178–9, 184
Berlusconi, Silvio, 163–5, 167
Bisacquino (town), 91
'Bloodhound' (police agent), 3, 4, 181, 224, 233, 252–7
Bolzoni, Attilio, 197
Bontate, Stefano ('prince of Villagrazia'):
    as member of Mafia commission, 25
    arrest, 26
    Riina's jealousy of, 26
    humiliated by Riina, 32
    murdered on Riina's orders, 38, 72, 226
    and Giulio Andreotti, 106

Borsellino, Paolo, 10, 65, 78, 104, 107–8

Borzacchelli, Antonino, 206, 210, 212, 214–15

Brancaccio (town), 74, 76, 120, 168, 172

Brusca, Bernardo, 36, 37

Brusca, Enzo, 122

Brusca, Giovanni ('the Executioner'; *also* 'the Pig'):
  and Bernardo Provenzano, 67, 72, 104–5, 115, 126–7, 140–2, 158–9
  and Salvatore Riina, 80, 109–10, 112–13
  and assassination of Falcone, 107, 141
  and Ciancimino, 114
  and murder of Giuseppe Di Matteo, 121–3
  convicted of Ignazio Salvo murder, 122
  attempts takeover of Agrigento (town), 136–7, 139
  becomes collaborator (*pentito*), 141–2, 180
  career as executioner, 195
  imprisonment, 199

Buscetta, Tommaso, 68, 70, 72, 98, 218, 262

Caccamo (town), 9, 54, 80, 209

Caldarozzi, Gilberto, 234, 257

Calderone, Nino, 26, 78, 104, 109

Calderone, Pippo, 78

Caltanissetta (town), 103, 130, 131, 133

Calvaruso, Tony, 125–6

Camilleri, Andrea, 5

Campanella, Francesco, 170–2, 219–21, 227, 229

Cancemi, Salvatore, 71–2, 107, 109, 166

Cannella, Tommaso, 87, 106, 174, 192, 203

Cannella, Tullio, 162–3

Capaci (town), 122

Capizi family, 185–6

Caponetto, Antonino, 70

Carnevale, Corrado, 79

Caruso, Damiano, 24

Caselli, Giancarlo, 109, 112, 114

Cassarà, Ninni, 64

Castellammare (town), 50

Castello, Simone, 58, 123, 132, 169

Castronovo (town), 22

Catania (town), 23, 26, 56, 78, 103, 132, 140

Catturandi (Palermo flying squad), 181–3, 233

Cavataio, Michele, 23–4

Chinnici, Rocco, 40

Christian Democratic Party, 73–7, 106–7, 155–7
  and Palermo dam project, 15
  and Salvo Lima, 28–9
  dismissal of Vito Ciancimino from party, 34
  and murder of Piersanti Mattarella, 37
  disbanding of party, 174

Ciaculli (Palermo suburb), 19–20, 23

Ciancimino, Massimo, 114

Ciancimino, Vito, 27–34, 102, 111

Ciminna (town), 56, 176

Cinà, Dr Gaetano, 164

Cinisi (town), 22, 25, 32, 43

Ciuro, Giuseppe, 210–12, 214–15

Colletti, Carmelo, 55,

Communist Party, 39, 59, 156

Contorno, Salvatore, 78–9, 124

Corleone (town), 4, 7, 14, 16, 85–9

Corleonesi (Mafia group), 19–20, 23–6, 28–42, 54–5

Cortese, Renato, 3–4, 233–4, 256

Cosa Nostra *see* Mafia
Craxi, Bettino, 75, 103
Credito Siciliano (Villabate), 219
Cuffaro, Salvatore, 170, 174–5, 211,
    213–16, 267
Cusimano, Mario, 171, 172, 221, 223,
    228

Dalla Chiesa, General Carlo Alberto,
    21, 39–40, 41
De Caprio, Sergio ('Capitano Ultimo'),
    114, 170
De Donno, Giuseppe, 111
Dell'Utri, Marcello, 163–6, 167
Denaro, Matteo Messina:
    hides out in Bagheria, 59
    as boss of Trapani, 80
    personality and character, 80
    loyalty to Salvatore Riina, 80, 103
    and Falcone assassination, 105
    and war on state, 120
    and Giuseppe Guttadauro, 168
    writes to Bernardo Provenzano,
       231–2
Di Carlo, Francesco, 26, 41, 164
di Cristina, Giuseppe, 35–6, 72
Di Gregorio, Rosalba, 265
Di Maggio, Balduccio, 112, 142
Di Matteo, Giuseppe, 121–3
Di Matteo, Nino:
    on Provenzano's friends and
       advisers, 102, 160
    on Mafia war against state, 102–3
    on Mafia 'submersion' strategy, 130,
       145, 167
    on Provenzano's leadership style,
       146–8
    Mafia business activities, 168,
       171–2
Di Matteo, Santino, 122
Di Noto, Dr Vincenzo, 181
Di Peri family, 124, 125–6

DIA (Direzione Investigativa
    Antimafia), 210, 212, 214
DiGati, Maurizio, 185–6
'Director, the' (police agent), 4
drug trafficking *see* Mafia: drug
    trafficking and money-laundering

Emilia (region), 227, 228
Episcopo, Nino, 176–7, 205
Eucaliptus, Nicolò, 81, 228

Falcone, Giovanni:
    anti-Mafia investigations, 49, 79,
       104–5
    and Mafia maxi-trial, 65
    use of *pentiti*, 78–9
    assassination, 104–7, 122, 199–200
    and law on maximum security
       terms, 167
Falsone, Giuseppe, 185
Ferro, Salvatore, 134, 136
Florence: Uffizi gallery bombing, 120
Fontana, Ezio, 221–3
Fontana, Nino ('Mister Millionaire'),
    58
Forza Italia (political party), 155, 157,
    163–4, 166–9, 174
    founding of, 157
    and Silvio Berlusconi, 167
    wins 1994 election, 168
Francese, Mario, 34–5

Gambino family, 38
Ganci, Calogero, 83
Ganci, Raffaele, 123
Gariffo, Carmelo (nephew of Bernardo
    Provenzano), 56, 62, 93, 173,
    249–50
Gariffo, Mariangela *see* Lo Bue,
    Mariangela
Gela (town), 69, 151
Genovese, Salvatore, 158–9

Geraci, Nené, 142
Geraci, Salvatore, 225
Giammanco, Enzo, 169
Giornale di Sicilia (newspaper), 35
Giuffré, Nino ('Little Hand'):
    comments on Bernardo Provenzano,
        8–10, 30, 54–5, 58, 72, 157, 159,
        168, 174, 203–4
    political corruption, 76–7, 155–7,
        167, 174–5
    comments on Salvatore Riina, 100,
        141, 162
    Falcone investigations, 105–6
    Provenzano's 'submersion' strategy,
        130, 145–8, 153–7
    keeps Provenzano's letters (*pizzini*),
        132, 211
    comments on Giovanni Brusca, 141
    comments on Benedetto Spera,
        178–80
    deteriorating relationship with
        Provenzano, 184–7
    arrest and collaboration, 207–11,
        261–2
Giuliano, Boris, 36–7
Godfather, The (film), 239
Gotha (anti-Mafia operation), 266
Grande Mandamento (anti-Mafia
    operation), 227–8
Grasso, Pietro:
    on Bernardo Provenzano, 8, 42,
        226–7, 230, 233, 262
    on Salvatore Riina, 105
    interviews Gioacchino La Barbera,
        110
    targeted by Riina, 110
    and Nino Giuffré as *pentito*, 208
    arrest of Provenzano, 257
Graviano family, 42, 74
Graviano, Filippo, 120
Greco family, 19–20
Greco, Carlo, 75, 117, 118

Greco, Leonardo, 53, 55, 56
Greco, Michele ('the Pope'), 33–4, 35,
    37, 40, 65–6, 79
Greco, Pino ('the Shoe'), 40–1, 59, 77
Greco, Salvatore, 19, 23
Gruppo Duomo (anti-Mafia
    investigation team), 233–5, 252
Gualtieri, Giuseppe:
    arrest of Bernardo Provenzano, 3
    on Provenzano, 6, 153, 235, 250
    on Provenzano and Saveria
        Palazzolo, 189
    streamlining of police investigative
        group, 234
Guttadauro, Giuseppe:
    home in Bagheria, 59
    appearance, 168
    as boss of Brancaccio, 168, 172
    successfully operates on Saveria
        Palazzola, 191
    receives protection from
        Provenzano, 192
    involvement in politics, 213–14, 216
    and Salvatore Cuffaro, 216
Guttuso, Renato, 53

ICRE (ironworks; Bagheria), 53–4
Ilardo, Gino:
    Provenzano and family life, 90
    mafioso pedigree, 130–1
    as police informer, 130–2, 140
    disillusionment with Cosa Nostra,
        131
    on Provenzano's communication
        methods, 131–2
    receives letters from Provenzano,
        132–4, 138–9
    murdered, 140
Impastato, Giovanni, 43–4, 46, 266
Ingroia, Antonino, 210, 211
Intile, Ciccio, 54
Inzerillo family, 38–9, 245, 266–7

Inzerillo, Totuccio, 36, 38, 42, 55
Italcostruzione (Mafia front company),
    50

John Paul II, Pope, 151

La Barbera family, 19–20, 29
La Barbera, Angelo, 19, 113
La Barbera, Gioacchino, 110
La Barbera, Nicola ('Cola Truppicuni'),
    136–7, 138, 181–3, 235
La Casamance (nr Marseilles, France),
    223
La Licorne Clinic (nr Marseilles,
    France), 222
La Repubblica (newspaper), 197, 238
La Torre, Pio, 39, 40, 41, 59
Liggio, Luciano:
    as Corleonesi leader, 6–7, 13
    early criminal activities, 12–13
    character and personality, 13
    murders Placido Rizzotto, 13–14
    murders Michele Navarra, 15–16, 25
    personality, 15, 21–2
    trial acquittals, 20–1
    involvement in kidnapping, 22
    activities in prison, 31, 35, 38, 65, 77
    appears in Mafia maxi-trial (1986),
        65–6
    appoints Riina and Provenzano joint
        leaders, 67, 69–70
    makes insulting comment on
        Provenzano, 152
    see also Provenzano, Bernardo;
        Riina, Salvatore
Lima, Salvo:
    and Giulio Andreotti, 28, 100
    and political corruption, 28–9, 73,
        100, 226
    and Vito Ciancimino, 30
    fails to fix Mafia maxi-trial, 106
    murdered, 106–7

Lipari, Arturo, 95
Lipari, Cinzia, 95, 242–3
Lipari, Giuseppe, 268
Lipari, Pino:
    and Provenzano, 60
    Sicilian public health system fraud,
        60
    charged with Mafia association, 63
    operates Palermo works cartel
        (Tavolino), 63–4
    paternalism towards Provenzano's
        sons, 90–1, 92, 94
    involves own family in Mafia, 95,
        152, 205, 242–3
    pretends to collaborate with police,
        205–6
Lo Bianco, Pieruccio, 74, 126, 178
Lo Bue, Giuseppe, 249–53
Lo Bue, Mariangela (*née* Gariffo), 249,
    251–3
Lo Piccolo, Salvatore, 244–7, 266–7
Lo Piccolo, Sandro, 267
Lo Verso, Stefano, 223–4, 228
Lupo, Salvatore:
    Mafia and social status, 17
    on viale Lazio massacre, 24–5
    on Luciano Liggio, 25–6
    on Corleonesi, 29–30, 67
    on Mafia leadership qualities, 154
    on Angelo Provenzano, 266
    continuing Mafia power struggles,
        267
'Lynx, the' (police agent), 254, 256

Madonia, Ciccio, 37
Madonia, Nino, 74
Madonia, Piddu, 80, 103, 130, 140
Mafia (*also* Cosa Nostra):
    methods of communication, 5,
        131–4, 158, 212, 237, 242, 243
    'submersion' strategy, 8, 144–61,
        171, 199

Mafia (*cont.*):
  ruling commission, 25
  culture, 25, 26, 68, 82–3, 134, 197–8
  drug trafficking and money-
    laundering, 29, 31, 49–53, 55,
    62, 266
  code of honour, 35, 48
  anti-Mafia laws, 39, 40, 162, 163,
    167
  wages war against state, 39–40,
    99–111
  'Mafia enterprise', 61
  the maxi-trial (1986), 65–6, 76–7,
    78, 79, 100, 106
  religious attitudes, 195–6
Mafia and political corruption *see*
  Christian Democratic Party;
  Communist Party; Forza Italia;
  Radical Party; Socialist Party (PSI);
  Southern League; UDC
Manca, Dr Attilio, 231
Mandalà, Nicola, 170, 171, 218–22,
  224
Mandalà, Nino ('the Lawyer'), 169
Mandalari, Giuseppe, 50
Mangano, Vittorio, 164–6
Mannoia, Agostino Marino, 77–8
Mannoia, Francesco Marino, 78
Marchese, Filippo, 78
Marchese, Vincenzina (wife of Leoluca
  Bagarella), 122–3
Marino, Giovanni, 236–7, 255–7
Martelli, Claudio, 77, 79
Marussig, Pierfrancesco, 172
Mattarella, Piersanti, 37, 106
maxi-trial, the Mafia *see* Mafia: the
  maxi-trial (1986)
Mazara del Vallo (town), 82, 84
Mercadante, Dr Giovanni, 173–4, 192
Mesi, Maria, 212
Mesi, Paola, 212
Messina, Leonardo, 47

Mezzojuso (town), 134, 135, 138, 176,
  180, 181
Miceli, Mimmo, 213, 214, 216
Misilmeri (town), 126
Moncada, Girolamo, 23–4
Mondello (town), 33, 110
money-laundering *see* Mafia: drug
  trafficking and money-laundering
Mongerbino ad Aspra (Bagheria), 59
Monreale (town), 56
Montagna dei Cavalli (nr Corleone),
  236, 253
Montalto, Francesco, 124–5
Montana, Beppe, 59–60, 64
Mori, Mario, 111, 113, 114
Morreale, Onofrio, 80–1, 228
Morvillo, Francesca (wife of Giovanni
  Falcone), 107

Navarra, Dr Michele ('Our Father'),
  14, 15–16, 21, 25
Nordrhein-Westfalen (Germany), 89

Orlando, Leoluca, 174
Orlando, Madeleine, 222
Ospedale Civico (Palermo), 173

Palazzolo, Paolo, 43, 48, 190
Palazzolo, Salvatore, 43, 46, 192
Palazzolo, Salvo (journalist), 5, 7, 45
Palazzolo, Saveria Benedetta
  (companion of Bernardo
  Provenzano):
  early life with Bernardo Provenzano,
    43–8
  convicted of money-laundering,
    49–52, 63
  life in Corleone, 85–91, 93–8, 188,
    193–4, 239
  rumours of life in Germany, 89
  Christmas trip to Germany, 97–8
  use of codes, 188

loving relationship with Provenzano,
189
health, 191–2
attitude to press, 196–7
and wish to marry, 263–4
Palermo University, 92
Palermo:
anti-Mafia street protests, 10
drug trafficking war, 19–20
rise of Corleonesi, 19–20, 23–5,
28–42, 54–5
viale Lazio massacre, 23–4, 47
corruption in city, 28, 29
Partanna Mondello (nr Palermo), 83
Partinico (town), 103, 142
Pasqua, Giovanni, 13
Pastoia, Ciccio, 59, 179–80, 184,
217–18, 224–9, 231
Pellegrini, Angiolo, 9, 49–50, 55–6,
61–2, 64, 157–8, 183
Pennino, Dr Gioacchino, 32–4
pentiti (Mafia defectors), 7, 47–9, 57,
71, 104, 108, 109, 121, 130, 155
Piana degli Albanesi (town), 83
pizzini (letters) *see* Mafia: methods of
communication
Porta Nuova (mafia group), 166
Prestipino, Michele:
comments on Provenzano, 5–6, 7,
149, 155
Provenzano's 'mediation' letter, 146
seizes Provenzano's health records,
230
Provenzano's arrest, 259
Principato, Teresa, 198
Prizzi (town), 35, 174
Provenzano, Angelo (father of
Bernardo Provenzano), 17, 89
Provenzano, Angelo (son of Bernardo
Provenzano):
personal life, 46, 88, 90–7, 182,
188–93, 196, 198–201

owns launderette, 94, 189, 194,
196–7, 240
relationship with father, 96–7, 191,
239–42, 264–6
use of numerical codes, 190–2
contacts with Giuseppe Lo Bue,
249–50
gives BBC interview, 265
Provenzano, Bernardo ('Binnu'; *also* 'the
Tractor'; *also* 'the Accountant'):
MAFIA LIFE:
final capture, 3–4, 249–58
and Salvatore Riina, 6–7, 27, 63,
67–78, 80–1, 98–9, 100–2,
113–15
power and influence, 6–8
rumours of death, 7, 123
skills at mediation, 8, 14, 15,
30–1, 32, 244–7, 266
escapes police ambush in
Castronovo, 22
as fugitive, 22, 236–9
nicknames, 25, 26–7, 34, 36
involvement in viale Lazio
massacre, 23–4
banned from public office, 27
rises to power in Palermo, 29–30,
35–6, 41–2, 55
as joint leader of Corleone
family, 31, 42, 67–73, 244
and Gioacchino Pennino, 32–4
accused of Dalla Chiesa
assassination, 40
and money-laundering activities,
49–52
convicted of Mafia association, 50
involvement in Sicilian public
health corruption, 56, 60–1,
62, 172–4
involvement in political
corruption, 57–8, 73–7, 163,
166–8

Provenzano, Bernardo
MAFIA LIFE (*cont.*)
controls public works cartel, 63–4
and Luciano Liggio, 67, 69–70,
152
wears bishop's robes as disguise,
103
involvement in Falcone and
Borsellino assassinations, 103–8
tensions with Leoluca Bagarella,
119–21, 124–6
takes leadership of Mafia (Cosa
Nostra), 123, 126–8
leadership style and 'submersion'
strategy, 129–30, 132–4,
138–9, 144–61, 171, 199
difficulties with Giovanni Brusca,
136–7, 139–42
murder of Gino Ilardo, 139–40
supports convicted mafiosi, 167,
243–4
break-up of political network,
168–9
attempts peace talks between
Benedetto Spera and Ciccio
Pastoia, 179–80
avoids police search near
Mezzojuso, 182–3
deteriorating relationship with
Nino Giuffré, 184–7
obsession with security, 202–4,
221, 235–7
Giuffré's collaboration with
police, 207–11, 261–2
mediates between Nino Rotolo
and Salvatore Lo Piccolo,
244–7, 266
imprisonment and trial, 261–3
wealth, 263, 268
see also Giuffré, Nino; Liggio,
Luciano; Mafia; Riina,
Salvatore

PERSONAL LIFE:
appearance, 4, 5, 12–13, 14–15
living conditions, 5–6, 258–60
personality and character, 5–6,
8–9, 67, 126, 148, 159
relationship with sons (Angelo
and Francesco), 9–10, 189–91,
239–42, 264–6
early influences, 13–14
birth and childhood, 17
meets Saveria Benedetta
Palazzolo (companion), 43–7
health problems, 67, 136, 181,
201, 210, 217–23, 230–1, 238,
264
disjointed family life, 90–9,
188–93
use of Bible, 151–2, 237
see also Palazzolo, Saveria
Benedetta; Provenzano,
Angelo; Provenzano,
Francesco Paolo
Provenzano, Francesco Paolo (son of
Bernardo Provenzano):
personal life, 48, 88, 89, 92, 198,
200, 265
relationship with father, 96–7, 191,
239–42, 264–6
Provenzano, Giovanna (*née* Rigoglioso;
mother of Bernardo Provenzano), 17
Provenzano, Maria Concetta (sister of
Bernardo Provenzano), 17
Provenzano, Michela Arcangela (sister
of Bernardo Provenzano), 17
Provenzano, Rosa (sister of Bernardo
Provenzano), 17
Provenzano, Salvatore (brother of
Bernardo Provenzano), 87, 88, 247,
269
Provenzano, Simone (brother of
Bernardo Provenzano), 89, 93, 97,
178, 247

Publitalia (advertising agency),
163–4
Puglisi, Padre Pino, 121
Punta Raisi airport, 32

Radical Party, 74
Riccio, Maresciallo Michele, 163
Riccio, Colonel Michele, 130, 131,
134–8
Riccobono, Rosario, 83–4
Riesi (town), 35
Rigoglioso, Giovanna see Provenzano,
Giovanna
Riina, Bernardo, 252–6
Riina, Giovanni (son of Salvatore
Riina), 113, 115, 119, 195, 198
Riina, Maria Concetta (daughter of
Salvatore Riina), 194–5
Riina, Salvatore ('Totò'; 'Shorty'):
as joint leader of Corleone family,
6–7, 27, 31–2, 67–73
and Bernardo Provenzano, 6–7, 27,
63, 67–78, 80–1, 98–9, 102
and Luciano Liggio, 13–15
appearance and character, 14–15, 26,
38
involvement in viale Lazio massacre,
24
rise to power in Palermo, 25–7,
35–6
banned from public office, 27
antagonism towards Vito
Ciancimino, 30–1
accused of Dalla Chiesa
assassination, 40
consolidates power in Palermo,
41–2, 55
marriage to Ninetta Bagarella, 47,
151
and political corruption, 73–7
faces rebellion against his rule, 77,
79
wages war against state, 99–101, 109,
110–11
involvement in Falcone and
Borsellino assassinations, 104–8
final capture, 111–15
and bungled police search of home,
113–14, 258
loathing for pentiti, 121–3
and Giovanni Brusca, 141, 142
see also Liggio, Luciano; Provenzano,
Bernardo
Riina, Salvo (son of Salvatore Riina),
194, 199–200
Riolo, Giorgio, 206, 210–11, 213–15
Rizzotto, Placido, 13–14
Rocca Busambra (nr Corleone), 18, 20
Rome:
San Giovanni bombing, 121
ROS (Ragruppamento Operativo
Speciale), 130, 138, 140, 202, 210,
214
Rotolo, Nino, 159, 160, 174, 244–7,
266
Ruffino, Giuseppe, 13, 21
Russo, Giuseppe, 35, 72

Sabella, Alfonso:
on Salvatore Riina, 41–2, 69, 71
hunt for bombers, 118
Salvatore Barbagallo's collaboration,
125
and Villabate feud, 125–6
issuing of arrest warrants, 129
and Vito Vitale, 142
Provenzano and Mafia prisoners,
244
Sabella, Marzia, 8–9, 257–9
Salvo family, 29
Salvo, Ignazio, 122
Salvo, Nino, 32
San Giuseppe Iato (town), 22, 30, 36,
112, 136, 142

Santa Maria di Gesù (town), 75, 80
Santa Teresa Clinic (Bagheria), 222
Santapaola, Nitto ('the Hunter'), 56, 103, 234
Santino, Umberto, 154
scappati (fugitives) see Inzerillo family
SCO (Servizio Centrale Operativo), 152, 233–4
Segno (Catholic magazine), 150
Sicilian Vespers (anti-Mafia operation), 108
Siino, Angelo ('the Builder'), 56, 63, 67, 108, 156, 222
Socialist Party (PSI), 74–6, 77, 156, 167
Southern League (political group), 162–3
Spera, Benedetto:
    as ally of Provenzano, 123
    struggle with Pieruccio Lo Bianco, 126, 178
    as fugitive, 176–7, 178
    rivalry with Ciccio Pastoia, 179–80, 225
    arrest, 182
Splendor (Angelo Provenzano's launderette), 94, 189, 194, 196–7, 240
Stanfa family, 209
Streva, Francesco, 17–18

Tavolino ('Round Table'; Mafia public works cartel), 63–4
Terranova, Cesare, 20, 37
Tolentino, Angelo, 176–7, 205

'Tractor, the' see Provenzano, Bernardo
Trapani (town), 49, 59, 74, 82, 89
Triolo, Ugo, 35
Troia, Gaspare, 220, 222, 224, 229, 230
Troia, Salvatore, 222–3, 224

Ucciardone prison (Palermo), 107
UDC (centre-right political party), 213
Umina, Carmelo, 202, 207
Umina, Salvatore, 207

Vaccaro, Lorenzo, 135
Vaccaro, Mimmo, 133
Valguarnera (town), 101
via Bernini (Palermo), 113
via Colletti (Corleone), 87
via Libertà (Palermo), 63
via Marconi (Ficarazzi), 226
via Scorsone (Corleone), 193
viale Lazio massacre (Palermo), 23–4, 47
viale Strasburgo (Palermo), 50
Vicari (village), 207
Villa Cattolica (Bagheria), 53
Villa dei Mostri (Bagheria), 57
Villa Valquarnera (Bagheria), 57
Villabate (town), 58, 124–6, 156, 169–72
Violante, Luciano, 118, 269
Virga, Domenico, 207, 208
Vitale, Giusy, 103, 114
Vitale, Leonardo, 103, 114
Vitale, Vito, 103, 114, 142–3

The author of *Mafia Women* and *No Questions Asked,* Clare Longrigg is perhaps the leading British expert on the Mafia. In this new biography, she draws on her vast experience and wide range of contacts to paint a portrait of a secretive and immensely powerful man, who for decades controlled the Mafia with an iron hand.